Charlie Peacock has written the definitive book on today's music and the church. Though the names and thoughts of stars such as Amy Grant, Michael W. Smith, Jars of Clay and Steven Curtis Chapman dot its pages, it is the Holy Spirit inspired, Scripture-based insights that grab and compel.

Bob Briner, Emmy Award-winning TV producer, author of *Roaring Lambs* and *Leadership Lessons of Jesus*

Bravo! If Charlie Peacock is pointing fingers, it's not at the Christian music industry, but to the holy light that can transform it. *At The Crossroads* is an intelligent analysis and a tremendous encouragement for any Christian artist bold enough to be a beacon in a dark and hungering world.

Lou Carlozo, *Chicago Tribune*

Charlie rethinks "Christian music" as I have been trying to rethink "Christian counseling." Before reading his thoughts, I knew I was stirred by some Christian music, turned off by some, and indifferent to much. Now my appetite is whetted for what God can do through music within the surprising boundaries He draws, and Charlie describes. A compelling, thoughtful discussion of music's power to be truly spiritual.

Lawrence J. Crabb, Jr., psychologist and best-selling author

At the Crossroads is a sincere plea for honest reflection and critical assessment of contemporary Christian music. Charlie Peacock calls for a new vision, a "comprehensive kingdom perspective" as a guide through the labyrinth of hype, conformity, worldliness and antiintellectualism that has plagued the enterprise.

William D. Romanowski, Calvin College, author of *Pop Culture Wars*

Charlie Peacock's book is an honest, informed and passionate critique of how evangelicals have created a musical ghetto grounded in thin theology, polluted piety, cultural claustrophobia, and corporate confusion. Every believer ought to read it, weep, and then take up Peacock's challenge to find a better way to transform worldwide culture for the God of the universe.

Quentin J. Schultze, Calvin College, author of *Internet for Christians*

A refreshing and challenging book for any Christian seriously engaged in the creative process.

Peggy Wehmeyer, Religion Correspondent, ABC News

AT THE CROSSROADS

An Insider's Look at the Past, Present, and Future of Contemporary Christian Music

CHARLIE PEACOCK

Nashville, Tennessee

© 1999
by Charles Ashworth pka Charlie Peacock
All rights reserved
Printed in the United States of America

0-8054-1822-9

Published by Broadman & Holman Publishers, Nashville, Tennessee
Acquisitions and Development Editor: Leonard G. Goss
Page Design and Typesetting: TF Designs, Mt. Juliet, Tennessee

Dewey Decimal Classification: 782
Subject Heading: CONTEMPORARY CHRISTIAN MUSIC
Library of Congress Card Catalog Number: 98-43996

Unless otherwise noted, Scripture quotations are from the Holy Bible,
New International Version, © copyright 1973, 1978, 1984.
Other versions are marked NASB, the New American Standard Bible,
© Copyright The Lockman Foundation, 1960, 1962, 1963, 1968,
1971, 1972, 1973, 1975, 1977, 1995;
NKJV, New King James Version, copyright © 1979, 1980, 1982,
Thomas Nelson, Inc., Publishers.

Library of Congress Cataloging-in-Publication Data

Peacock, Charlie.
At the crossroads : an insider's look at the past, present, and future of contemporary Christian music. / by Charlie Peacock.
p. cm.
ISBN 0-8054-1822-9 (hardcover)
1. Contemporary Christian music--History and criticism.
I. Title.
ML3187.5P37 1998
782.25--dc21

98-43996
CIP

1 2 3 4 5 03 02 01 00 99

Contents

Acknowledgments

I must begin by acknowledging my debt to the writing of Francis and Edith Schaeffer. Next, a special thanks to Louis and Mary Neely and all those involved with the Christianity and culture experiment that was Exit Records, including Mike Roe, Daryl Zachman, Jimmy Abegg, Steve Griffith, Steve Scott, Aaron Smith, and others no less important. Thanks and appreciation to Steve Turner, who was there before I arrived. Dan Russell, you were a great encouragement to me in those early years as well.

Many thanks to Billy Ray Hearn, Bill Hearn, and all the folks at the EMI Christian Music Group, especially Peter York, who became my musical champion in 1989 and carefully ushered me into the full embrace of the Christian music community. Brown Bannister, you were there too. Thanks.

Thank you, Scotty Smith for your teaching and for the Art House years. To all those who supported the AH mission, thank you, especially Nick Barré, Doug McKelvey, Russ Ramsey, David Dark, Christ Community Church, and all the students, financial supporters, and volunteers. It was good.

Special mention must be given to Dr. Leland Ryken, who first suggested I write this book, as well as to Edith Schaeffer and Frederick Buechner, who both sent words of encouragement in the early days of the Art House. Glenn Kaiser and JPUSA, Andy and Sue Boyer, you were there as well. Thank you.

To R.C. Sproul, R.C. Jr, Dick and Mardi Keyes, Quentin Schultze, William Romanowski, Michael Horton, Os Guinness, thank you for your teaching and your encouragement. Ken Hefner, keep up the good work.

I owe a huge debt of thanks to the kind people who have supported my music throughout the years. Thank you for caring and for saying so. I'm privileged to walk in community with you.

To Molly Ashworth Nicholas, April Hefner, and Greg Rumburg (all gifted writers), thank you for figuring the statistics, early proofreading, and offering helpful suggestions. Len Goss, thank you for sweeping the tangential under the rug. Wes Yoder, thank you for guarding the vision. Mike Butera, thank you for your obedience in telling me the truth—it set me free. Thank you, SCC and Jars for your faithfulness. Many thanks to all the artists who participated in the interviews. Respect to the pioneers of CCM.

To my son Sam and to my new son Mark Nicholas, this book is for you both. You're the future of the music. Choose well.

To my wife and best friend Andi: I love you so much. Thank you for your great patience and for not letting me quit when I wanted to. Kiss me like a . . .

A final word of thanks to my friend and mentor Bob Briner, who has championed me since the moment we met. I could not have written this book without you, Bob. Knowing you has helped to make me a better man. You make the invisible kingdom visible.

Terminology

Origin and Acknowledgment

One of the more confusing parts of writing about music created and marketed by Christians is what to name it. *Christian music* would seem the obvious choice, but are we talking about music created by Christians for Christians such as Gregorian chants, a Monteverdi oratorio, Bach's cantatas, or Handel's Messiah? Or are we talking about Charles Tindley and Tommy Dorsey? Or, are we talking about all of it, from the psalms of King David to dc Talk? What about gospel music? What about southern gospel? What about black gospel? Why all the gospels? You can see the challenge here.

I knew I wanted to write about something that happened with Christians and music starting back in the late sixties—something which is today a $500-million-a-year industry. And though it has included black gospel and southern gospel, and even some Gregorian chants, the music and industry I needed to put a name on had always been more about a kind of Christianized pop/rock music—music which changes with the pop music of the surrounding culture. This music and the community of artists, industry workers, and audience members it represents is usually referred to today as contemporary Christian music, or CCM for short. Though many of the music's earliest pioneers perpetuated this terminology (and derivations of it), a magazine named *Contemporary Christian Music/CCM* set the name in stone, and has continued to help refine its meaning for more than twenty years.

CCM® is a registered trademark of CCM Communications, home to *CCM Magazine, CCM Update,* and other concerns important to the nurture and growth of this unique musical form. It is with the kind permission of *CCM Magazine* founder John Styll that I make use of the CCM acronym throughout the pages that follow. This permission does not in any way indicate an endorsement of *At the Crossroads* by CCM Communications. In addition, the opinions expressed in *At the Crossroads* by this author or any other parties do not necessarily reflect the opinions of CCM Communications.

Foreword

by Steven Curtis Chapman

I don't remember what it was that originally inspired me. Perhaps a sermon, or maybe a discussion in my church youth group, or possibly a time of personal Bible study. What I do remember is that I was mowing the yard on my Dad's tractor when I began to write my first song. But what was it that stirred me to race suddenly from the yard to find a pen and a piece of paper to compose those lyrics?

Undoubtedly, the message of Jesus' parable in Matthew 25, commonly called the "parable of the talents" awakened a new passion in me. In pondering the story in which several servants are entrusted with certain "talents" by their master to be used in a way that would honor him and show good stewardship, I was struck with a deep desire to simulate the "good and faithful servant" who heard those treasured words of his master, "Well done." After a few hours with my guitar, and with a trash can full of crumpled sheets of paper, I emerged with the first of my many musical "cries of the heart," which I hoped would be pronounced "Well done." While this wouldn't prove to be my most creatively crafted song, it was as sincere a lyric as I have ever penned, and one to which I have referred many times through the years as my "mission statement" on the art that God has allowed me to share. It read:

Before he left this earth for heaven, Jesus commanded us to go
And bring all people to him, by letting His love through us show
When Christ comes I just want to hear Him say
When Christ comes I just want to hear Him say "Well done."

At the tender age of fifteen, I had little notion of the significance of Christ's challenge. What would it really be to live in such a way that he would be able to say those words, "Well done, good and faithful servant?" Now, twenty years later, I am still considering the implications of that parable, and that is the reason why I think the book you are holding in your hand is so important.

To think, that Almighty God would give us the sacred trust of the message of reconciliation and send us out as ambassadors through whom his appeal would be made (2 Cor. 5:19, 20) is a truth that should humble and astonish us. And when we realize that the Artist and Creator of all things has invited us into the creative process and entrusted us with unique artistic abilities to use for his glory, we should truly feel awed, and yet, sobered by a sense of our own responsibility and need for wisdom.

I know of no one who has wrestled more profoundly with these issues and how they may relate to the arts, especially Christian music, than Charlie Peacock. I can't help but think how invaluable a book like this would have been to me as I took my first steps in serving my Master by using the gifts and abilities he had given me. The relationship between the importance of theology and the goals of Christian music found in the chapter entitled "In the Beginning" are alone worth the time invested in reading this book.

This book does not answer all of our questions about Christian music and how it should be "done." Instead, it allows the Holy Spirit to guide us to solutions, however different and unique they may appear to be. I believe God will use it in the lives of his children, like you and me, who are "compelled by the love of Christ" to use our gifts and talents in such a way that our Master might say, "Well done, good and faithful servant."

Introduction

Contemporary Christian Music at the Crossroads

Contemporary Christian music (CCM) is at a crossroads, the crossroads between what was and is, and what's yet to come. This book is a compass check, a way of setting aside time to look back, to assess where CCM is currently, and most importantly to choose a true and faithful future direction. As a Christian and a sixteen-year veteran of contemporary Christian music, I have a vested interest in seeing that we do choose faithfully. The Contemporary Christian music community is my community, one that I am very much a part of, and gratefully so.

I believe that books ought to be written for the benefit of people and communities, and this book (or compass check) is no exception. All along I've imagined it being of benefit to anyone and everyone connected with contemporary Christian music: artists, industry, *and* audience. I have also hoped that professors, teachers, parents, youth workers, and pastors would find it helpful as well. I have tried to write in such a way that young musicians just starting out might find answers to their many questions, regardless of whether they use their talents in church, contemporary Christian music, or the mainstream music business. All in all, this book was written to benefit anyone concerned with the future direction of contemporary Christian music, or interested in the intersection of Christianity, music, and the music business.

It's important to note that this book frames the words of an artist and not a journalist, and as such reflects only my experience—what I have seen and known. Even so, that experience has been extensive, both in mainstream music and within the Christian music industry, and it's this twenty-plus total years of experience which informs the book. I secured my first major label artist development deal with A&M Records in 1980 and I went on to make recordings for Exit, A&M, Island, Sparrow, and re:think. As a record producer I have had the privilege of working with many talented artists including the 77's, the Choir, Avalon, Margaret Becker, Out of the Grey, Michelle Tumes, Al Green, Sarah Masen, Rich Mullins, Michael Card, Bob Carlisle, and CeCe Winans, to name just a few. Songs I've either written alone or cowritten with others have been recorded by numerous artists such as Amy Grant, ("Every Heartbeat"), Russ Taff ("Down in the Lowlands"), and dc Talk ("In the Light"). In addition to the callings of artist, producer, and songwriter, I have also experienced the joy and challenge of founding my own record label, re:think (now a part of the Sparrow Label Group). All told, there is little concerning the music business or the ministry of Christian music that I have not experienced, and again it is out of this experience that I have written.

Robert Johnson and Jesus

On November 27, 1936, blues musician Robert Johnson recorded his now famous song "Cross Road Blues." Blues lore has it that the lyric of the song describes Johnson's encounter with the devil at a country crossroads early one evening deep in the Mississippi delta. According to blues historian Robert Palmer, "The crossroads is the place where aspiring musicians strike their deal with the devil, and Robert [Johnson] claimed to have struck such a deal."[1]

In chapter 4 of the book of Matthew we read about Jesus at a crossroads. The devil comes to him while he is fasting in the desert. The Scriptures tell us that Satan led Jesus up to a mountaintop and showed him all the kingdoms of the world in all their splendor. Then the devil offered to strike a deal with him, saying, "All this I will give you if you will bow down and worship me." Jesus refused, saying, "Away from me, Satan! For it is written 'Worship the Lord your God and serve him only'" (Matt. 4:8–10).

As it was for Robert Johnson and Jesus, so it is for the men and women of CCM. The crossroads is always about choosing between the kingdoms of the world and the kingdom of God. For CCM it's also about choosing between subjective ideas having to do with music, the church and the culture, and God's objective kingdom ideas concerning these same things. Positively speaking, the crossroads represents the opportunity for CCM to begin to approach music, ministry, and *yes,* industry, in a far more comprehensive and faithful manner.

While there are Christians who believe that CCM is controlled by the devil and his evil spirits, I for one do not. I know of no CCM legend, lore, or otherwise which tells the story of a contemporary Christian musician who sold his soul to the devil for talent, or fame, or fortune. What I do know is that all human endeavor is problematic, and no Christian enterprise is beyond the stain of sin. Are there problems we need to address at this crossroads? Yes, there are many, and this book addresses them head-on. "Too often," David Wells asserts, "the quest for answers is driven by impatience, by a refusal to do the hard work in taking the measure of the problem first."[2] Not so with this book.

Please note that I'm aware that for every problem and example of poor stewardship of talent and resources, remarkable exceptions do exist, and for these faithful exceptions I'm grateful. Perhaps you're one of them. With this admission in mind, I kindly ask that as you read this book please look past my use of generalizations to the very real problems these generalizations seek to expose. Truthfully, I've desired to write as a peacemaker and not a troublemaker. A peacemaker reconciles people to the gospel and the kingdom of God, and it is fidelity to the gospel and the kingdom that drives both book and writer. My mission is to stress the truths of Scripture. It isn't to dress down people who have erred or with whom I am not in agreement. Borrowing words from Eugene Peterson, I pray that my writing will reveal me, not as a *bystander criticizing or a turncoat propagandizing, but rather, as an insider agonizing.*[3] As it has been said, "He has the right to criticize who has the heart to help." I have the heart to help.

The Purpose of This Book

This could easily have been a book about the tremendous good that's come of CCM, a volume jam-packed with testimonies from artists, audience, and industry. But such a book, I believe, would have been premature and arguably less helpful. Despite what some critics report, significant good has come of CCM, and God has received glory and honor and praise as a result. Even so, I still cannot stress too strongly that the mission of this particular book is *not* to tell the history of CCM or to testify to the good, necessarily. Instead, the primary mission of this book is to explain the need for repentance, rethinking, and reimagining in spite of evidence of jewels scattered among the dross.

The purpose of this book is to isolate from CCM's historical beginnings those theologies and ideologies which have shaped and influenced artists, industry, and audience demonstrably more than all others. Once isolated, the aim of the book is to reveal how these powerful and enduring ideas have essentially formed an ad hoc philosophy of Christian music, informing and defining CCM artistry, industry, and audience from the beginning to the present. Throughout the book I try respectfully and lovingly to critique these notions, making clear that these foundational theologies, philosophies, and ideologies do not sufficiently reflect a comprehensive kingdom perspective or the whole story of the Christian mission—a perspective and mission from which the CCM community is in no way exempt, and which it must in fact embrace. In the context of this book a *comprehensive kingdom perspective* is mentioned often, as is the *Christian mission*. While both of these will be explored in detail later, a *comprehensive kingdom perspective* is a perspective which sees life as God sees it (as much as is humanly possible). It is a phrase very much akin to *biblical worldview*—a way of thinking about life and the world that is informed by the Scripture. The *Christian mission* denotes those activities which God has called his people to, specifically, spreading the gospel, loving our neighbors, acts of mercy, and managing the creation he left us in charge of.

It is my opinion that CCM's foundational ideas, the ones that started it and still fuel much of it today, do not accurately reflect a comprehensive kingdom perspective or the Christian mission. I believe that CCM's foundational ideas are insufficient and incomplete and, as such, fail to provide the participants of CCM with a sufficient theological or ideological foundation from which to create music, ministry, and industry. In the course of the book I will offer a counter-philosophy built on what I believe is a stronger foundation.

There is undeniable zeal and love for Christ in those of us who make up the CCM community. To me this is beyond debate. Unfortunately, as I hope to make clear, our methods cannot and will not withstand critical examination. Though our intentions are often exemplary, our methods and undergirding ideologies are insufficient. Our lack of a sufficient foundation works against us, keeping us from living out the purposes of those who are called by God. My desire is to remind us of what we are called to do and who we are called by.

The purpose of my analysis and assessment of the theology and ideology behind CCM is not to engage in the unproductive throwing of stones, or even to emphasize successful choices worthy of repeating. It is, instead, to accurately identify exactly where we are in order to recognize which direction is, in fact, *forward*. This is important, helpful information to have when you're standing at the crossroads.

My hope is that this kind of in-depth analysis will give those of us who still haven't found what we're looking for regarding the intersection of Christian faith, music, and the music business, the necessary ammunition with which to battle the apathy, complacency, and unwanted conformity common to all human organizational systems. Like most organizational systems, CCM promotes conformity. Some conformity and bias is built into the system and necessary to its survival. Good conformity within a system produces an ordered and stable environment where good can flourish. For example, conforming to many of the conventions of business helps one to stay in business and to make a profit. The Sparrow Label Group, the company I work with most, has been very profitable. As a result, they've been able to fund many good causes through The Sparrow Foundation. In their case, conformity to good business practice resulted in a profit, profit which is now used in part to contribute to the good of others.

There is, however, another kind of conformity which is not good. It is the type of conformity which is born of fear and lack of faith in God. This kind of conformity produces legalism, performance-based acceptability, and stunted, uninspired imaginations. It is a conformity that breeds apathy and complacency. Wherever there is an abundance of this type of conformity, there is little chance for diverse, faithful, and imaginative business, music and ministry. Unfortunately, CCM possesses this type of conformity as well.

Creation conforms to certain norms and conventions, yet does so without taking away from its astonishing diversity. Conformity to some standard is what creates the foundation for imaginative growth. Conformity which cultivates more conformity, season after season, is anti-human, anti-creation, and ultimately, anti-kingdom. Regarding conformity, the CCM community would do well to take its cues from God's creation. There are reasons why it does not, chief among them division, lack of unity, and an arrogant disrespect for diversity.

CCM and the Mothership Connection

CCM mirrors the mothership of evangelicalism from which it was launched some thirty years ago. Like evangelicalism, CCM is a fragmented lot composed of special interest groups. In CCM these groups center around either individual artists or groups of artists which share a common focus. Each special interest group is fueled by a particular theological/ideological bias or denominational/non-denominational tie which affects its thinking and its appeal. Some of these special interest groups are acting out of obedience to the doctrine of the body of Christ. They know and understand that they are set apart to do a unique work specific to their calling. Because of this, they respect those who've been called to something altogether different from them. They work in loving cooperation with their brothers and sisters and do not tear down their different but still equally important work. Unfortunately, other special interest groups are not so healthy. Some groups believe that they alone model the way authentic contemporary Christian music ought to be done. Often, the ideas and positions held by these groups are reinforced not so much by a kingdom perspective or a biblical way of thinking, as by the vote of the Christian at the cash register, the ticket counter, and unfortunately, even the altar. In other words, the more positive votes a special interest group like this can acquire, the more justified they feel in taking the position they do regarding Christian music. Even though this kind of market-driven view of success produces a certain arrogance, a lack of votes is no guarantee of humility. Some special-interest groups rationalize the failure to secure support for their position and methods by maintaining that their particular spin on Christian music is so right and powerful that the enemy is fighting to keep it from the people.

The presence of this type of separatist, uncharitable position within the larger CCM community diligently works against achieving anything other than the most narrow consensus as to what Christian music is. Instead of an ocean of possibilities we are often left with islands of conformity, and as a result we miss vital opportunities to be God's people carrying out God's mission for the purpose of his kingdom. As I hope to make clear, neither a positive nor negative reception of our ideas and methods concerning music represents the starting place for thinking about music in light of the gospel and the kingdom of God. Our agendas for music must be informed by God's perspective. Only by conforming to the image of the Son will we have the eyes to see the diverse purposes music created by Christians can and should have.

Living Under the Truth Requirement

My intent is to inspire and to stir within you a desire for the truth in all things, not necessarily to convert you to my point of view. Along the way, if you do become convinced that a position I've taken is truthful, then choose it freely, as one who *is* convinced, not coerced. Above all, seek the truth and settle for nothing less. Live in the glorious freedom of what Os Guinness has referred to as Christianity's *truth requirement*. The world's way of thinking does not include this requirement. On the contrary, the world accepts as true that which feels right, or that which works or gets the job done. In the world's way of thinking, subjectivism and pragmatism replace the truth requirement of Christianity. Christians who live under the truth requirement live in the light of objective truth, where feelings and methods get checked against the brightness of God's Word. Checking our feelings and methods against the sure Word of God is a full-time activity for Christians who are serious about taking hold of the life which is truly the kingdom life. This is, in fact, an activity which defines us. Consider J. I. Packer's words:

"What is a Christian? . . . he is a man who acknowledges and lives under the word of God. He submits without reserve to the word of God written in 'the Scripture of truth' (Dan. 10:21), believing the teaching, trusting the promises, following the commands."[4]

On Problems and Solutions

For many readers, I suspect this book will provide a whole new way of looking at Christian music, and beyond that, to life generally. Though it's necessary to face the problems head-on, this book is also about proposing solutions. In addition to listening to and analyzing the critical and exuberant voices within our community, I endeavor to offer solutions to the problems which the voices have brought to our attention. Second, I offer solutions to problems which are, frankly, seldom identified as problems in CCM. Last of all, I offer my own ideas about the future direction of a community at the crossroads.

For some readers, the problems I address will simply articulate what they have always suspected, but may not have put into words. My hope is that the solutions I've proposed will for many closely represent their own good dreams for CCM, or at least offer a starting place from which we can rethink and reimagine Christian music together. Still, others may be disappointed to find that the problems they perceive to be the most critical and the solutions they thought obvious have been played down or are missing altogether. This is the inevitable outcome of writing a book which is not meant to be an exhaustive study of its subject.

Defining True Need

Throughout the book you will notice that I emphasize the need to:

1. Recover a comprehensive knowledge of God's Word to the end that we know and understand God's thoughts about himself as well as God's thoughts about his creation, his kingdom at hand, and his kingdom coming.
2. Renew our love for God and begin to live in response to his grace in every sphere of existence from prayer and praise to music-making and marketing.
3. Recover the Christian mission as defined as:
   (a) Evangelism and discipleship, as in proclaiming the gospel of grace through word and deed to the end that unbelievers are converted to Christ, and that believers are taught to obey the Word of God (Matt. 28:19–20; Luke 24:46–48).
   (b) Love for one's neighbor demonstrated by servant acts of kindness and mercy (Mark 12:31).
   (c) Fulfillment of the divine calling to care for God's creation as his sole representatives and image bearers (Gen. 1:28, Ps. 8:6–8).
4. Cultivate a comprehensive kingdom perspective—God's people, in God's place, under God's rule—and make life choices based on this perspective.

The Price of Repentance, Rethinking, and Reimagining

The future direction of Christian music is in the hands of the people who decide for it—the artists, the industry leaders, and the audience. For some, the crossroads will be a time of assessment, repentance, and renewed dedication to God's kingdom purposes. For others it will be a time of scrambling, positioning, and dealmaking. The direction we decide to take at the crossroads, today or in days to come, will ultimately be determined by what we understand our calling to be and what we know and understand of God's kingdom.

Initially, the idea of repentance, of rethinking, and of reimagining CCM could garner tremendous support from artists, industry and audience. Yet because CCM is now so fragmented (less and less consensus as to its mission) and so individualistic (less and less sense of the body of Christ working together), we should expect the idea to lose its appeal when it affects personal and corporate financial scenarios, or challenges deeply held presuppositions about the purpose and work of CCM. Even if your own study of the Scripture does prove to you that problems are authentic and change is needed, fear of others and the love of money and self can easily steal the desire to embrace the solutions and future direction this book advocates. Only a love for God and a fearful reverence of him can empower any of us to respond to the Spirit with an authentic desire to let go of our fears, our worldliness, and our pride.

Conclusion

I have been thinking about the subject of Christian music since 1982. You now hold in your hands my sincerest and most heartfelt thoughts on the subject of contemporary Christian music after sixteen years of serving God and my community as a musician. I have prayed to write with grace, charity, and an overriding concern and love for others. Where I have missed the mark, I humbly ask my reader's forgiveness.

For some readers, tackling this book will represent a first effort at really thinking this subject through. Don't be afraid to take it in bite-sized chunks or to skip around. Since this book delivers a dual theological message, one for life and simultaneously one for Christian music, I would imagine readers returning to this book and to various chapters (paragraphs even) at different seasons of life. Use this book for good.

I'm aware that much of this book is very philosophical. It's not a tell-all exposé of Christian music and it's not a "how-to." It's a book which is meant to encourage faithful responses to the grace of God. Whether good comes of this book through your reading one chapter or the whole book does not concern me. May good come. That's what matters.

It is doubtful that this book represents my last thoughts on the subject of Christianity and music. I fully expect God to continue to renew my mind and shape my thinking on this important topic. This being so, it is likely that I will return to this topic again and again. And when I do, I trust I will return having been gently corrected by the Spirit, and my brothers and sisters in Christ, for any errors I commit in this, my first go-around.

Chapter I

Voices at the Crossroads

Christian music has enjoyed unprecedented popularity and success in the 1990s. Total sales of popular Christian music in 1996 reached a new high of $538 million (33 million units). In 1997 sales were up again with 44 million units sold—a 30% increase from the year before.

In 1997, Christian singer and songwriter Bob Carlisle had the top-selling recording in America—not the number one Christian CD but the number one CD period. "Butterfly Kisses" became a smash hit on adult contemporary radio stations, driving album sales to more than three million units. At one point the recording was outselling its nearest competitor, the Spice Girls, by 50,000 copies per week. Amy Grant, dc Talk, Jars of Clay, Kirk Franklin, and other

Christian artists have seen similar success in the mainstream market, and the trend continues.

Given this kind of success, what is there to imply that contemporary Christian music is at a crossroads?

The problem isn't concert attendance or cash flow—at least not yet. The problem is with the spiritual foundation of a musical form that is completely dependent on that foundation for artistic direction and ultimate commercial success. From modest beginnings in the 1960s, contemporary Christian music, or CCM, has grown exponentially both as a business and as a ministry. But today it stands on shaky ground. Artists, promoters, record companies, radio stations, and millions of listeners are deeply divided over the purpose of CCM, its mission, and even its exact musical definition.

As the Cheshire Cat told Alice in Wonderland, "When you don't know where you're going, any road will do." Until we lock onto a God-breathed direction for our music, we're stuck in the middle of the intersection tapping our feet. Spiritually, we're at the most important crossroads in the history of the industry.

A Din of Voices

Contemporary Christian music is filled with the sound of many voices offering opinions and shouting questions. Like the music of the church throughout the ages, CCM is subject to the criticism of the church and the culture. For many Christians, CCM is a blessing—a gift from God. For some, it's an embarrassment. Others have never heard of it. CCM fans, parents, teachers, cultural critics, pastors and priests, people eager to be a part of the CCM community, and gifted young artists committed to taking their music to an unbelieving culture—all are looking for answers.

Many simply want to know where Jesus fits in amidst all the show-biz buzz and hype. In response to this kind of questioning, record companies spend a good deal of time and money to assure listeners that Jesus *is* at the heart of the music and of the artists they promote.

Others argue that CCM is nothing but vapid Christian subculture clichés set to the beat of what they term "secular" culture. Often their mission is to redirect CCM lovers back to the riches of hymnody and to warn their listeners and readers that CCM is substandard and trivial. Others are even less charitable. For them CCM is nothing short of the devil's handiwork. As one Christian mother has said, "You will never convince me that this [CCM] is of the Lord."[1]

Which road leads to the truth?

Over the last few years, the CCM community has addressed key issues in various public forums to a greater extent than any time in its thirty-year history—issues such as the near-wholesale buyout of Christian record companies by mainstream corporations, and the debate over what makes one lyric "Christian" and another not. Questions are everywhere. Opinion is queen of the world. Competing voices of people within the church cry out, hoping to capture hearts and minds. Listen. Can you hear the voices of criticism saying in no uncertain terms that money, success, and business have become the only bottom line that CCM respects? Can you hear them say that evil spirits plague and control us and that we've all but abandoned Christ? Who and what are these voices? These are not imaginary voices. They are the voices of real people—people wanting to be heard.

What's That Sound?

The voices of criticism are those which simply cannot affirm CCM as it is presently constituted. Their criticism is meant to lead to greater faithfulness. Other voices say CCM has drifted so far from the shore of truth that it's time to abandon the cursed ship. Still other voices come from critics outside the church.

If we listen further we'll hear *voices of debate* wrestling with two ongoing issues that have defied resolution: the crossover debate over the present means by which CCM companies market their artists to the mainstream pop audience; and the lyric debate concerning the role of the lyric in contemporary Christian music. The fact that we've continued to debate these questions is a good sign. Debate allows us time to learn from one another, challenge each other, and test our own understanding against true understanding—the voice of God revealed in the Scriptures.

Finally, there are the *voices of success* trumpeting ministry faithfulness and the recent achievements of CCM, telling of awards and honors, arenas filled to capacity, souls saved and lives changed, Christian artists at the top of the pop charts, unprecedented market share, and much more.

Caught between the voices of criticism and the voices of success, it's no wonder we have so many questions. Before we can get to the truth, we have to get our hearts and minds wrapped around the ideas that shape the Christian music community and the issues that concern it. We must listen to the voices, and be prepared to rethink and reimagine our own image of Christian music.

Not Enough Songs Mention Jesus Anymore?

In April 1996, the board of directors from the WAY-FM Media Group Inc. placed a full-page ad in *CCM Magazine* titled "An Open Letter to the Christian Music Community." The letter focused largely on the importance and historical precedent of using CCM as a tool for "winning young people to Jesus and discipling them in their walk."

"Not enough songs mention Jesus anymore," observed the writers of the letter. "Has the 'J' word all of the sudden become non-hip, or have we found that 'you' or 'he' has more power?"

"Yes . . . we believe there is a place to address social issues and love between two people occasionally. However, we hope that all of us involved in CCM will remember that our first priority is to be a lighthouse of truth in an ever increasing spiritual fog."

Live concerts gave WAY-FM reason for concern as well: "In our opinion, the gospel also has been diluted to some degree in live concerts. We have been disappointed in the last few years with some of the concerts our stations have promoted. In some instances, there has been little or no ministry throughout the entire event."

The letter closed with this request: "We are asking all of our friends in this 'industry' and the body of Christ at large, to pray for the songwriters, artists, managers, producers, labels and radio stations. Pray that we will experience a fresh anointing and that the message in our music will clearly and creatively communicate the gospel."

Evil Spirits Plague and Control CCM

In early 1997, Scott MacLeod, a musician associated with a "prophetic teaching, vision and worship" ministry, published a forty-six-page book titled *Snakes in the Lobby.* The book, mailed out free to many industry insiders, described in MacLeod's words, "a vision that I received and the interpretation that unfolded regarding it." MacLeod published the vision hoping that it would help those who "have been confused, disillusioned and wounded by the condition of what is now called the Christian music industry." According to MacLeod, "The vision was received while a small group of us were praying about this condition, and against the powers and principalities that have, and still do, control and manipulate much of what is called Christian music."

The lobby in MacLeod's title refers to the lobby of the Nashville hotel/convention center where the annual Gospel Music Association convention is held each April. MacLeod recalls his vision: "The people were busy talking and going on with their business (what is commonly called schmoozing), each one dressed up in appropriate music attire, when much to my astonishment and horror I saw what looked like a massive snake lying on the lobby floor." MacLeod described the lobby as "full of people who were busy 'lobbying' for position, power and their own agendas."

The snake, MacLeod says, represents "the powerful evil spirits that plague and control much of the Christian music industry and much of Christendom." The Snake Keepers are described as "the people who have been in power and have, knowingly or unknowingly, let the ways of the world enter into Christian music."

The Bottom Line: Money and Success

In November 1997, the People's Church of Salem, Oregon, announced its plans to terminate Jesus Northwest, the Christian music festival it had operated for the last twenty-one years. The announcement came in the form of a letter of repentance written by People's Church pastor and festival executive director, Rev. Randy Campbell. Seeking forgiveness, Campbell wrote: "We humbly repent before the Lord and ask the forgiveness of the body of Christ for inadequately representing Christ in our ministry, message, and methods."

While the letter clearly expressed responsibility for specific sins for which the People's Church claimed guilt, the letter also revealed that problems with CCM and others were contributing factors in the decision to terminate the festival: "Although the Lord is changing us, many problems still remain in the greater working of the contemporary Christian music industry, the Christian publishing industry, and independent ministries we have worked with over the years. These issues prevent us from being involved with the type of festival we've been providing. We feel that within these industries and ministries much of what is done (for example, ministry direction, decision-making methods, even the message itself) is often driven by marketing—not the mind of the Lord. It is driven by analyzing demographics, not His anointing, by audio/visual production, not His power or presence. Money, success and business have become the bottom line."

Reform and Return the Money

On October 31, 1997, veteran CCM recording artist Steve Camp, describing himself as "burdened and broken over the current state of CCM," released an essay in poster form accompanied by 107 theses entitled "A Call for Reformation in the Contemporary Christian Music Industry." Of all the voices of criticism, Camp's is arguably the most provocative. Along with studiously detailing CCM's shortcomings, Camp outlined specific steps he felt must be taken as well: "True revival is marked by repentance; true repentance brings restitution; true restitution demands that Christian music be owned and operated only by believers whose aim is the glory of God consistent with Biblical truth. *This means that the current CCMI (contemporary Christian music industry) labels must return all the money that they have received to their respective secular counterparts that purchased them and divorce alliances with them"* (emphasis mine).

To further illuminate his position, Camp explains in Thesis 86 that separating from the world does not mean avoiding the use of an unbeliever's services or skills:

"For instance, it is not unbiblical to consult non-Christian experts in matters of business, craft or trade . . . but we can never engage in intimate binding—indissoluble relationships, alliances or partnerships that result in shared responsibility or authority for ministry purposes" (Deut. 22:9–11; Phil. 2:14–15).

On the subject of music itself, Camp, citing 1 Chronicles 15:37, 42, takes a definitive position: "Music, by biblical definition, is a ministry." He concludes his essay by urging the reader to "come away from an industry that has all but abandoned Christ and forge, by God's grace, what it was always meant to be . . . a ministry. Pray on this. Pounding on Wittenberg's Door, let us come together to make history—to make Contemporary Christian Music . . . Christian again."

Debating the Lyric

On September 8, 1997, *CCM Update* published an article entitled "Album Lyrics Raise Questions: Lack of 'Christian' content complicates Dove Award eligibility, chart placement decisions." The article served to make public a number of issues the CCM community had struggled with since Amy Grant's 1991 recording, *Heart in Motion.* Chief among them was what makes one lyric "Christian" and another not, and when, if ever, does the work of a Christian artist cease to be categorized as "Christian"? Predictably, Amy Grant received prominent mention, beginning with the lead paragraph: "Amy Grant's new album *Behind the Eyes,* and others like it that don't necessarily reflect 'evangelical' lyric content, have spearheaded an industry discussion." The article also noted that the "Gospel Music Association (GMA) and Christian Music Trade Association (CMTA) have recently taken action to create new criteria and re-evaluate existing guidelines used to determine placement on sales charts and Dove Award eligibility."

Sales chart placement and Dove award eligibility are important and complex issues to many industry insiders, especially when mainstream artists are starting to find their way onto the CCM charts. Nevertheless, the issue for people like Rick Anderson, music buyer for Berean Christian Stores, is very simple: If there's no Christ, it's not Christian. Anderson appraised Grant's album *Behind the Eyes* by saying: "It's not a Christian album. A Christian album should be clear on the person of Christ and these lyrics are not." The directness of his statement illustrates the intensity of the lyric debate: People have strong opinions about what makes something Christian, especially when it comes to lyrics. As further example, consider that both the WAY-FM Network and the AIR 1 Radio Network declined to play Grant's single, "Takes a Little Time," citing a lack of "lyrical relevance" and failure to meet "lyrical criteria."

The GMA contacted a list of people "with diverse expertise and experience" in hopes of gathering various working definitions of *gospel music.*[2] Frank Breeden, GMA President, told *CCM Update:* "I have no prediction for the outcome. It could be anything from 'we can't arrive at a definition' all the way to 'here it is.'"[3]

In July of 1998 the GMA Board of Directors and the Dove Awards Committee approved the following definition:

"Gospel music is music in any style whose lyric is: substantially based upon historically orthodox Christian truth contained in or derived from the Holy Bible; and/or an expression of worship of God or praise for His works; and/or testimony of relationship with God through Christ; and/or obviously prompted and informed by a Christian world view."[4]

Release of this definition unleashed a new round of criticisms and concerns. A sincere effort to resolve the question only added more fuel to the debate.

Debating Crossover

The issue of whether the music of Christian artists should cross over into the mainstream, and by what means, continues to stir debate. In a *Billboard* guest editorial, Mark Joseph called the CCM industry "the modern-day equivalent of the Negro Leagues." If that's true, then like baseball's Jackie Robinson and Roy Campanella, there is a deserving new generation of CCM artists aptly described by Joseph as "artists of faith who refuse to be silenced or sidelined."[5]

Drummer David Carr of Atlanta rock band Third Day spelled out his band's desire to take their music outside the Christian community. "We want to see people who aren't gonna get the gospel anywhere else; they're not gonna go to a church . . . or to a Christian festival, or walk into a place where the gospel's getting preached. We want to see lives changed, lives that haven't come close to seeing God."[6]

Third Day, and other younger Christian artists who have tried or are presently trying to contribute to mainstream pop music (for example, Sixpence None the Richer, Sarah Masen, Jars of Clay, Flick, and MxPx) realize "lives that haven't come close to seeing God" are not generally found sitting next to them in church. These newer artists, in the same way as Amy Grant, dc Talk, Michael W. Smith, The 77's, Vigilantes of Love, Over the Rhine, and others before them, believe that reaching people with the gospel, with compelling music, with a conversation, or with anything that is simply good, requires taking it to them. While most Christian labels do some limited marketing of select artists to the mainstream community, it is neither their mission nor their priority, a stance to which *Billboard* columnist Deborah Evans Price takes exception. "I can't tell you how many interviews I've asked about mainstream plans for a particular artist or song and get the response that the company is 'exploring options,' and nothing ever happens."[7]

"It seems," says Matt Slocum of Sixpence None the Richer, "like the Christian community doesn't really understand what it means to go over into the mainstream and try to be a light in that market."[8]

Yet the leadership of Christian music *does* understand what it means to go over into the mainstream, even though it's not necessarily to "try to be a light." Music critic Tom Roland of *The Tennessean* reports that "Christian executives attribute much of the growth (in 1997) to increased exposure in mainstream outlets." According to Roland, "Nine of the year's Top 10 albums received exposure on mainstream radio."[9]

A Flood of Success

That leads us to the other side of the discussion. While some voices are those of woe and warning, others celebrate CCM's robust financial health and growing popularity. Publicity and promotional muscle have secured Christian artists major national media exposure through *The Wall Street Journal,* National Public Radio, *Time, USA Today, Live With Regis & Kathie Lee, Good Morning America, The Tonight Show with Jay Leno, ABC World News Tonight,* and others. Marketing to ancillary markets has also played an important role in CCM's success. For example, partnerships with record clubs Columbia House and BMG, and TV shopping programs such as QVC and the "Keep the Faith" infomercials have all proven profitable, increasing the consumer base of Christian music. God's Property with Kirk Franklin scored a big hit in 1997 with the single "Stomp," receiving radio play across the board as well as strong video exposure on BET and MTV.

Music publishing has done its part as well. The 1996 Grammy Award for Song of the Year went to three of Christian music's most gifted songwriters, Wayne Kirkpatrick, Tommy Sims, and Gordon Kennedy, for their song "Change the World," recorded by Eric Clapton for the *Phenomenon* movie soundtrack. The 1997 Grammy Award for Country Song of the Year was awarded to Bob Carlisle and Randy Thomas for "Butterfly Kisses." Through music licensing agreements and writing for specific feature films, songs by Christian artists have appeared in films such as *The Apostle, Speechless, Dr. Dolittle,* and *That Thing You Do,* on television's *Party of Five,* and even the Super Bowl telecast.

Live performances by Christian artists have had considerable impact as well. Christian concerts have become increasingly more professional and competitive with their mainstream counterparts. For sheer numbers alone, both Carman (Texas Stadium, 71,000 attended) and The Young Messiah tour (1.25 million attended over 18 dates in '95) have set remarkable attendance records. Moreover, Kirk Franklin, Amy Grant, dc Talk, Jars of Clay, The Newsboys, The Brooklyn Tabernacle Choir, Michael W. Smith, and Steven Curtis Chapman draw thousands of people a night to their concerts, selling out major venues from the Tacoma Dome to Madison Square Garden to the Hollywood Bowl. Jars of Clay racked up a remarkable 300 tour dates in 1996 alone.

A Million First Time Commitments

Finally, artists like Carman, Geoff Moore, Rebecca St. James, and NewSong continue in the tradition of Keith Green and Mylon LeFevre—they are musicians, but musicians who share the gospel from stage and who offer altar calls at their concerts. Some, like Carman, receive a large response. According to Carman Ministries Inc., headquartered in Nashville, from the inception of Carman's ministry to date, they have registered "a million first-time commitments" to Christ.

Conclusion

There are many voices eager to be heard in the CCM community—voices of criticism, debate, and success. Many other examples of representative voices could have been used. I chose these specific examples because I believe them to be definitive, in that the ideas contained within them define the general ideological climate of CCM. These are, I believe, the ideas which have influenced CCM from its beginning to the present. It is these ideas that I want us to hear, transcribe, analyze, and test for truthfulness, quality, and kingdom perspective.

Chapter 2

The Path of the Teachable Sinner

In 1981 I was a struggling twenty-four-year-old musician. I'd been married for six years and anesthetized for every single one with drugs and alcohol. All my attempts at being a spiritual person were failures. Zen seduced me but could not hold me. Neither could the Tao. Transcendental Meditation worked for a drummer friend but not for me. Dianetics?—merely interesting science fiction. Krishnamurti held me for a moment but only because Marc Johnson, the respected jazz bassist, had suggested him to me. Rudolph Steiner and anthroposophy turned out to be nothing more than a minor flirtation with something I couldn't even pronounce. And so it went.

At the beginning of year seven I entered a recovery program where I was encouraged to believe that a power greater than myself could restore me to sanity. Sanity, I came to realize, was the ability to think accurately and truthfully about the reality of life. I had not been thinking accurately or truthfully. I'd been following my feelings without checking them against the facts. The recovery program taught me a life-changing truth: feelings aren't always facts. Feelings need to be checked against facts. Somehow, in my first twenty-four years of life I'd failed to develop a fact checker for my feelings, and as a result, ended up with an unreal life composed of too little truth. This made it very difficult for me to live in the world.

The Really Great Sinners

Looking back over this strange and rocky period, I can point to the exact moment my sanity began to return. It was when I took what is known in recovery as a "fearless moral inventory." In a notebook I wrote an inventory of all the wrong I had done in my life (at least what I was conscious of at the time) and of all the people I had harmed in some way or another. It made me sick to my stomach. My life seemed to be an unbroken chain of miserably foolish choices, one after another, and I was reaping the full consequence of those choices. I read the notebook aloud to God and to a friend. God made no audible comment. The friend muttered, "That ain't nothing." But he was wrong. It *was* something. It was convincing evidence that something was wrong. I was humbled to find out that most of what was wrong began and ended with me. I had been thinking, speaking, living, and acting entirely for myself. It was time to repent, rethink, and reimagine life.

My notebook was instrumental in proving to me the biblical concept of sin. When I eventually heard the gospel I was undone, because I understood myself to be a sinner in need of a savior. In similar fashion, I have encountered all kinds of convincing evidence throughout my career that CCM is made up of true, false, insufficient, and glorious ideas—ideas that ought to be wholeheartedly affirmed and ones that demand immediate repentance. Yet this information will only be of real value to people who consider themselves sinners. Why? Because people who understand themselves to be sinful, yet forgiven image-bearers, are open to the possibility of having missed the mark in some way. *They are more afraid of not knowing the truth than having been found in error.* They regret naming anything false that is in reality true, or anything true that is in reality false. The really great sinners in the church are like that.

Ideas Have Consequences

If we remain humble and contrite, we will in turn remain teachable, and God certainly delights in the teachable sinner. If we want God in our midst, and I believe our community does, we'll have to admit our sin and helplessness. The self-sufficient, as I know from past experience, have no need of God. When correction comes with grace (and it will—count on it), we will not regret its arrival. Only a person who doesn't know God regrets being brought closer to him.

Years ago when an article in *The Times* of London proposed the question "What's Wrong with the World?" the late G. K. Chesterton, an extremely imaginative and teachable sinner replied, "I am. Yours truly, G. K. Chesterton."[1] Chesterton understood that all ideas have consequences, and that each individual human error, whether large or small, contributes to what's wrong with the world. This principle applies to the world of CCM as well.

Amnesiacs Traveling the Spiritual Map

I have a sense that many artists, industry people, and supporters of CCM are still traveling the spiritual map, searching for something more fantastic than the God of Scripture, all the while conducting their search in the name of the God which Scripture alone describes. I also have a sense that our musical community is suffering from a prolonged attack of amnesia. It has caused us to forget that we're sinners, and in turn we've thought too highly of ourselves. To forget that we're sinners is to forget how easily we can be fooled into feeling or thinking we're right about something, when in truth we are terribly wrong. Our amnesia has also caused us to forget that we're a people being renewed in the image of God, and as a result we've thought too lowly of ourselves. To forget this is to forget that we're called to be God's direct representatives on earth, a distinctive people deeply and inextricably connected to their Creator and his purposes.

Fortunately for us, the beauty of the body of Christ is that, when we do fall victim to amnesia, there are always a few brothers and sisters still in possession of their kingdom memory. This is good news. It means there's always someone to show us the way home. If I lose my memory tomorrow, if I forget who I am in Christ, I can count on someone to remind me. In this way the body of Christ is like the human body—given the presence of spiritual truth and love, time and nurture, it will often heal itself. This gives me tremendous hope for the troubles which plague the CCM community. Healing begins with the truth, whether it be blood cells acting true to their function, or the powerful truth of Scripture. When brothers and sisters do become lost and forgetful, we serve them best by lovingly telling them the truth about their condition. No glossing over is needed, just the truth in love.

Listen to the Voices

It's by listening to the voices of the people in and near our community that we'll find the ideas and issues that make up contemporary Christian music. These voices are singing hundreds of individual melodies, often all at once. As a result, there's as much *cacophony* as there is counterpoint. There are astonishingly glorious moments when many of the voices come together to create intricate unifying harmony. Yet, there's still too much dissonance, even for the most left-of-center listener. Granted, some of the dissonance is there because the composer put it there. He thought it would keep the composition interesting and its listeners awake. Most of it, though, is a result of voices either singing out of tune or singing the wrong notes altogether. By listening to the voices, we learn that the Christian music community is composed of wanted dissonance (unity in diversity), harmony (goodness, truth, and beauty), unwanted dissonance (strife and disunity), and unwanted harmony (choices which work to some degree, but are either unnecessary or misapplied).

Listen for the Truth

In my work as a record producer, one of my responsibilities is to oversee the recording budget. This means I pay all the bills that come in, such as invoices for musicians, studio time, and recording engineers. From time to time there's a problem. Something doesn't add up. Its usually up to me to analyze the accounting data, project files, and the record company's own in-house report to see where and why things don't add up. The fact that every choice is documented helps me get right to the business of analyzing all the invoices and checking them against the data entry reports.

On occasion the record company and I disagree about something having to do with the budget. Often the deciding factor is the thoroughness and accuracy of the data as well as the analysis of it. If a compromise is reached, it's the data and the analysis of it that help us come to an agreement.

Analyzing ideas and viewpoints about the present position and future direction of CCM works the same way. By carefully comparing the voices of criticism, debate, and success, we'll be able to find out where and why things don't add up. We'll find out why there's such a discrepancy between the voices of criticism and the voices of success. Most importantly we'll be able to see whether or not we are being good and responsible stewards of what God has entrusted to us.

This is not a matter for guesswork. If you build a life on assumptions, rather than what you can know for sure, you risk missing the only life worth living—a truth-informed life. It's one thing to guess while playing a board game, another to guess at life.

Christians do not, should not, surmise when it comes to living life. We're people in relentless pursuit of truth. And we're people who submit our ways of thinking to God's ways of thinking, in order that ours might be checked for untruths. Once we've considered the many voices in the CCM debate, once we've identified and extracted the core ideas, it's time to test those ideas for truthfulness. We first test them against God's Word and the testimony of his creation, then against the consensus of the saints in history. There is no other way. Our best guess, hunch or feeling, just will not do.

Truth Misapplied and Insufficient

Once all false ideas are rejected, we are left with true ideas that are then tested for quality. But aren't all true ideas quality ideas? No. For example, I might say to Mike, "You've got a quality idea there, friend." When I speak in this way, I communicate to Mike that his idea is good or excellent. Yet, if I say to Mike, "You've got a quality idea there, friend, but it won't work in this particular situation," what have I communicated? I hope I've communicated that I think his idea is good, but that it cannot be applied to the situation at hand, even though it's true. For this reason, one goal in the testing of ideas is to identify *misapplied truth.* Once identified, we can work towards replacing misapplied truth with the right truth for the right job, so to speak. This is the only way to make the best things happen.

Another essential goal is to identify *insufficient truth.* This is any truth which, when put into action, is by itself insufficient to help a person live in faithfulness to the whole of the Christian life. For example, 1 John 3:9 says, "No one who is born of God will continue to sin, because God's seed remains in him; he cannot go on sinning, because he has been born of God." This is true.

But we do sin, don't we? For a young Christian, unfamiliar with the Word, a verse like this taken by itself could be devastating. An obvious and honest response to this verse is to think that you might not be born of God after all.

Additional verses offer a more accurate and truthful picture, and we need to know them in order to avoid taking passages out of context and recklessly misapplying them. Listen to 1 John 1:9–10 and 2:1: "If we confess our sins, he is faithful and just to forgive us our sins and purify us from all unrighteousness. If we claim we have not sinned, we make him out to be a liar and his word has no place in our lives. My dear children, I write this to you so that you will not sin. But if anybody does sin, we have one who speaks to the Father in our defense—Jesus Christ, the Righteous One."

Now that's good news. And together these Scriptures form a complete description of the teaching. Together they are the full and sufficient truth, whereas the passage from 1 John 3 alone is true but insufficient. All of us involved with CCM, from the artist to the audience, should seek to bring the full and sufficient truth to bear upon the subject of music, ministry, entertainment, and business.

Created in God's Image

We've much to profit from by analyzing and testing the ideas contained within CCM. When we fail to build times of analysis and assessment (testing) into our lives, we fail to take up the tools of stewardship our Father so purposefully created in us. Like our Creator, we're made to imagine, create, analyze, and assess. We possess these abilities because we bear God's image. The catch with being human and not God is that we're just as apt to imagine and create a mess as we are a masterpiece. Often we don't know what we have until we make time to stand back, analyze, and assess it.

In analyzing and testing the ideas within CCM, we're taking a close look at the imagination and ideology of a community, our community—artists, industry, and audience. We are testing our choices to see if they're consistent with the voice of the Word. Secondly, we're testing our ideology to see if it is congruent with who we are in Jesus Christ. When our choices are consistent and congruent, we give God glory and we know true success. When they're not, we repent, which is a path to true success as well. Out of the joy of repentance comes Spirit-inspired rethinking and reimagining. If this leads to greater faithfulness, and it will, we will be thankful, even if it stings a little in the process.

Spirit, Come Flush the Lies Out

The Christian music community has existed without the full game plan of the kingdom of God for too long. Few people know and understand more than a few elementary plays in the play book. Football metaphors aside, we've emphasized mission without any consensus or understanding as to what a true comprehensive mission for music might be in light of the kingdom of God. The mission will not be clear or unified until we recover that which Packer defined for us earlier. We must live under the Word of God, submitting without reservation to its truth, "believing the teaching, trusting the promises, following the commands."

We dare not forget this in all our busyness and work for the Lord. To do so is to cut ourselves off from clear instructions for our mission—the full game plan. To cut ourselves off from the instruction of Scripture is, by default, to accept instruction from the father of lies. Such a choice is the choice of fools—not the clear-thinking, teachable sinners we desire to be.

Who will I be today, a fool or a teachable sinner? Who will you be? The shape and future of Christian music and its ability to contribute good and truth to the church and the world rests with our choices.

Spirit, come flush the lies out. Bring truth. Help us to repent, to rethink, and to choose well for the future. Help me, the neediest, most of all.

Chapter 3

The Source of the Truth

After we've heard the din of voices, after we've separated misapplied and insufficient truth from all the rest, after we've considered our own personal experience and feelings about contemporary Christian music, we come to the point where we have to decide on one direction or another. As I said before, this is no time for Christians to rely on guesswork. If we will turn humbly and with teachable hearts to God's Word and allow it to guide us, it will always lead us down the right road.

God's Creation Is Good

We begin with the understanding that everything created by God is very good. After creating, "God saw all that he had made, and it was very good" (Gen. 1:31). Our creational parents, Adam and

Eve, were created in such a way as to perfectly reflect their Creator, mirroring his image faithfully. They were fully functioning creative beings, in a perfect relationship of dependence upon God, thinking, speaking and creating only good all the time. That is, until the Fall.

The story of the Fall is the story of humanity's introduction to ideas which contradict the ideas of God. The source of these contradictory ideas is Satan, a fallen angel. He is the author of suspicion and so holds the power to make God's word suspect to the human. People continue to be deceived today. We believe Satan's lies and then turn and feed them to one another as Eve fed Adam the forbidden fruit. Sin has brought the curse of God on humankind. But God always preserves that which he loves, and loves what he has created. With the Fall, the Creator became the Redeemer. The history of redemption had begun.

In this New Covenant time in which we live, God is calling and equipping his adopted children (the church) to live with him and for him under the kingdom pattern of Eden once more, wherein *God's people are in God's place under God's rule.* Though we are not yet living in the fullness of the kingdom of God (the new heaven and new earth), we do have the "firstfruits of the Spirit" as the guarantee of our final redemption (Rom. 8:23). By grace through faith in Jesus, we've been saved from the penalty of sin. All Christians, including those who create, market, and enjoy CCM, have been called by God, and equipped by the Holy Spirit to live as God's people, in God's place, under God's rule, right now, in these, the in-between-times. To live as God's people, in God's place, under God's rule is both a present and future kingdom mission and reality.

The Kingdom Perspective

I'm highlighting this idea because I'm convinced that *a comprehensive kingdom perspective* will be of great help to the CCM community. To gain a kingdom perspective is to get at reality. It is to see things as God sees them, that is, as much as any human can. It is to get the story straight—to have a sufficient and accurate picture of God acting in history on behalf of that which he created. For pastor/author Scotty Smith, a kingdom perspective is seeing the kingdom of God as "the proper context for our knowledge and experience of the gospel of God's grace." To see the kingdom "is to be overwhelmed with awe and joy at the enormity and glory of God's dominion."[1]

A kingdom perspective is not a religious perspective. It is so much bigger than that. A kingdom perspective informs us and teaches us that privatized ideas about salvation, such as accepting Jesus as your personal Savior, are so incredibly small that they cannot begin to do justice to the re-creation and transformation of humankind and creation that God has initiated in Christ. As Scotty Smith enthusiastically states, "Forgiveness is not the end, it's the beginning!"[2] In Adam we died, but in Christ we are made alive again, and "just as we have borne the likeness of the earthly man, so shall we bear the likeness of the man from heaven" (1 Cor. 15:49). We are at the beginning again. For we "are being transformed into his likeness with ever-increasing glory, which comes from the Lord, who is the Spirit" (2 Cor. 3:18). The new is here, and the old is passing away. The image of God in humankind is being renewed, and God's people are once again called to be in God's place under God's rule. This is the kingdom perspective which I believe the CCM community must come to embrace.

The Church

As significant as the church is to us, it should not be confused with the kingdom. Christians, who make up the church, are subjects in God's kingdom. The kingdom itself is something far more vast than the church. It is a huge reality composed of God's dominion. The church is a community of humbled worshipers who know through grace the object of true and ultimate worship—God the Father, God the Son, and God the Holy Spirit. Contrary to some notions, the church is not comprised of those who escape the real world to fuel up on an hour of worship in order to reenter real life. Instead, it consists of those who begin with the idea that true worship is real life, a life of doxology in which God is exalted, glorified, and proclaimed in the sanctuary and in every sphere of existence. The church is not meant to be a retreat from culture, but is instead called by God to shape it by virtue of its distinctiveness—its saltiness, its brightness.

Our day of worship is meant to frame and inform the intensity of vision for the thinking, speaking, living and acting we will do the rest of the week.

The Calling

Disciples of Jesus are, as Os Guinness so succinctly puts it, called by him, to him, and for him.[3] This is our primary calling. We have

returned to the kingdom pattern of Eden. We are God's people again and, as such, are called to live for him under his rule. We do his work, in his way, in his time.

We've been appointed by King Jesus to carry out a kingdom mission of bearing witness to him and to his kingdom. Guinness defines this mission as "everyone, everywhere, and in everything" thinking, speaking, living, and acting "entirely for him."[4] This kingdom mission is our secondary calling. Here again you can see a return to the kingdom pattern of Eden. We are called to be God's people in God's place, which is no longer the garden, but now defined as everywhere and in everything. This is the calling to be salt and light in every sphere of existence from the church to the boardroom. These two concepts: God's people, in God's place, under God's rule, and everyone, everywhere, and in everything, accurately reflect a comprehensive kingdom perspective of calling and mission.

If the CCM community is composed of Christians who truthfully desire to live in response to God's calling, then we must see ourselves as subjects in God's kingdom. We must see ourselves as one among many communities of Christian enterprise, thinking, speaking, living, and acting entirely for Jesus. The contemporary Christian music community is not just a group of individuals who listen to CCM, who earn money from it in some way, and who claim a personal relationship with Jesus Christ. This is far too weak a description. Like the church, the CCM community is made up of people whom God has chosen and grafted together as a new humanity. They are a part of the body of Christ of which Christ is the head. The members of the body of Christ are dependent on Jesus and on one another.

Before we can hope to tell good and true stories through music, which is our secondary calling, we must first acknowledge and live in light of our primary calling as followers of Christ. It is foolish and dangerous to reverse the order. For example, I have several callings in my life. I'm called to be a son, a husband, a father, and a friend. I'm also called to write music and produce recordings. As important as each of these are, they must be seen in the light of my primary calling as a disciple of Jesus. Remember, I've been called by him, to him, and for him. Everything else in my life is meant to be lived out in response to this central truth. The truth that Christians have a primary calling by God, to God, and for God is the starting place for thinking about all secondary callings, including contemporary Christian music.

Secondary Callings

A secondary calling is a God-appointed calling. God has given us meaningful secondary callings through which we can use our imaginations, express our creativity, and mirror his holiness. Here, calling is connected to the biblical idea of dominion or ruling. Like God, whose eternal kingdom is his reign, realm, authority, and dominion, humankind has been given dominion over the earth. Dominion, introduced in Genesis 1:26–27, should not be confused with negative images of dominating. Rather, it is the God-given role of ruling over creation by caring for it and developing it. Don't think small, though. Caring and developing God's creative work is a vast undertaking—it is as comprehensive an undertaking as the word can withstand. It includes everything from procreation to composing music to proclaiming the gospel.

In giving humankind dominion, God appointed us governors over creation. As with any high office, there is accountability and responsibility which comes with the position. Humans are accountable to the Sovereign for the way they govern. God has equipped us to rule with love and wisdom, and we are not permitted to exploit creation for selfish purposes. To be anything but careful with what God has made is to mishandle his creativity. To mishandle his creativity is to misunderstand the seriousness of our role as his representatives on earth. Everything that has and will continue to develop out of this stewardship role must be seen in light of our primary calling. Everywhere we go and in everything we do, we should purpose to live by the truth that we are called by him, to him, and for him. We are not called by ourselves, to ourselves, and for ourselves. This describes the old way of self-perspective and not the new way of kingdom perspective.

Full-time Christians

The importance of a person's calling is not determined by whether or not it resembles full-time Christian service. As Elton Trueblood wisely pointed out years ago, "It is a gross error to suppose that the Christian cause goes forth solely or chiefly on weekends."[5] In reality all Christians are in full-time Christian service. A few callings, primarily those of pastors and missionaries, have defined this phrase for us and, as a result, have limited the impact of God's people everywhere and in everything and have led to confusion over the idea of ministry. The church in general, and the people of CCM specifically, must commit to restoring the idea that all secondary callings are important and that they all have the potential to minister or to serve. We cannot afford to relax our grip on this truth. To do so is to invite a double-life view in which callings are divided into the sacred and the secular. The danger with this kind of dualism, says Os Guinness, is that it narrows "the sphere of calling." Instead of everyone, everywhere, and in everything, you quickly end up with a few people, in a few places, doing a few things entirely for God.

Any teaching which narrows the scope and sphere of calling by promoting certain ones as more important, more spiritual, or more pleasing to God than others must be dismissed outright. The scope and sphere of calling is vast and never narrow. It is *comprehensive* in its service to the saints and the watching world. This is a truth which many musicians within the CCM community understand. Unfortunately, they are outnumbered by those who advocate a much narrower view of calling when it comes to music.

Dan Haseltine of Jars of Clay believes his band's portion of this vast calling (as it pertains to music and lyric) is to "prepare people to hear the Word of God, to start down the path of thinking about eternal things."[6] The members of Jars of Clay do not, however, advocate this for everyone and are in full support of musicians who directly proclaim the gospel from stage. Charlie Lowell, keyboardist for the band, puts it this way: "Some seem to have a view of the body of Christ as this head and twenty-eight arms. We see it as different kinds of people with various gifts, doing different services, having different careers, and using their specific gifts differently. We wish the church would be open to this and encouraging of it, instead of questioning it or trying to redefine it."[7] One Christian who isn't trying to redefine it is Russ Lee of NewSong. "Music is a vehicle that we use to share the gospel of Jesus Christ, but we don't hang that sign on another brother's or sister's neck. They don't have to do what we do if they are not called to it. We take [music] into the church and use it as a tool . . . but we're probably much more broadminded than those who say that that's all music should and can do."[8]

Our mission should be to faithfully answer to our own calling and not tear down the callings of others. In this way Jars of Clay and NewSong have modeled for us a kingdom perspective. Faithfulness to individual callings while keeping our primary calling—being followers of Christ—in focus is the starting place for cultivating a comprehensive kingdom perspective of ministry and music.

God Inspires Those Who Serve Him

At some point early on in my artistic development, I realized that while I was indeed responsible for my talent, I had not created it. Neither had I invented the raw elements which make up music. I know now that they have their origin in God, but I still can't get in front of them. I can only get behind them. And it's from this position that I imagine, create, and produce the music that I do. I cannot claim to have created the idea of melody and rhythm, but I can be creative in the sense that after I've finished writing and recording a song, there is something of truth and of beauty and of good use in the world that would not have existed apart from my creating it. This truth was never more clear to me than when my wife and I traveled to Venice years ago.

In the Basilica of the Frari, Venice, Italy, there are one hundred and twenty-four elaborate, wood-carved choir stalls—all created by the Cozzi family, wood carvers of Vicenza. The choir stalls are stunning and even more remarkable when you find that it took several decades and several generations of Cozzis to complete them. The family, young and old, worked together to bring something of beauty *and* use into a fallen world. Who but God could inspire people to make such a radical commitment? Only people who are called by him, to him and for him make these kinds of radical choices. Perhaps Psalm 90:17 was a verse they prayed, meditated on and sang while they carved and polished to God's glory.

> And let the beauty of the LORD our God be upon us,
> And establish the work of our hands for us;
> Yes, establish the work of our hands.

If we desire to think, speak, live, and act entirely for him "everywhere, and in everything," then our secondary calling must remain intertwined with our primary calling. We are first called to him, to his presence. The psalmist asks that the presence of God be upon the people of God. He asks for something of God's quality and character to begin the work, to establish it, to be its starting place. The psalmist understands that it is God who inspires the work of hands that serve him *and* that it is God who has the power to give the work eternal significance.

When I think of the Cozzi family spending decades carving the choir lofts in the Basilica of the Frari, I think of people whose calling speaks of the presence and beauty of God. How else could this beautiful and useful art have come to be except with the power and presence of God? How much of contemporary Christian music elicits this kind of response? I would guess very little. Phil Keaggy's guitar playing perhaps. Still, shouldn't there be more? Living in response to our calling is the key. In response to God's grace, we ought to be more and more thinking, speaking, living, and acting entirely for him. In order to do this, though, we will have to begin to think of life in terms of our primary and secondary callings, rather than what we do for a living, or what our jobs or professions are.

By placing all of our thinking, speaking, and doing under the banner of calling, all of life is infused with true meaning and purpose. Life becomes something far bigger than our own personal happiness and survival. A kingdom calling also inspires an integrated life and works against the disease of dualism and compartmentalization. The banner of kingdom calling is huge. It includes, says Ken Meyers, "not just a person's occupation from 9 to 5, but also his or her role as a spouse, parent, citizen, and neighbor—in short, the whole of one's identity under God."[9]

The Called One

John Henry Newman had this to say about his own calling: "God has created me to do Him some definite service; He has committed some work to me which He has not committed to another. I have my mission. Therefore I will trust Him. Whatever, wherever I am, I can never be thrown away. If I am in sickness, my sickness may serve Him; in perplexity, my perplexity may serve Him; if I am in sorrow, my sorrow may serve Him. My sickness, or perplexity, or sorrow may be necessary causes of some great end, which is quite beyond us. He does nothing in vain."[10]

This is the perspective God has called the artists, industry, and audience of contemporary Christian music to take. The kingdom perspective of a called one is fueled by faith freely expressing itself through love in response to the grace of God.

Faithfulness to one's calling is ultimately the only true measure of success. By your faithfulness you will change people and creation according to God's plan. Write these words on your heart:

"So do not throw away your confidence; it will be richly rewarded. You need to persevere so that when you have done the will of God, you will receive what he has promised. For in just a very little while, 'He who is coming will come and will not delay. But my righteous one will live by faith. And if he shrinks back, I will not be pleased with him.' But we are not of those who shrink back and are destroyed, but of those who believe and are saved" (Heb. 10:35–39).

Set Free to Start at Good

One reason for respecting a life lived by faith is the freedom that comes with not having to have every choice you make produce an immediate tangible result. The result may not even be seen in your lifetime. Faith in God and his will for our lives frees us from faith in man and the lie of pragmatism. Oh, how our community needs this! Oh, how I need it. Instead of living as people pleasers, we can live for God in response to his grace and love. Instead of living under the lie of pragmatism, thinking that whatever works must be good, we are a people set free to start at good, and whether good choices cause us to fail or succeed by the world's standards of success is of no importance.

May God give us present and future grace to live as his called people, everywhere and in everything, under the banner of his kingdom and to his glory.

Sin at the Crossroads

How do we begin to understand accusations of sin in the CCM camp? At this crossroad between claims of unprecedented success and faithfulness, and claims of unprecedented failure and disunity, there are fixed ideas under which we can proceed. No enterprise in which Christians participate will be free from sin and error. This being true, there is one fact we can know for certain. Regardless of our genuine concerns that CCM may no longer be about winning young people to Jesus, or that demons control the Christian music industry, or that non-"Christian" music is at the top of the CCM charts, or that Christian music is at the top of the pop charts, or that money and success have become the bottom line, or whatever the problem might be, one thing remains absolutely constant: the truth of God's Word, and its timeless ability to sufficiently explain our past, present, and future struggles.

The book of Hebrews speaks of our struggle against sin (Heb. 12:10). The book of Galatians tells us that "the Scripture declares that the whole world is a prisoner of sin" (Gal. 3:22), and Romans reminds us "there is no one righteous, not even one" (Rom. 3:10). And in case we've forgotten, there is 1 John 1:8, "If we claim to be without sin, we deceive ourselves and the truth is not in us."

Some members of the CCM industry have taken a heroic stance when convicted they acted in error. Let's look at one of our representative

voices, the executive director of the Jesus Northwest Festival, who wrote regarding the closing of the festival: "Although the Lord is changing us, many problems still remain in the greater working of the contemporary Christian music industry, the Christian publishing industry, and independent ministries we have worked with over the years." He went on to ask forgiveness of the body of Christ for providing "a ministry that has been a blessing to some but for others has opened a door to commercialism, focus on man and not on Christ and appealed to the flesh more than the spirit."

Though their public act of contrition is to be respected and admired, the idea that the Lord is changing the people who comprise the ministry of Jesus Northwest, but letting the sin problems of other Christians remain unchecked and unchanged, is an idea without merit. We may not like where other people are in the process of sanctification, but if they indeed belong to Christ, you can be assured that sanctification is taking place. It's important to remember that sanctification is an ongoing process. It is true that Christians cooperate with the process, but nevertheless they remain God-dependent at all times in the process. You can be assured that God is committed to changing every human being who has trusted in Jesus Christ for the forgiveness of his or her sin. Amazingly enough, he's changing people whom I don't like and whom I disagree with! There will always be sin problems in CCM as long as there are people in CCM, myself included. This admission should not be confused as a license to sin. It is an acceptance of our present kingdom reality—not the kingdom coming, but the kingdom at hand.

Is anyone really surprised that sin, error, misplaced priorities, confusion, and disunity can be found in CCM? If we're to be surprised about anything, it ought to be that there is still grace for people with such short memories. How quickly we forget the gospel and what necessitated it.

Speaking the Truth in Love

Are we not to put off falsehood and to speak the truth to one another in love? Are we not to speak only what is helpful for building others up according to their needs, that it might benefit those who listen? Are we not to rid ourselves of all bitterness, rage and anger, brawling and slander, along with every form of malice? Yes, yes, yes. But this is difficult stuff. It's hard to tell a brother or sister in Christ that they've sinned. And it's hard to accept someone pointing out our own transgressions. Well, relationship is messy. For that matter, the kingdom life at hand is extremely messy.

Christians are not spiritual free agents. They are called by God, to God, and for God. For this reason we must take accusations of spiritual unfaithfulness and visions of partnering with the devil very seriously. And, we must take accusations of having sinned against brothers and sisters as serious cause for self-examination and repentance.

None of us can afford to blow off our critics. We cannot avoid entering the debates or speaking the truth in love. And we don't dare become too impressed with ourselves and our symbols of success. All accusations of sin, conflicts, criticisms, and debates ought to cause us to cry out to God, begging him to examine our motives and expose our self-deception. This is not, however, to say that ideas shouldn't be debated, prophecies tested, or accusations challenged. Don't be afraid to hear the sound of your voice answering these accusing voices. Part of taking them seriously is debating, testing, and challenging them when necessary. It also means treating any person, and especially a fellow believer who takes issue with you personally or with CCM in general, with the dignity and respect due to a fellow image-bearer of God. Pray to speak or write in such a way that love for God, his truth, and his church outweighs self-interest and wrong motives. Mocking, despising and ridiculing belong to someone other than Christ. Reject them.

A Huge Story

It is my belief that the Christian music community must come to understand that the significance, and ultimately the quality of the work we do and the lives we live, will be determined by our understanding of the biblical story that is our legacy, and the kingdom story of which we are a part today. It is a huge story. It is not a small story about the American church. Neither is it a small story about the importance of contemporary Christian music. The story given to us to live out is the only good and true story worth living: to be God's man or woman in God's place under God's rule. It is to live for God everywhere and in everything. There are no small roles in this story. We cannot and must not put borders around it. The question is, will we, the artists, the industry, and the audience of CCM enter into the story with faith and imagination, with sufficient reverence and awe? Ten years ago my friend Margaret Becker sang these simple but essential words: "I commit." And so must we all.

Chapter 4

In the Beginning

Jesus himself said of the Sadducees two thousand years ago, "You are in error because you do not know the Scriptures or the power of God" (Matt. 22:29). The same can be said of us who labor in Christian music, as well as of those who buy it, listen to it, and champion it. We can trace the reasons for this back to the earliest stirrings of the CCM industry.

Contemporary Christian music was born of the Jesus movement of the late 60s and early 70s and was in fact originally known as "Jesus music." This revival among young people was by most accounts a tremendous sovereign work of God, a unique time of God calling out his children from among the massive tribe of youth, ranging from suburban young people to disenfranchised hippies. In a 1972 article in *U.S.*

News & World Report, Billy Graham declared it "by and large a genuine movement of the Spirit of God."[1]

Reflecting on the "street" element of the Jesus movement, social critic Ken Myers wrote, "The Jesus People were essentially Christian hippies, an unorganized assortment of relatively new believers who were adamant in their eagerness to construct their fellowship and worship according to the sensibility of the counterculture."[2]

U.S. News & World Report further expanded on this idea: "Many Jesus people—or Jesus freaks as they sometimes call themselves—once belonged to the youth revolt and a counterculture aimed at tearing down adult values. Today, they are emerging, disillusioned, from that experience. But they retain from the revolt's credo a passion for experience, not rationalism. Their biggest meetings often are held in large churches that offer them hospitality—but their suspicion of institutions extends to the institutional church."[3]

There was indeed a strong suspicion of institutions among many of the new converts. They sincerely believed that God was working in a new way through the Jesus movement and, as such, was not about to pour new wine into old wineskins. In this climate non-denominational fellowships flourished. These fellowships had a look and sound unlike any of the mainline denominations, or any Christian fellowship before them. Many of the young people who came to Christ during the Jesus movement eventually found their way back to mainline denominational fellowships, yet many more helped to establish the new, largely charismatic, non-denominational fellowships, including communes modeled after the life of Christians as recorded in the book of Acts (2:44). The well-known and respected Jesus People USA commune is still thriving today in downtown Chicago, though it is now affiliated with a denomination.

More than anything, the Jesus movement focused on these four elements:

(1) The imminent return of Jesus in the form of the Rapture.
(2) The worship of God using the contemporary instrumentation and style of the time.
(3) Evangelism, and the use of music in evangelism, especially evangelism targeted at youth.
(4) Charismatic renewal.

The Charismatic Influence on CCM

The Jesus movement and the charismatic renewal movement were deeply intertwined. Though not synonymous, the charismatic movement and the "street" element of the Jesus movement were for the most part an inseparable, synergistic pair. Thus the theological ideas common to the Jesus and charismatic movements were common to CCM's beginnings as well.

Within the non-denominational fellowships, two influential theological positions took root: (1) a renewed dependence and emphasis on the work of the Holy Spirit and the manifestation of the gifts of the Spirit, and (2) an eschatology (view of the end times) emphasizing the pretribulation rapture of the Church. The idea of the church being raptured, or suddenly taken out of the world by Christ, is directly related to 1 Thessalonians 4:16–17.

Survey Says: Same as It Ever Was

A survey of thirty-five popular CCM artists and groups taken in April of 1998 revealed that fellowship in a non-denominational setting is still very attractive to CCM artists. When asked, "What faith tradition best describes you?" twenty-five percent of those polled chose the term *non-denominational.* Another twenty-five percent chose the term *Baptist.* The next largest block, atypical of CCM's past, chose the term *Presbyterian* to describe their faith tradition. This shift is largely due to the number of popular Christian artists who attend the Presbyterian Church of America (PCA)-affiliated Christ Community Church in Franklin, Tennessee. The fact that twenty-five percent of the artists surveyed chose *non-denominational* as descriptive of their faith tradition is instructive in that it shows the continuing impact of the early suspicion of institutions. However, it does not directly substantiate a continuing charismatic influence. Only five percent of the artists polled aligned themselves with charismatic denominations such as Four Square or Assemblies of God, and no artists chose to describe their faith tradition as charismatic. This is not surprising to me though. For six years, starting in the early eighties, I attended two non-denominational charismatic churches. At neither one did we ever first refer to ourselves as charismatic. Our first impulse was to emphasize that we were *non-denominational.* We might have added the qualifying terms *born-again,* or *Spirit-filled.*

The Charismatic Influence: From Thinking to Feeling

Though the charismatic movement's renewal of the Spirit's role in the believer's life was positive in many ways, this emphasis had its downside. By emphasizing the work and gifts of the Holy Spirit, especially spontaneous revelational prophesying and speaking in tongues, the focus shifted from knowing God through His Word to knowing God through experience. This in turn shifted the focus from thinking to feeling, wherein for many believers their experience became as much the measure of truth as the sure Word of Truth. Subjective, private experiences—hunches, spontaneous prophecies, intuitions, visions, and hearing God speak inside one's head—were often given equal authority with Scripture, and in some cases more. For some Christians, the desire for charismatic experiences gradually eclipsed their desire to learn of God through the Bible. Charismatic experience came to be perceived as a more personal, tangible, and valuable encounter with God than the encounter which comes by reading and meditating over the Spirit-inspired Scriptures. The fallout from this view of life in the Spirit was substantial. When anything like a Christian world and life view was articulated in the public arena, it was likely to be in the form of a severely truncated witness such as, "Hey, man. Do you know Jesus Christ as your personal Savior?"

People might have been bold enough to ask the question, but few were bold enough, or adequately equipped, to witness to the lordship of Christ over every sphere of life. While evangelism brought people into the church, biblically informed ways of thinking and doing were seldom brought to bear upon the ideas driving culture outside the walls of the sanctuary. Very few Christians understood the necessity of cultivating a comprehensive theology.

Misplaced Emphasis

This emphasis on experience contributed to an already existing suspicion of and disrespect for the word *theology,* especially as it might relate to education received at seminary. For many, theology meant dead orthodoxy, and a seminary education was largely considered to be useless. The depth of distrust of the formal study of Scripture among many of CCM's pioneers is probably best characterized by Keith Green's reference to seminary as something more akin to a *cemetery*.[4]

Green's remark, though flippant, accurately reflected the suspicion that words like *seminary* and *theology* inspired. While Bible studies were viewed by most as essential in order for God to speak in the believer's life, many charismatics were taught, directly and through the modeling of leaders and other believers, that God was eager to speak to them through the still, small voice inside their heads, through tongues and interpretation, and through the prophesying of church leaders.

Seminary training was considered unnecessary for the most part. However, Pastor Chuck Smith of Calvary Chapel, Costa Mesa, a charismatic *and* a gifted Bible expositor, has boldly admitted that "one of the greatest weaknesses of the charismatic movement is its lack of sound Bible teaching."[5] This is not an affordable weakness. Neither is it a weakness common only to charismatic brethren.

The charismatic movement's emphasis on the important work of the Holy Spirit has helped to remind millions of believers of the Spirit's role in the Christian life. This emphasis by itself is not the issue. The difficulty is in our human propensity to emphasize one important idea to such a dramatic degree that others, equally important, are excluded. When what is excluded is sound Bible teaching, God's children are left standing on very shaky ground.

If the fullness of God's revealed truth in the Bible is not taught and applied to the fullness of life, if our experiences and our God-thoughts are not interpreted and corrected by God's own thoughts, then it is certain that our ways of thinking and doing will be insufficient to speak to life's challenges, especially the challenge of engaging with culture. Our faith journey must be founded on the Scripture. If it is not, it is certain that we will stray from the path of faithfulness to Jesus and the mission and kingdom perspective he has given us. Such was the case with CCM pioneer Tom Stipe.

Subjectivity vs. Scriptures

Stipe, by his own admission, has stated that he personally veered from the path of faithfulness by allowing "subjectivity to reign over reasoning from the Scriptures."[6] Until recent years, Stipe, pastor of the Crossroads Church of Denver, had been actively involved with one of America's largest and most popular non-denominational network of churches, the Association of Vineyard Churches (AVC)—a ministry developed out of the Jesus and charismatic renewal movements. While Stipe alone is responsible for his own sin, it is worth examining the ideological bias of the leadership under which

he served. Various statements made by John Wimber, the network's leader and founder, suggest that Stipe had submitted his ministry to the authority of someone who seemed to favor subjectivity over reasoning from the Scriptures. Wimber, now deceased, was a gifted and highly revered pastor/teacher in charismatic circles worldwide. Certainly thousands of Christians would testify to the impact John Wimber has had on their lives. Nevertheless, with no disrespect intended, his zeal for subjective experience caused him to take theological positions which fell quite wide of the truth of Scripture, including these words to his fellow charismatics in the Calvary Chapel network of non-denominational churches:

"Calvaryites are sometimes a little too heavily oriented to the written Word. I know that sounds a little dangerous, but frankly they're very pharisaical in their allegiance to the Bible. They have very little life and growth and spontaneity in their innards. Sometimes they're very rigid and can't receive much of the things of the Lord."[7]

This not only sounds dangerous; *it is dangerous.* Such comments from a dearly loved leader are unfortunate. It pains me to reprint them. The only reason I've included them is because of Wimber's association with the Jesus and charismatic renewal movements, and because he's been so incredibly influential in non-denominational charismatic circles worldwide. And because his comments characterize in general the kind of skewed thinking which so often occurs as a result of emphasizing spiritual spontaneity over the stirring up of a faithful hunger for what God has plainly revealed about himself in his Word. I have been guilty of the same error myself. I can remember an interview I did with *Cornerstone* magazine ten years ago where I grossly misrepresented the truth. In my zeal to communicate the power of God's Spirit, I offered the opinion that God could and likely would reveal himself to unsaved people and bring them to salvation through music and lyric whether the lyric contained a detailed account of the gospel or not. In my attempt to communicate that the Holy Spirit could do this if God so desired, I left out the fact that this is the exception. I left out the truth that people do not regularly call on the name of the Lord to be saved unless someone shares the gospel with them. Romans 10:14 reminds us of some questions to take seriously: "How, then, can they call on the one they have not believed in? And how can they believe in the one of whom they have not heard? And how can they hear without someone preaching to them?"

Unfortunately, the type of thinking exemplified by Wimber's comments and my own story have negatively influenced CCM, often leaving it biblically bankrupt to address the critical issues and challenges it has faced over the years—and those we face at present. To our detriment, we have at times relied more heavily on spontaneous "spiritual" hunches than the clear and reliable instruction of the Spirit-inspired Word. And when we've reached for scriptural knowledge, we've often come up short because we have not studied in such a way as to apply God's Word to the whole of life. This has contributed to our lack of biblically comprehensive theologies for the enjoyment and use of music, and for faithfully interacting with capitalism and the corporate world.

Continue in What You Have Learned

Perhaps the "Calvaryites" Wimber criticized were simply Christians trying to do their best to present themselves to God as disciples of Jesus, disciples who do not need to be ashamed and who correctly handle the word of truth (2 Tim. 2:15). Their heavy orientation toward the Word and their allegiance to the Bible may have been inspired by Paul's reminder to Timothy:

"But as for you, continue in what you have learned and have become convinced of, because you know those from whom you learned it, and how from infancy you have known the holy Scriptures, which are able to make you wise for salvation through faith in Christ Jesus" (2 Tim. 3:14–15).

Paul goes on to remind Timothy that all Scripture is God-breathed. "Above all," he writes, "you must understand that no prophecy of Scripture came about by the prophet's own interpretation. For prophecy never had its origin in the will of man, but men spoke from God as they were carried along by the Holy Spirit" (2 Pet. 2:20–21).

A High View of Prophecy

What many contemporary believers who prophesy words of foretelling or prediction often miss is that the Scripture also speaks of prophesying as proclaiming or declaring truth. Contrary to popular ideas, the prophets of old prophesied not as much in the role of foretelling as in the role of proclaiming what God had personally taught and instructed them to proclaim. New covenant believers have this same role with regard to Scripture. To proclaim Scripture is to prophesy. In other words, a high view of prophecy and a high view of Scripture are not mutually exclusive positions. In Malachi 4:5 the prophet foretells the coming of John the Baptist. In Acts 2:1–38 we have

the record of Peter, filled with the Holy Spirit, proclaiming the Scriptures with power. To prophesy is to declare truth under the guidance of the Spirit, whether it is by predicting, foretelling, or some other means.

The Scriptures Are the Work of the Spirit

Only God can search the motives behind a person's allegiance to the Bible. This being so, I would think it better to give any believer who shows allegiance to the Bible the benefit of the doubt. This position gains strength when you consider that the same benefit of the doubt *cannot* be given to someone who shows *greater allegiance* to receiving "the things of the Lord" via spontaneous spiritual revelation. Why? The Scripture does not allow for it. All our thinking and doing, whether we believe it to be Spirit-inspired or not, must be tested by our present understanding of the Word and, when necessary, corrected by it. Without the starting place of God's Word, the Christian life would be a subjective free-for-all composed of far too little truth to be of any significance. The same applies to contemporary Christian music.

Am I saying that God does not guide his children by the Spirit with feelings and impressions of his will? Absolutely not. However, just because God can guide his children in any way he chooses does not mean that his children should abandon careful study of his Spirit-inspired Word. Regardless of whether we call ourselves cessationists, charismatics, Pentecostals, or advocates of the third wave, none of us can afford to carve away at the authority and necessity of Scripture by equating those who have, as Wimber said, "life and growth and spontaneity in their innards" as being men and women who somehow "receive much of the things of the Lord," while men and women who read, meditate on, and pray the Scriptures do not. This kind of thinking does not serve to build up the church. And it certainly does not help those of us in CCM equip ourselves with the knowledge necessary to faithfully engage with both the church and the culture at large.

The Equipping Role of Scripture

I really have to wonder how much more of the things of the Lord any of us need to be seeking beyond what the Scripture has already clearly revealed. Didn't Paul tell Timothy in 2 Timothy 3:16–17 that the Scripture is "useful for teaching, rebuking, correcting and training in righteousness, so that the man of God may be thoroughly equipped for every good work"? And yes, I'm using Scripture to make the point that Scripture is important.

But for this I make no apology. What is my alternative? What is yours? I came to Christ through the preaching of the Word. Naturally, I'm inclined to acknowledge the Scriptures as God-breathed words of eternal life. I'm inclined to see them as instruction and correction. Should I now abandon the very words which the Spirit used to bring me life? I wonder sometimes if many of us aren't looking for something other than training in righteousness. How about you, are you looking for something other than to be thoroughly equipped for every good work? For that matter, have any of us finished our training, completed every good work, and are now so bored with life that we're twiddling our thumbs awaiting instructions from on high? Absolutely not! We are not through with Scripture because God is not through with us. He is still using it to train and equip us for kingdom life and for kingdom work.

In 2 Timothy 4:3–4, Paul continues his letter: "For the time will come when men will not put up with sound doctrine. Instead, to suit their own desires, they will gather around them a great number of teachers to say what their itching ears want to hear. They will turn their ears away from the truth and turn aside to myths."

We must do all we can to avoid having this passage of Scripture describe contemporary Christian music. In doing so, we will not only keep ourselves from sin and error; we will positively affect the church, leading many brothers and sisters toward the truth and away from that which scratches their itching ears but hardens their hearts to the Spirit of Truth.

Chapter 5

The Jesus Movement

In spite of the good which came from an emphasis on the work and gifts of the Spirit during the Jesus/charismatic movement, CCM became the product of an environment where, not only was it acceptable to de-emphasize learning of God from his Word, such foolishness was (and still is) sometimes encouraged. Again, it is impossible to have a high view of the Holy Spirit, his gifts and his work, and not have a high view of Scripture. Scripture is his work.[1]

Our Thinking and Doing

Without the Word, we are left to take our best guesses on how to proceed with artistry, ministry, and commerce. And our best guesses are far from the best. How can any of us in the CCM community possibly choose to continue in this way, allow ourselves to be influenced in this way, or support this kind of thinking when to do so is to willfully ignore God's thoughts and God's words? This is our crossroads. It's time to face the consequences of our subjectivism and make better, more faithful choices. One helpful way of achieving more faithful choices in the future is to study history, especially the history of Christians in centuries past.

The Great and Standing Rule

The writings of eighteenth-century theologian Jonathan Edwards have been a great help to me in shaping what I hope is a charitable and balanced view of the role of Scripture, the Holy Spirit, and the Spirit's gifts in the Christian life. In his treatise *The Distinguishing Marks of a Work of the Spirit of God,* Edwards wrote:

"My design therefore at this time is to show what are the true, certain, and distinguishing evidences of a work of the Spirit of God, by which we may safely proceed in judging of any operation we find in ourselves, or see in others. And here I would observe, that we are to take the *Scripture* as our guide in such cases. This is the great and standing rule which God has given to his church, in order to guide them in things relating to the great concerns of their souls; and it is an infallible and sufficient rule. There are undoubtedly sufficient marks given to guide the church of God in this great affair of judging of spirits, without which it would be open to woeful delusion, and would be remedilessly exposed to be imposed on and devoured by its enemies. And we need not be afraid to trust these rules. Doubtless that Spirit who indited the Scriptures knows how to give us good rules, by which to distinguish his operations from all that is falsely pretended to be from him."[2]

Having established that the Scriptures are our only trustworthy guide, Edwards also observes: "The Holy Spirit is sovereign in his operation; and we know that he uses a great variety; and we cannot tell how great a variety he may use, within the compass of the rules he himself has fixed. We ought not to limit God where he has not limited himself."[3]

From here Edwards plainly states that in his experience of revival and dramatic manifestations of the Spirit, there are certain kinds of behavior and imaginings that are neither evidence for, or evidence against, a work being of the Spirit of God. These kinds of behavior and imaginings range from the extraordinary way in which minds are affected to the extraordinary effects on the bodies of people "such as tears, trembling, groans, loud outcries, agonies of body, or the failing of bodily strength."[4]

According to Edwards, "We cannot conclude that persons are under the influence of the true Spirit because we see such effects upon their bodies, because this is not given as a mark of the true Spirit; nor on the other hand, have we any reason to conclude, from such outward appearances, that persons are not under the influence of the Spirit of God, because there is no rule of Scripture given us to judge of spirits by, that does either expressly or indirectly exclude such effects on the body, nor does reason exclude them."[5]

We are created to imagine after that which has captivated us and "we cannot think of things spiritual and invisible, without some exercise of this faculty."[6]

So What's the Attraction?

If the Scriptures are so foundational to the Christian life and to ongoing faithfulness, how is it that we've so often invested more in extraordinary experiences than the extraordinary which is found in the study of God's Word?

Christians should be open to the fullness of God, submitting to the truth that God can make his presence known at any time, in any way he chooses, whether it fits our present understanding of him or not. We are not to quench the Spirit and we are not to despise prophecies (I take this to mean the canon of Scripture, as well as any Christian who soberly and sincerely makes a claim to divine prophecy).

We are to engage our minds in service of the truth. We test, we hold on to that which is good, and we abstain from every form of evil (see 1 Thess. 5:19–22). But how do we test all things? First, by recognizing that the measure for what is or isn't good cannot be left up to what John Wimber called "the spontaneity of our innards." Second, we must rely on the Scripture as the only trustworthy means available for testing the quality of our experiences, our work, and our ideas. Without this reliance, we risk being left with nothing more than impressions, feelings, and hunches. Or, we're left holding onto unchecked ideas we've assimilated from the larger culture around us and from whatever part of the Christian subculture we call home. Only the Word and the Spirit working together will adequately equip us to test all things, hold on to the good, and abstain from evil. Nothing else will do, no matter how convincing it appears at first.

According to author and pastor John Piper, one possible explanation for why many of us "feel attracted in a disproportionate degree to the extraordinary spiritual gifts" is that "these gifts are, by and large above the ordinary processes of objective observation and reasoning."[7] I think it is fair to say that their other-worldliness is one of the things we like about them. Many of them seem to exist in a state beyond rational verification, which contributes to a kind of comfort—they're so out of the ordinary they must be from God. When we experience God in this way, we often feel as if we've been removed from the humdrum of normal life and brought a little closer to heaven perhaps. We feel as if we've been lifted out of this world into the presence of God where we expect the unexpected. He might speak to us like an intimate friend, or lay us out flat on our backs. The unpredictability is both frightening and exciting.

If this is in fact a worthy and accurate explanation for our behavior, there is something very important which cannot be left unsaid: The gifts of God and powerful, emotional encounters with God (see Isa. 6 and Acts 9:1–9) are never meant to be used as a retreat from reality. On the contrary, they are to prepare and equip believers for ever more reality, never less. And even if they are "by and large above the ordinary processes of objective observation and reasoning," they are not meant to replace the image-bearing ability to observe and reason which God has given to humans alone.

Engaging in study, thinking, and reasoning will not prevent me from experiencing charismata or revival, *or* diminish my high view of the present work of the Holy Spirit in any way. On the contrary, they prepare me to carry out the ministry role assigned to me by the defining nature of the spiritual gifts given me. In reality, every true believer in Christ Jesus is a charismatic, for the Scripture makes plain that "the manifestation of the Spirit is given to each one for the profit of all" (1 Cor. 12:7 NKJV).

Time to Choose

It's time to listen to the ideas that shape us, analyze them, and test them for truthfulness. Each of us in CCM must give honest consideration to where we stand on our view of Scripture and our view of the work of the Holy Spirit. A high view of both is essential. We must put aside labels such as charismatic and noncharismatic, anointed and not anointed, revivalists and dead churches for a moment. Take a vacation from your enculturated surroundings and go to God's Word. Find out *why* it is that you believe the way you do. Have you framed your Christian life by what the Bible says, or are your choices simply enculturated responses to your present worshiping environment? If you are in an environment which emphasizes the Word, but seldom speaks of the Spirit's role and power, would this explain your inclination to speak and act the same? Likewise, if you are in an environment which emphasizes the gifts of the Spirit and learning of God through subjective experiences, could this explain why you tend to embrace similar views? We are called to worship God in spirit and in truth. Both are necessary in acceptable worship.

One CCM veteran concerned about the balance between the two is songwriter/vocalist Wayne Watson. "I think one of the reasons we have so many subjective definitions as to what our faith is," says Watson, "is because there seems to be very little consequence for being subjective. I think if there were consequences for some of this subjectivity, maybe it would be lessened."[8] I agree. We may never be called before the church to suffer disciplinary consequences for our errors, but we've suffered consequences just the same, and continue to suffer them. At this point, true church discipline would be welcome, since its purpose is not to shame the guilty, but to orchestrate a safe and forgiving environment for repentance and restoration.

CCM and the Rapture

While the Jesus/charismatic movement's emphasis on gifts of the Spirit set the stage for learning of God through experience rather than scripture, a concurrent view that the Rapture was imminent pushed the study and formulation of a comprehensive biblical framework for CCM, and the calling to care for creation, to a very low point on the list of priorities. As a result, very few Christians gave much thought to Jesus' admonition to be salt in the world—to be, as my friend author Bob Briner says, a Roaring Lamb. And with good reason. It's difficult to be a Roaring Lamb, concerned with living for God everywhere and in everything, when you are preoccupied with being caught up with Jesus in the clouds.

The Rapture is a premillennialist doctrine especially common to the people of the Jesus movement, the non-denominational churches of the era, and to charismatics in particular. It is a doctrine which refers to the church being caught up to be with the Lord in the clouds at his Second Coming (see 1 Thess. 4:15–18). Premillennialists in general are divided over when the rapture will occur. Some say before the great tribulation, others mid-way through, still others believe it will occur after the tribulation period. The view most common to CCM's Jesus movement/charismatic roots is the first view, known as pretribulationism, or "pretrib" for short. The pretrib view divides the Second Coming of the Lord into two stages. First, Jesus will come for his church before the great tribulation via the rapture. During the tribulation the saints will remain with him. Following the tribulation victory, the church will appear with Jesus at his Second Coming (which under this scenario would actually be a third coming). According to the *Dictionary of Christianity in America,* "This view gained ascendancy in American premillennial circles before World War I, thanks in large part to *The Scofield Reference Bible,* and (later in the 1970s) with . . . Hal Lindsey's best-selling *The Late Great Planet Earth.*"[9]

One cannot underestimate the influence Scofield and Lindsey had on the Jesus movement, the charismatic renewal movement, and on CCM's earliest beginnings. The key to understanding their effect on CCM lies in one very important assertion common to both, that all prophetic events previously impeding the return of Christ have been fulfilled and that Christ's coming for his church is imminent. CCM veteran John Fischer underscores the effect and consequences of this idea on contemporary Christian music.

"One thing that's important I think in grabbing the mood of those early days was that there was really absolutely no thinking of careers. That was not in our minds. At least it certainly wasn't in mine. There was this idea that you were on the edge of the world, and you're not thinking about tomorrow. You're thinking about now, and the only thing we knew about tomorrow was the Lord's coming back. And sing it now, and get the word out now, and change the world now, and we don't have much time. That's exactly what we all thought."[10]

While focusing on the imminent rapture seemed to create the feeling of being absolutely sold out to Jesus and ready for his summons, history has proven that faithfulness and readiness are not as conveniently predictable or easily defined as CCM's pioneers once thought. Fischer commented on this as well. "What happened with the late '70s was kind of slowly creeping in the idea that, *Wait a minute, we do have the rest of our lives here.*"[11]

The Second Coming and the Rest of Our Lives

CCM's originators learned what Christians throughout the ages have discovered—no person can know the day or the hour of Christ's coming. We are to be prepared for his coming, but in no way should a by-product of this preparedness be a failure to prepare for and to carry out cultural engagement. CCM's pioneers made this exact error, and as a result were left without directions on how to proceed with the future. The idea of becoming an industry fully integrated with international entertainment corporations would have been absolutely unimaginable to them.

Living Out the Kingdom Mission

In order to preach the gospel we must know the gospel. Not just the message of salvation but the entire gospel story of redemption, from Genesis to Revelation. Not only must we know it; we must prayerfully seek Spirit-wisdom to apply it in our daily lives. By learning the whole of Scripture we are able to construct truthful, sufficient theologies of everything necessary to life, from culture and music, to parenting and business. In this way, whether at home or in Nepal, at church or in the workplace, the gospel we live, the gospel we speak and the gospel we sing, will by its truthfulness and authenticity be attractive to those who do not know Jesus. Love of God and neighbor requires us to cultivate this kind of gospel preparedness. People who possess this kind of preparedness are ready to be Roaring Lambs, and a Roaring Lamb is as equally prepared to be salt and light in the world as he or she is to meet Jesus in the clouds. This is a kingdom perspective.

The preparation necessary to live the gospel and share the gospel is far more complex than the preparation necessary to meet Jesus in the clouds. In the latter, I must know Jesus, and be known by him in order to be included in his Second Coming. In the former, I must know Jesus, be known by him, *and* be learning of him from his Word. In the time I'm given, I must learn and study the Scripture in order to accurately bring the Word of Truth—in everything from human sexuality, capitalism, and child-rearing, to music and retail merchandising—to bear upon all of life. Until Jesus summons his church, I should do nothing but live the good life, a life so good, so imaginative, so thought-provoking, so truthful, so compelling that it shouts to the world, "Hey world! The gospel is alive in me!"

Having become convinced that this lifetime would indeed be cut short by the Rapture, many of CCM's pioneers failed to develop a comprehensive biblical framework for CCM artistry, industry, and audience. Zealous for Jesus' return, they thought it only necessary to prepare themselves and others for the afterlife. Armed with this conviction, many of these brothers and sisters believed that the primary purpose of contemporary Christian music was to take the message of salvation to young people. They quickly discovered they were not alone, finding sympathetic support from an unusual place—the Recreation Department of the Baptist Sunday School Board, now LifeWay Christian Resources of the Southern Baptist Convention.

Chapter 6

CCM's History: Of Baptists and Folk Musicals

The Southern Baptists, like their Jesus movement and charismatic brethren, came to recognize that contemporary rock and pop music could speak to young people in powerful ways. While the largely non-denominational charismatics were busy using music to fill churches with new young believers (for example, Calvary Chapel, Costa Mesa), the Baptist mission became to use music both to evangelize and to keep Baptist youth interested and involved in the Baptist church. The idea of introducing contemporary music to Baptist youth was not a collective decision on the part of the Southern Baptist Convention. It was, however, given birth under their roof by a handful of Baptists led by a young music minister named Billy Ray Hearn. It all started with the creation of the first Christian folk musical, *Good News.*

Something for the Kids

In the summer of 1997, thirty years after *Good News* was first produced, I revisited this historic event with three of the men who made it happen, Billy Ray Hearn, Ralph Carmichael and Elwyn Raymer.[1] Hearn recalled how *Good News* got its start: "When *Good News* was created I was a minister of music at the First Baptist Church in Thomasville, Georgia. The Recreation Department of the Baptist Sunday School Board (now LifeWay Christian Resources of the Southern Baptist Convention) was interested in bringing music into their recreation programs for youth, and I was the guy who knew about that stuff and could do fun music for the kids, so they asked me to come speak about how I thought I could incorporate music for youth into their recreation programs. This was during the time when churches were building gymnasiums and trying to show that the church could meet a lot of the needs of families, including recreation. The music they wanted me to do wasn't supposed to be church music; the church already had its own music. This was supposed to be music for outside the church."

I asked Hearn why they settled on the idea of a youth musical, and not something in keeping with the pop music of the time such as the Rolling Stones or the Beatles.

"About this same time," replied Hearn, "along came this group called Up With People that did a youth musical kind of thing. They were emphasizing God and Country; I saw that and the reception it was getting and thought, 'Do what Up With People does, but only with more gospel in it.'"

"So it was really through the Recreation Department," confirmed Hearn, "that youth-oriented music made its way into the Baptist churches, starting with a musical we developed at Ridgecrest® and Glorieta® called *Good News.*"

Good News, composed by Billy Ray Hearn, Bob Oldenburg, Cecil McGee, and others, was first performed in 1967 at Glorieta® Baptist Assembly, a retreat and conference center in New Mexico, and shortly after that at Ridgecrest® Baptist Assembly in North Carolina. The Sunday School Board was eager to make the musical available to all the churches in the denomination. Hearn recalls, "Elwyn Raymer from the Baptist Sunday School Board came to Glorieta® to write it down and put it in a form that could be sent out to the churches so they could perform it."

Raymer remembers being none too happy about his assignment: "I worked for the Church Music Department and this was coming out of the Department of Recreation, so I came to it a little snobbish."

Snobbish or not at the outset, Raymer recalls his change of heart: "It was my job as a music editor for the Sunday School Board to get the music for *Good News* into print and onto disc. We took some equipment down to a big youth music gathering at Glorieta® over Christmas and stayed up all night recording it in a rough fashion. *Good News* changed my life, because I had to face that God had his hand on it, and that I was wrong about it."

Good News was hugely successful, with the Sunday School Board selling about 300,000 copies. Raymer noted, "The Baptists as a denomination did have a great organization in order to disseminate things. So once something was noticed as good and worthwhile it could be disseminated throughout thousands of churches. The old hierarchy kind of gave us our chance to do music that was for youth and was fun."

This was just the beginning. The Recreation Department of the Baptist Sunday School Board had sparked something big. Hearn tells it this way: "People really started getting excited about this kind of thing when I brought 1300 vocalists and 50 orchestra members, all kids, to do *Good News* at the Southern Baptist Convention that year in Houston. We performed right before Billy Graham spoke. Some of the Word Records people were there, and saying afterwards, 'we gotta do this kind of thing.' Later Word wanted to know if I would leave the church work I was doing to come to their headquarters in Waco, Texas. I was hired as their Director of Music Promotion and right away started developing another musical with Ralph Carmichael and Kurt Kaiser."

Kaiser, a composer employed by Word Records, flew in to attend the Houston event and to meet with Hearn. With enthusiasm high, Kaiser and Hearn decided to phone Ralph Carmichael, a respected composer/arranger for Bing Crosby, Peggy Lee, and Nat King Cole, to discuss the possibility of creating more youth-oriented musicals for the church.

Carmichael, a friend of Kaiser's, and already a partner with Word through his own Light Records, recalls the telephone conversation. "One night I got a call from Billy Ray Hearn about doing something for the kids. He wanted to see if I'd be interested in experimenting, with doing some things musically to see if we couldn't get the kids interested. Out of that came *Tell It Like It Is.*"

For *Tell It Like It Is,* Carmichael remembers, "We wanted the ring of honesty, cutting through the churchy vernacular. We first recorded it with The Baylor Religious Hour Choir at a studio in Dallas."

Downplaying his own contribution, but emphasizing his mission, Carmichael told me, "I can't stress enough that Billy Ray came up with the concept. My dream was to give the kids their own music."

The Musical/Cultural Gap

Some readers will have begun to suspect a gap between the music kids were listening to on pop radio, or on *The Ed Sullivan Show,* and the music these three men had in mind. In 1967-68 a handful of the artists and songs popular with "the kids" were: "Ruby Tuesday," The Rolling Stones; "Light My Fire," The Doors; "Hey Jude," The Beatles; and "Mrs. Robinson" by Simon and Garfunkel.[2] Of these, only Simon and Garfunkel were even remotely close to what these men had created or were intent on creating.

There are at least two good reasons for this discrepancy. First, Billy Ray Hearn, Kurt Kaiser, and Ralph Carmichael were and are gifted musicians, arrangers, composers, and conductors whose musical interests range from fronting a swinging big band or performing the most noble of hymns to conducting a classic symphonic or choral piece. They are not, and never have been, rock 'n roll musicians. Theirs was a different musical voice.

The second reason, and probably the more important, is the context. You cannot understand the musical gap between *Good News* and "Hey Jude" unless you have some sense of the context and setting of the denominational church in 1967-68. What Christian groups like MxPx, dc Talk, and Plankeye take for granted today, men like Ralph Carmichael, Billy Ray Hearn, and Kurt Kaiser fought very hard to attain. If today's voices of debate center around lyrics and crossing over, yesterday's earliest voices were concerned with electric guitars and drums. If you were a church kid in the late sixties and early seventies attending a mostly white, mainline denominational Protestant church, these men were on your side, fighting for your right to plug in a guitar and pound the drums.

Hearn and others had to introduce rock instrumentation slowly and carefully, almost one sound at a time. First it was acoustic guitars (emulating folk music more than rock) with perhaps an electric bass, maybe a tambourine. Later drums—but not too loud! Then maybe an electric guitar, but certainly not one played through a wah-wah pedal with a big stack of speakers, a la Jimi Hendrix. Carmichael proudly summarized the instrumentation changes they pioneered in these words: "We fought for, and won, the liberty to experiment."

Keep in mind also that this music—the earliest glimmerings of CCM—was introduced to the mainline churches through choir directors. Thousands of churches purchased musical scores of *Good News* and *Tell It Like It Is* in hopes of putting together a new and exciting contemporary gospel presentation for their youth group kids. The only problem, as Hearn relates, was that "the choir directors were not trained in this music; they were frightened by it." Carmichael, Hearn, and Kaiser began winning the Baptists (and others) over by putting on workshops surrounding the churches performance of a musical.

These pioneers were up against tremendous obstacles. Can you imagine being frightened by a youth musical? Well, perhaps you can, but I don't think it's for the same reasons that these choir directors were frightened. Apparently CCM's trailblazers had reason for fright a time or two themselves. Carmichael told me a story about an encounter he had with voices of criticism prevalent then:

"Some time after *Tell It Like It Is,* I went up to the National Religious Broadcasters convention where I was asked to talk for half an hour about my dream to give the kids their own music. I pled for the idea that things themselves (electric guitars and drums) are not inherently good or evil, that we'd been able to use radio for good, so why not the kids' music? Someone stood up and denounced me as 'making that rock-n-roll sound.' Scott Ross, one of the earliest Jesus music DJ's, then stood up to defend me, but they shouted him down. For a while there I thought there might be a stoning."

Despite their struggles, these men had important and influential allies. Carmichael made it clear that "the Graham organization, Youth For Christ, and the Southern Baptists were supportive. They said 'we're gonna try this, 'cause it's working with the kids.' "

The Journey from Musicals to Jesus Music

Although Kaiser, Carmichael, and Hearn went on to write and promote other youth musicals, the influence of two of the men was just beginning. By the early 1970s, both Ralph Carmichael's Light Records, distributed by Word Records, and the new Myrrh label owned by Word and run by

Billy Ray Hearn, were releasing CCM albums by artists such as Randy Matthews and Andrae Crouch and The Disciples. There were other important figures entering the field by this time, including Calvary Chapel's Maranatha Records, Larry Norman's Solid Rock label, and Benson Records. But Carmichael and Hearn were largely responsible for building an infrastructure for contemporary Christian music within the existing gospel music framework. Having started with youth musicals, Hearn and others quickly transformed their companies into advocates of a more authentic rock sound, signing Jesus movement musicians mostly from out of the non-denominational charismatic tradition.

Hearn went on to start Sparrow Records in 1976, creating a home for CCM artists Barry McGuire, Keith Green, the 2nd Chapter of Acts, and others. Today Hearn is the Chairman of the EMI Christian Music Group, home to dc Talk, Steven Curtis Chapman, The Newsboys, Twila Paris, and many other prominent artists.

The Consequences of Insufficient Truth

Several ideas which fueled the early youth musicals are still with us today. They were ideas important to their time, ideas which God used to add to his church, ideas which brought him glory. Yet as comprehensive theologies of music, ministry, and commerce, they are insufficient to the needs of CCM today.

Derivative music, inspired by Up With People for use outside the church to attract the kids, does not give us a sufficient starting place for thinking about music, ministry, or the business of music. Granted, it gets us somewhere, but it is not enough. And it's not enough to prepare us for the future, for faithful integration with culture, or for even faithfully creating music for the church.

Music based on a vision of kids who like pop and rock music, but who need to be saved or discipled, is not music which represents a kingdom bias. Music with a kingdom bias allows for this type of use but in no way is it limited to it. A kingdom bias is an ideological bias which favors a comprehensive and diverse picture of musical faithfulness. It is music created by musicians called by God, to God, and for God, everywhere and in everything musical. This is what is meant by a comprehensive view of the role of music in the church and in the culture. It is a calling that is huge. Unfortunately, the Baptist influence set the tone for CCM's cultural disengagement from a world infatuated with Mick Jagger and Janis Joplin. We have been hard pressed to recover from this fundamental schism ever since. CCM became music for "the kids" instead of God's musical people everywhere and in everything. It emphasized retreating from the cultural sphere by creating a Christian version of popular music just for Christians.

It is biblical and essential to communicate the gospel. In this, Billy Ray Hearn, Ralph Carmichael, Kurt Kaiser, Elwyn Raymer, and the Southern Baptist leadership were indeed faithful. All Christians, even the nastiest critics of CCM, must acknowledge that God has used these enthusiastic and imperfect men to add to his kingdom. This is reason to give God praise and honor and glory. And, it is reason to honor these men and their contributions to the church and to contemporary Christian music.

The Jesus and charismatic renewal movements carried with them an urgency to evangelize young people, tell the truth about Jesus' return for his church, and initiate fresh experiences of God among young converts. It's biblical and essential to emphasize evangelism, the return of Christ, the worship of God, and the ministry of the Holy Spirit. In this, these movements were tremendously faithful. Here again, all Christians, even the staunchest critics of the Jesus movement and of charismatics, must acknowledge that God used these enthusiastic and imperfect movements to add to his kingdom.

Getting at Kingdom Reality

As essential as it is to communicate the gospel in its fullness, the Scriptures on the whole do not teach that a faithful Christian life is constructed only of the evangelism of youth, anticipation of the Rapture, worship services, and hunger for the more extraordinary spiritual gifts. It most definitely teaches that evangelism and spiritual, truthful worship are at the core of what it means to live a faithful Christian life. Still, these essentials on their own do not flesh out the complexities of a comprehensive and faithful life. Though evangelism is foundational to our mission, and worship and obedience are our only appropriate responses to the gospel, there is more to the living out of life in Christ and the kingdom mission than these incredibly important ideas support. They are sufficient ideas unto themselves and central to the Christian life, but they are insufficient in helping us to understand the many ways that one aspect of creation, namely music, can be enjoyed and used in service of God, the saints, and the unbelieving world. As important as evangelism and worship are, they do not represent the starting place for thinking about, producing, or marketing music.

The Consequences of Overemphasis

I do not believe that musicians, record companies, churches, teachers, pastors, and young converts set out at the beginning of the Jesus movement with some master plan to purposely exclude important doctrines and scriptural principles applicable to life and music. Neither do I believe that they necessarily failed in the preaching and teaching of the whole of God's Word. What I do believe is that corporate worship, the evangelization of young people, the gifts of the Spirit, and the belief in the imminent return of Jesus were emphasized to such a degree, over and above everything else, that all other ideas seemed small and almost unnecessary by comparison.

CCM, being both a proponent of and partially a result of the Jesus movement, embraced this same set of emphases. As a result, Scriptures and doctrines applicable to CCM and necessary to the construction of a broader, more comprehensive biblical foundation for music in the kingdom at hand were largely overlooked. Few influential people ever widened the lens enough to see music for anything other than a fantastic tool for evangelism, worship, and something for the kids.

I doubt that the pioneers of CCM had any idea their creative choices were laying the foundation for what is today a $500-million-dollar-a-year industry. Had they understood the challenges that lay ahead, it's likely they would have searched the Word for a more complete foundational theology. As it was, they did not; the consequence being that for nearly thirty years, contemporary Christian music—the artists, the industry, and the audience—have operated under many of the same insufficient theologies that fueled CCM's beginning.

Sharing Highs, Lows, and In-Betweens

Every true believer eventually learns that life in Christ is full of highs, lows, and in-betweens, and that Christ is no more or less present in the highs than he is in the lows. Life in the kingdom at hand is about sharing the gospel, prayer, time in the Scriptures, and hands lifted high in worship. But it's also about changing diapers and taking children to softball practice, about dealing with the pain of having a Christian friend commit suicide, about making distribution deals with mainstream record companies, about moral failure and restoration, about overcoming anxiety attacks, and about thanking Jesus when you kiss the bride of your youth. And this is just the beginning.

Chapter 7

In Search of Theology

When contemporary Christian music began, its ideological and theological influences were very limited. The Baptist influence was mostly one of a denomination loosely defining a mission and opening up the door to possibilities which CCM founders such as Billy Ray Hearn ably walked through. And while it's true that the Jesus/charismatic renewal movements of the late 1960s did touch a diverse group of Christians, including Catholics and Episcopalians, no group of believers felt the influence of these more than the non-denominational church—the worshiping environment of choice for so many of CCM's founders.

The Checks and Balances of Diversity

A lack of diverse influences in contemporary Christian music has contributed to a shortage of checks and balances—checks and balances which the body of Christ is designed to provide in everything related to its mission. One of the most important doctrines found in Scripture is the doctrine of the body of Christ, which affirms that the church is indeed a diverse group of people, and that we need each other's diversity to be healthy. CCM's resulting lack of diversity begs the question: While the Southern Baptists, along with many non-denominational charismatics, were opening their arms to the new contemporary sounding Jesus music, where were the other conservative denominations? The Billy Graham organization was there, along with various important campus ministries, but where were the other evangelicals who placed a high premium on the Scripture as the central voice in the believer's life? Unfortunately, they were largely absent from any charitable, meaningful, ongoing dialogue concerning the creation of CCM, its mission, and its infrastructure. If the errors and sins of CCM's primary founders were in building an industry upon narrow and insufficient ideological and theological bedrock, then the errors and sins of those absent from any influence or dialogue are of the "omission" variety—they didn't show up to contribute.

Even though rampant liberalism was good reason to avoid many of the mainline denominations in the 1960s, there were men and women who could have helped CCM flesh out a more comprehensive and faithful understanding of music, ministry, and commerce. With the exception of Francis and Edith Schaeffer, and a small handful of others, very few of them brought comprehensive theologies to bear upon contemporary culture, or upon the early dialogues regarding contemporary Christian music.

What conservative Presbyterians and people of the reformed tradition (the tradition of Luther, Calvin, and the Puritans) in particular could have contributed to CCM was a reasonably fleshed-out theology of vocation or calling. Some in this tradition could have spoken to music's utilitarian use, as well as to the Christian's freedom to simply enjoy music as a gift from God. Others could have offered the truth that Christians are free and called to enter into the musical dialogue of culture and faithfully contribute biblically sound and aesthetically beautiful music to the church. In short, the knowledge necessary for formulating a comprehensive kingdom perspective of music was within our reach.

Failure to Walk the Talk

Various problems kept these reformed thinkers from taking hold with any kind of measurable influence. One problem was a general arrogance on the part of those who could have contributed—an arrogance which dismissed the importance of pop culture. This turning-up-of-the-nose at the counterculture and the music of youth was a huge miscalculation. The result was a general failure to anticipate the kind of impact these forces would have on the church in the very near future.

In addition, any positive ideological or theological contribution caretakers of theology past might have made was severely stunted by their failure to model important truths and propositions in their own lives, or, in the vernacular of the time, to walk the talk. In spite of the powerful truth claims of Scripture, in spite of traditions of finely tuned theologies of art and music, work and calling, many of these believers were at a loss to live out these ideas and ideals in the world between Sundays. In the eyes of the average unsaved young person, most of these mainline believers appeared to be just as sold out to empty platitudes, shallow lives, and relentless materialism as their unsaved neighbors. More often than not, these traditional models also lacked the vitality and enthusiasm that always accompanies the joy of being known by Jesus and being commissioned as a co-worker in the kingdom. I think this was the main reason why Jesus people and the charismatic non-denominational churches often referred to many such believers, their churches, their denominations, and their theology as being "spiritually dead." Their apparent dullness and conformity was one very substantial reason why the vitality and excitement of the new charismatic non-denominational fellowships held such an attraction for new young converts. As I noted before, they felt that God was not about to pour new wine into old wineskins.

Suspicious Minds

Another important reason for the lack of ideological and theological integration between CCM's primary founders and other possible contributors was an unfortunate suspicion of one another. Anyone vocal about laying claim to a theology rooted in the reformed theology of Luther and Calvin was automatically suspect in the eyes of the average charismatic non-denominationalist. The reasons for this reaction center around an enculturated misunderstanding of the reformed view of predestination (see Rom. 8:29–30) and its relationship to evangelism. Whereas reformers say that because God has predestined people to be saved we can evangelize with confidence, charismatics often viewed reformed types as being lax on evangelism—since God has predestined, why bother evangelizing? This misunderstanding led to a general caricature of reformed theology as being antievangelistic. The principal founders of CCM, who placed a very high priority on evangelism, often viewed brothers and sisters in this faith tradition as ivory tower thinkers far more committed to arguing over doctrine than saving sinners.

In like manner, many mainline churches and teachers, including those of the reformed denominations, were strongly suspicious of the Jesus people, the charismatic non-denominational churches, and their evangelists and teachers. In his popular book *Dynamics of Spiritual Life,* Richard Lovelace notes, "Critics of the Jesus people have included not only liberals upset by Neo-Fundamentalism but also Evangelical spokesmen who have attacked the shallow theology and sensational tactics of the movement's leaders and vigorously repudiated its claims to be the onset of a major spiritual awakening."[1]

Men and women within the mainline denominations, keepers of rich theological traditions, frequently reduced Jesus movement charismatics to holy-roller caricatures. Throughout the history of CCM, both camps have been less than kind to one another. Instead of bringing tensions, criticisms, and disagreements to light in charitable dialogue, they have more often than not resorted to backstabbing and throwing stones—often with full media coverage.

Something's Missing

What's missing from CCM is a comprehensive theology of music in general, and a theology of CCM artistry, industry, and audience in particular. In order to begin to rethink contemporary Christian music, we'll first have to recognize the necessity of developing a comprehensive theology. Christians, particularly young Christians, often dismiss theology because they simply feel no need for it. Yet, it's this dependence on feeling over thinking which leaves us reaching for the world's ideas when it's time to apply a kingdom perspective to every subject under the sun.

As CCM artists, industry, and audience, with thirty years of hindsight to guide us, it's now inexcusable for us to continue on with CCM as it was and as it is. The hour has arrived for us to get serious about promoting unity and developing a sufficient and comprehensive theology for our callings, for our appreciation of music, for our ideas about ministry, evangelism, and worship, and frankly, for the call to life itself. It's impossible in the kingdom at hand to have an exhaustive theology, but a sufficient theology is within our grasp.

I'm aware that some people in CCM are still a little suspicious of the word *theology.* According to artist Wes King, "When we say theology there are automatically going to be those people who say 'Oh those eggheads.'"[2] For Brian McSweeney of Seven Day Jesus, the word *theology* definitely has a negative connotation: "When I hear the word theology, I think of becoming stale. I think of a bunch of people saying, 'This is the right way. This is the way it was and this is the right interpretation.'"[3] Brian's bandmate Chris Beaty reacts differently to the word. For him it simply means "knowing about what God intended for us to realize and know in the Bible."[4]

Wes King acknowledges that some negative responses to the word may be justified. "I definitely think theology can have bad connotations," King asserts, "when it becomes a pedantic approach composed of rights and wrongs and lists of rules. I think there's credence in criticism of this variety of theology."

Defining Theology: The Insufficient and the Sufficient

At its simplest and truest, theology is God thoughts, God knowledge, or the study of God thoughts. Since every cognizant person has some thought or opinion about God, they in turn possess a theology of some kind, good or bad. According to J. I. Packer, "God-thoughts are only right when they square with God's own thoughts about himself; theology comes good only when we let God's revealed truth—that is, Bible teaching—penetrate our minds."[5] Wes King makes the musical connection: "If we don't hate what God hates, and love what He loves, and hope for what he hopes for, then we're going to have bad theology, bad music, shallow music, and we're probably going to look more to what the world is doing."

Unfortunately there's no "probably" about it. It is what we do. From music to marketing, CCM takes its cues from the world. This is due in part to the fact that CCM has many leaders who simply will not lead, either out of fear or for lack of a sufficient theology for their calling. "What often happens," Os Guinness says, "is that Christians wake up to some incident or issue and suddenly realize they need to analyze what's going on. Then having no tools of their own, they lean across and borrow the tools nearest them."[6] On this point Scott MacLeod's prophecy appears to be correct: "The people who have been in power have, knowingly or unknowingly, let the ways of the world enter into Christian music."[7] I do not know if this is because powerful evil spirits plague and control much of the Christian music industry, as MacLeod claims God has revealed to him they do. What I do know is that Christian leaders who attempt to lead without having committed to the ongoing development of a sufficient theology are certainly cooperating with the overall mission of Satan's evil spirits. And the disciples they make along the way are no better equipped than they are.

If Satan cannot have a Christian's soul, and he can't, then he will at least try to see to it that the Christian lives an ineffective and unproductive life. He must acquiesce to the fact that Christians are in the kingdom, but he doesn't have to make it easy for us to cultivate a comprehensive kingdom perspective. And he doesn't.

To operate under an insufficient theology, above all else, is to possess too few of God's thoughts about himself. When a theology is constructed of too few of God's thoughts about himself, as well as too many God-thoughts which don't square with the Bible, that theology too is insufficient. Also insufficient are theologies constructed of misapplied truth.

A sufficient theology is one composed of God-thoughts regarding every area of life, carefully checked against, and ultimately constructed of, God's thoughts as revealed in his Word. This comprehensive and sufficient theology is made up of hundreds of smaller theologies, such as a theology of music, a theology of culture, and a theology of work or calling. These theologies are meant to be constructed of truthful ideas applicable to the subject. If the subject is the audience, then you set about to frame a truthful theology about what it means to be a member of the audience.

Our theologies often miss the mark, not because they're necessarily riddled with untruths, but because the truths we've emphasized are insufficient to the task at hand. Our theologies also miss the mark when they're composed of ideas incongruent with our core beliefs. This is what ultimately ails the CCM community and keeps us from living out a comprehensive version of the Christian mission in the kingdom at hand.

Without God's thoughts and God's ways, we are left with our own dim and insufficient ideas. If we willfully choose to neglect the work of building truthful theologies for our callings, we will find ourselves waving good-bye to the brightness which illumines life. We will find ourselves stumbling blindly down the way which seems right to a man but leads to nothing but darkness.

Theology is what informs mission. A mission without good theology is no mission at all, regardless of whether your mission is good business or good vocational ministry. Here, leaders in the CCM community must take special note. A man or woman in leadership who fails to make the connection between good theology and good business is one who has yet to enter into the fullness of what it means to lead. Faithfulness for a Christian business person is not defined solely by faithfulness to good stewardship principles. Granted, stewardship urges us to make the most of what we receive. If this results in increased profits, it's a good thing. However, we can only call it truly good when the means and methods of achieving the profit have not violated God's good thinking. In order for us to get near this goal, God's good thoughts must precede good business. Good business is never defined by business achievement according to the principles of the world. On the contrary, the best of good business always begins with God's notion of good. And the only way to get at his ideas regarding good is to know what he has said. The only place recognized by Christians throughout history, to faithfully get at what he has spoken, is the Scripture.

Theology Lite: Tasty and Less Filling

I once heard of a young band who, in an attempt to appear relevant to the prevailing Christian culture, declared that they were "into Jesus but without all the theological baggage." The point I hope to make is that it's impossible to be into Jesus and not be into theology. Every believer has a theology whether or not they recognize it or can articulate it, whether or not it is cogent, real, truthful, and sufficient. This being so, our goal in CCM ought to be to pursue the most comprehensive and faithful understanding possible of Scripture and its application to our lives.

There is a contingent of believers who would like to see knowledge, the thinking component, relegated to a much smaller role in the construction of Christian theology. To quote David Wells, they desire a theology in which "any cognitive elements are strained through the sieve of what appears to be 'practical,' so that what is felt becomes as important as what is known or believed."[8] Wells goes on to identify this reconfiguration of theology as therapeutic.

There are many sincere CCM artists who would declare with a hint of pride that their mission is not to present music which causes people to think so much as to feel, and specifically to feel that everything's going to be all right. God's in the driver's seat, so don't give up hope and keep your eyes on the prize. This approach is indeed therapeutic in that it ministers to the felt needs of the audience. Rather than wrestling with what they've yet to grasp, it reminds the audience over and over of what they learned in the first week of being a Christian.

Certainly music reaches the emotions, and reaching emotions and relieving anxiety is not necessarily a bad thing. Where the problem lies is in thinking that making people feel good about being a Christian, or relieving pain and anxiety, is the ultimate focus and purpose of Christian music. Especially problematic are songs which stress to listeners that they made the right choice by becoming a Christian and that they need to just hang in there, everything's going to be all right, Jesus is on the case.

One popular group that's come to realize there is a bigger, more serious reality at stake is Point of Grace. "I think God is putting this urgency in all of us," says group member Shelley Breen, "to see that what we're doing with our group is more serious than we ever thought it was. We've always taken it seriously, but in the past it was sort of more on the feel good, it's O.K., encouraging side of things."[9]

Shelley is correct. God's kingdom purposes are serious and they are huge. The music of God's people should, as much as possible, reflect this truth.

What About Theological Disagreements?

This discussion of the importance of cultivating a comprehensive theology is not meant to infer that all Christians must be in agreement on all things at all times. We will certainly have differences of opinion when it comes to theology and its doctrinal particulars. Nevertheless, this does not mean that we should avoid formulating convictions on debatable issues. On the contrary, as author Mark Shaw points out, "Though these other [debatable] matters are secondary to the primary truths of salvation, they cannot be ignored, because they are addressed in the Word of God."[10] Study of the Word with regard to debatable matters is something I hope to encourage every reader to invest time in ever so faithfully.

It is our responsibility to know the Word of God and to seek, as best we can, to formulate truthful and informed ideas about what the Word says, and how its teaching applies to our primary and secondary callings. Again, we know there will be differences of opinion as to exactly how the Word is directing us; still, these inevitable differences never excuse us from the work of being a student of the Word. As disciples of Christ we should always seek to understand ever more truth and to remain open to the possibility that we have misunderstood some portion of Scripture.

Bringing differences to light can be profitable. It helps us to identify what is complimentary in our thinking. Our contrasting opinions are of help as well. They can help us to refine our positions and give careful consideration to whether someone else's position might actually be more accurate than our own.

Most important, we should never forget that theology is for the church. God's thoughts, and what we glean from the study of them, are meant to serve the church and the creation. None of us who truly loves the church and God's creation can afford to become so attached to our personal theological formulations that we forget theology is meant to be used as an act of love and service to the church and the watching world.

People for whom theology is a vocational calling wisely recognize that the training and ability to rightly divide the Word of God is God's gift to them, and all God's good gifts are to be used for the building up of the church. All the rest of us, the "little theologians," also need to recognize that our theologies ultimately make up our ideas about what we think it means to be a Christian and how life is to be approached and how we should live out our calling to Christian music. To the degree we think biblically sound thoughts about artistry, industry, and the role of the audience, we proportionately increase our chances of living as biblically informed and faithful people.

Good Theology as a Response to God

Finally, developing truthful and comprehensive theologies is a way of responding in love to God. It is, as Miguel DeJesus of Smalltown Poets says, "loving God with your mind."[11] Jesus said that the first and greatest commandment is to "love the Lord your God with all your heart and with all your soul and with all your mind" (Matt. 22:37). This is the starting place, our primary calling. Only by beginning here will we ever be able to fulfill the second greatest commandment—our secondary calling to "love your neighbor as yourself" (Matt. 22:39). Loving God's thoughts and loving his kingdom story of creation and redemption are what spark the spiritual

imagination to dream well and choose well for the church, for the creation, and for your neighbors who make up the watching world. Living in loving response to God, who first loved us, absolutely defines the Christian life, and as such, ought to define contemporary Christian music as well. To think this way is to have a good theology. To do it, to live it out, is to live in response to God's love. It is to show that you clearly understand the theology you profess. You are making the invisible kingdom of God visible to the world. This should be the goal of everyone involved with the care and stewardship of music and musical artistry.

Chapter 8

Music and the Voice of the People

Christians have long debated the theological content of lyrics and the issue of musical accompaniment—whether congregational singing should be supported by musical instruments or not, and if so, what kind of instrumentation and what style of accompaniment. History shows that disagreement and debate over musical matters in the church are not unique to our time, or to the CCM community. What is unique and peculiar to CCM is the pool of opinion specifically concerning:

(1) The genre known as contemporary Christian music.

(2) The industry which funds, markets, promotes, and otherwise disseminates contemporary Christian music to the church and the world primarily as a form of

religious pop music.

(3) The role and use of contemporary Christian music in the life of the individual Christian, the church, and in the culture at large.

Exploring the Complexity of CCM

Prior to the advent of the contemporary Christian music industry, there was lively debate within Christian music or church music circles over issues such as style and instrumentation. These disagreements had been going on in one form or another for centuries. Today for many Christians, these issues have either been resolved, or are no longer as volatile as they once were. As a result of the commercialization and popularity of contemporary Christian music, other far more complex issues have surfaced.

In order to participate intelligently in the contemporary Christian music dialogue, Christians need more than an opinion on whether a cappella voices are more pleasing to God in worship than guitars and drums. No serious fan, inquiring parent, concerned youth pastor, or industry participant can pretend to understand the phenomenon of contemporary Christian music and its issues without having invested time in exploring the complex system of intentions, ideologies, methods, and technologies it has become. The ability to tolerate the complexity of CCM is an essential prerequisite for understanding it and making the right decisions about it.

Opinion Is Queen of the World

Our opinions regarding the enjoyment and use of music are shaped by musical taste, theology, and enculturation. Most of us possess various biases when it comes to music. That's perfectly reasonable. Often the reason we tend to think a certain way about music is because of the denomination or fellowship in which we were raised. Unfortunately, we often voice our biases in less than charitable tones.

Often our opinions, positions, and convictions take on the tone of "thus saith the Lord." If and when they do, it usually means that our hearts and minds have hunkered down and dug in. It means we are ready to defend what we've come to believe is the highest and best use of music—or what we've come to believe is the most faithful expression of music or its most faithful role. Since we are prone to believe we've accurately identified the highest and best use, we often err by trumpeting it as the only use, or at the very least, the primary use. Here are some different opinions of what music is:

Voice One

"Music, by biblical definition, is a ministry."

"Music is a powerful tool from the Lord Jesus to his church intended for worship, praise, encouragement, edification, evangelism, teaching, admonishing, and exhorting God's people to holiness—with always our chief aim 'to glorify God and worship Him forever.'"[1]

Voice Two

When CCM was developed, "albums were recorded and concerts were held with the purpose of winning young people to Jesus and discipling them in their walk. It was and still is a great tool, using the familiar to discuss the spiritual."

"Yes . . . we believe there is a place to address social issues and love between two people occasionally. However, we hope that all of us involved in CCM will remember that our first priority is to be a lighthouse of truth in an ever increasing spiritual fog."

"We are asking all of our friends in this 'industry' and the Body of Christ at large, to pray for the songwriters, artists, managers, producers, labels and radio stations. Pray that we will experience a fresh anointing and that the message in our music will clearly and creatively communicate the gospel."[2]

Voice Three

"Music is multipurpose. It can be for praise of God, it can soothe the savage beast, it can help enhance a joyful and celebratory attitude such as at a wedding."

"Even though we can communicate with one another with our voices, I think the best thing we can do with our voices is praise God. I think music is the same way."[3]

These are three strong positions on the purpose and use of music, all of which contain definitive theological ideas worthy of our best thinking. Let's examine them.

Analysis of Voice One

1. The Bible defines music as ministry.
2. Music is a powerful tool given to the church by Jesus Christ with these intended uses in mind: worship, praise, encouragement, edification, evangelism, teaching, admonishing, and exhorting God's people to holiness.

3. The chief aim or purpose of every use listed in point number 2 is "to glorify God and worship Him forever."

Analysis of Voice Two

1. Music is something familiar to everyone, and as such is useful as an effective tool for winning young people to Jesus and discipling them in their spiritual journey in Christ.
2. Though music on occasion may be used for the purposes of addressing other topics and issues (other than those traditionally associated with Christianity), the first priority of CCM is to clearly and creatively communicate the gospel.

Analysis of Voice Three

1. The best thing we can do with our music is praise God.
2. Even though the best thing we can do with our music is to praise God, God created music in such a way that it is good and useful for communicating important thoughts and emotions between human beings in a variety of settings for a variety of purposes.

Each voice has its own biases and assumptions. I think that the first two voices characterize the general ideology of CCM and the opinions of many people within the CCM community today. You may be among them. If so, then you understand firsthand that there are many voices that claim a core use, or priority use, for music—one which supersedes all other uses. All other uses (if they are even acknowledged) are minor and insignificant by comparison.

The third voice sets itself apart by its resistance to exclusive or near-exclusive positions regarding the uses of music. Yet like the other voices represented it, does recognize the high calling of music as a means of praise and worship to God.

These three representative voices contain three categories of ideas and biases:

(1) Voice one contains ideas and biases which define the faithful use and purpose of music by carefully limiting them to a narrowly defined ministry role, using such designations as praise and worship, evangelism, and discipleship to define its role. This category promotes exclusivity with little or no tolerance for exception.

(2) Voice two contains ideas and biases which define the faithful use and purpose of music by prioritizing them to a ministry role

using designations similar to category one. This category allows for exceptions to the priority on occasion, but never to the degree that exceptions begin to outweigh narrowly defined priority uses and purposes. This category promotes near-exclusivity with a limited tolerance for exceptions.

(3) Voice three contains a bias which defines the highest and best use of music without limiting other good uses and purposes. This category promotes an inclusive view of the use and purpose of music while recognizing that music directed toward God is the most excellent use of music.

By analyzing these voices we can arrive at workable categories which accurately represent the primary ways in which the CCM community thinks about music. There are certainly exceptions to the ideas and biases we've considered, and people will resonate with these in varying degrees. Nevertheless, these three get close to the truth of what most of us perceive the uses and purposes of music, specifically CCM, to be.

The Defining Moment

Since voices one and two are more alike than voice three, as an experiment let's see what sort of definition of contemporary Christian music emerges by combining the ideas and biases from voices one and two:

Contemporary Christian music is both a ministry in and of itself, and a powerful tool for ministry. This music has been given by God to the church, to be used for the purposes of praise and worship, encouragement, edification, teaching, admonishing, exhorting God's people to holiness, and especially as a tool for evangelizing and discipling young people.

My purpose in including the words "contemporary Christian music" in the definition is to draw attention to CCM as a specific musical genre. In order to accurately represent a ministry emphasis which has also characterized CCM from its beginning, I've singled out young people as the primary target of evangelism and discipleship.

Overall, this definition forcefully communicates that no matter what anyone else is doing with popular music, no matter what uses are being made of music, no matter what issues and topics others choose to sing about, CCM's priority mission remains clear. When it comes to CCM, music is ministry. Music is a powerful tool for ministry as well. It's a God-given tool to be used for the purposes of praise and worship, encouragement, edification, teaching, admonishing, exhorting God's people to holiness, and especially as a tool for evangelizing and discipling young people.

My guess is that many readers will agree with this mission statement, but that an equal number will either be unsure, or say that voice three more accurately represents your position. In a survey I conducted, I asked thirty-five CCM artists and groups whether they would characterize their work as music or music ministry. Fifty-seven percent (57%) chose music ministry, 23% chose music, and 20% chose both. While the designation music ministry did receive the most votes, the majority of artists polled (49%) do not believe that music, by biblical definition, is a ministry.

A Closer Listen

As you can see from the survey results, there is a near-even split between those artists and groups who define their calling as a call to music ministry, and those who define it as a call to music. Many of those who say it's both are simply looking for a way to express the truth that they are musicians, but Christians first, and that all Christians must be involved in and concerned with ministry (i.e., serving). If it's true that, on the average, 57% of CCM's artists consider their work to be music ministry, they are right in line with CCM's historical ideology. The remaining 43%, those who consider themselves to be musicians (with varying ideas regarding the nature of ministry, calling, and their definitions) are people more likely to find a fit within voice three. Let's give their voices a closer listen:

"I've seen the marriage of the enjoyment of music and the desire to reach people for Christ come together in a really cool way. Yet in other instances I've seen music really compromised and the gospel cheapened because the music is used purely as an evangelical tool."[4]

"I feel like the phrase *music ministry* almost separates what it is you do from the rest of life. If I was a doctor I would still think being a doctor would be my calling, my career, and my ministry. But I wouldn't have to call it a medical ministry, because as a Christian your life should be a ministry, because you should be serving people, period. Ministry is serving."[5]

"God made music. He didn't make Christian music and secular music and all that. It's really kind of sad. I wish it could just be music, and since you're a Christian, you're naturally going to write songs with Christian content."[6]

"All five of us see the music business as a way for us to do what we love to do, music, to become better at our craft, to share art that we feel like

God has inspired us with, and by doing so, hopefully provide support for our families. The great thing about it is that just like anything else in life, we can do this to the glory of God. It's incredible."[7]

"We want to play a show and be seen as a good band. We're not afraid of being called Christians or of expressing our beliefs, but we do it in a different way than some people like."[8]

A New Model of Artistry

Like the other representative voices we've heard, these voices have a great deal to say. Especially since they represent a new model of artistry emerging from within CCM—one which includes its own list of core ideas and biases:

1. Often when music is used *purely* as an evangelical tool, both music and the gospel are compromised and trivialized in the process.
2. Your calling does not have to be tethered to the word *ministry* in order to be ordained of God, or to be ministry. The idea of calling is deeply connected to the idea of ministry or serving, something which all Christians are called to regardless of their secondary callings (or vocations). The whole of the Christian life is about the imitation of Christ's servant model of ministry. Christians are called by God to serve his purposes everywhere and in everything. This allows for a great deal of diversity in the uses and purposes of music created by God's people.
3. With the exception of music written by Christians specifically for churches to use in corporate worship and discipleship settings, perpetuating the idea of "Christian" pop music and "secular" pop music tends to contribute to an unhealthy dualistic view of life. God has called his people to an integrated life which takes into account, and actually calls for, a holy and Spirit-led interface with the world.
4. The calling to music is broader and much bigger than the majority of the CCM industry and audience allows for. There is a longing among many of God's people to see the CCM community commit to funding, developing, and supporting a diversity of ways in which music might serve the church and the watching world.

5. Involvement in the mainstream music business is a legitimate God-ordained calling. It is a tangible expression of musicians living for God everywhere and in everything. To accept this call is to be an artist who crafts inspired and truthful music which God graciously uses for a multitude of purposes. These purposes include provision for the artists and their families (for which no apology need be made), the artist's pleasure and enjoyment, pushing back the effects of the fall (adding "salt"), entertainment, and evangelism.
6. Since we do our work as unto God, it is a good and honorable thing to be a musician who commits to doing good, image-bearing musical work as unto the Lord. Though free to do so, God does not require Christian musicians to add other secondary callings such as pastor, teacher, or evangelist in order to live out their primary calling to serve him and live for him in all things.

Conclusion

Having heard from a cross-section of representative voices within the CCM community, we see how a number of ideas and biases shape the ways people think about the relationship between Christianity and music. Acknowledging the influence of these ideas and biases is an important first step in understanding them. Each one of us must decide for himself or herself whether any of these voices ring true with the voice of God's Word.

Chapter 9

Getting at the Truth

Music is the soundtrack to the story we're telling through our lives and our communities. Through emotion and word it documents our journey. It looks back at past grace and in gratitude gives God worshipful praise. It looks forward in faith to future grace and gives God praise as well. Music is present when we're born and when we're buried, when we learn our ABCs and when we graduate from high school, when we celebrate birthdays, baptisms, Christmas and Easter, when we first hear the gospel, when we share our first dance, our first kiss, and when we marry. Music is both a quiet song in our hearts and a thundering symphony that takes our breath away. Our enjoyment and use of it seems to know no end. It is literally the sonic backdrop to life and culture. All in all, it's possible to say that music is everywhere and not risk exaggeration.

As Francis Schaeffer and others have so ably pointed out in the past, music needs no justification. It can simply be. It doesn't need to do anything to justify its existence any more than water, wind, and clouds do. The fact that God included music in the totality of his creation is all the justification it needs. This is an idea which Christians throughout the history of the church have advocated, yet seems to run counter to much of CCM's ways of thinking and doing.

Many of the voices I've analyzed so far talk about the use and purpose of music in ways that suggest taking action of some kind. These voices are telling us that music created by Christians should do something. They seem to imply that contemporary Christian music cannot be allowed to just be—to exist without some justification.

Here's where the battle is joined. If music is indeed the powerful tool many say it is, they can't leave it idle when there's a job to do. If something powerful is not accomplishing its powerful purpose, then its power is being wasted. If they feel strongly about the waste, they're likely to feel anger, regret, grief, or frustration. They're ready to pledge to God and the church to do all they can to prevent future waste and misuse. In similar fashion, those who believe that the musical energies of God's people should be spent on praise and worship, evangelism, and discipleship with very few exceptions will likely be angered and frustrated when that energy is redirected.

A sincere commitment to this position fuels much of the criticism which sounds out in our community. Voices such as these are not alone in their zeal to protect powerful tools. History shows that Jesus' disciples also shared this propensity.

Jesus and the Beautiful Thing

Jesus was in Bethany at the home of a Pharisee known as Simon the Leper. While Jesus reclined at Simon's table, a woman named Mary came and stood behind him at his feet and began to weep. She carried a pint jar of very expensive perfume. As her tears began to drip down upon the feet of Jesus, Mary took the alabaster jar of perfume and poured it on his head, and on his feet, mixing the perfume with her tears. Kneeling down, she kissed Jesus' feet and wiped them with her hair. When the disciples saw this, they grumbled indignantly among themselves, saying, "What a waste of perfume."

One disciple named Judas objected loudly. "Why wasn't this perfume sold for money and the money given to the needy? That perfume was worth at least a year's wages. It could have been put to good use." After hearing this rebuke, Jesus spoke. "Leave her alone," he said. "Why are you bothering her? She has done a beautiful thing to me."

This story illustrates our propensity to error regarding the use of music in two critical ways. First, despite our best intentions many of us become consumed by an overwhelming need to shape and control the uses of music for what we truly believe to be admirable purposes. Often our voices, like the voices of the disciples, are fueled by the heartfelt desire to see some perceived wrong made right. Our error is in trying to right a wrong that is not wrong and therefore does not need to be fixed. Instead of building up and helping those who want to do a beautiful thing for Jesus, we often grumble and tear them down for their seeming lack of practicality.

God's Economy

The disciples misunderstood the economy of God. Though every one of us should remain open to the good and practical uses of music, we want to guard ourselves against repeating the errors of the first disciples. We want to remain open to the idea that Jesus may be saying to some of us even now, "Dear friend, leave this sister's music alone. Why are you bothering her? She has done a beautiful thing to me." Not only do we want to remain open to this possibility; we want to be very careful to avoid the sin of Judas. Judas saw the perfume as a means to a selfish end, yet pretended he was concerned with a higher and better use of it.

If the sin of Judas applies to anyone reading this book, and you know it, then my heart breaks for you a thousand times. In John 12:4–6, the Scripture teaches that Judas was not upset about the waste of perfume because "he cared about the poor, but because he was a thief; as keeper of the money bag, he used to help himself to what was put into it."

As a sinful man, it's possible for me to approach the use of music wearing the heart of a thief, while masquerading as someone deeply concerned with using music as a powerful tool for disseminating the gospel. I may be deluded into thinking I'm the "keeper of the money bag." This is the way a fool thinks. But if I'm thinking spiritually, then I will remember that all money belongs to God. I'm simply a steward, a manager over anything he chooses to put in the bag. My work is to invest it wisely for his

kingdom purposes—purposes which I know to be extremely diverse and more comprehensive than I will ever begin to understand in this lifetime.

He wants our ways of thinking to be connected to his higher ways of thinking about use and purpose—ways that make our understanding of what is practical seem so incredibly small.

At the heart of the thief resides the idea that he is accountable to no one and dependent on no one. Because no one else is going to take care of him, he must fend for himself in any way he can. Christians, on the other hand, are accountable to everyone, especially God. And we are wholly dependent on him for everything, including the breath we breathe.

It's a fool who steals from God, then runs to those who do not know Jesus to negotiate for worldly riches he does not need, only to end up hanging himself with the weight of his spiritual emptiness. I repent of this sin. If this sin is yours as well, then avail yourself of God's grace and go, as Jesus said, and sin no more.

God's Record of Success

It is important that the Christian music community grab hold of the truth that God's success is assured and therefore not determined by the success or effectiveness of contemporary Christian music. This is a difficult truth for many of us to live by, but it is one that all of us—artists, industry, and audience—need to seek and make our own.

It is just as important to understand that it's not the financial success of Christian music that ensures our provision. It's not our clever thinking, our business deals, our sacrificial work for the Lord, our position in the community, our market share, or our scratching of itchy ears which assures us we will be O.K., that we will be taken care of, that we will have enough. It is God and God alone who ensures this promise. To believe it requires faith and trust. May God graciously give it to us.

Same Old Song

You will not often hear anyone aligned with the CCM community specifically say that the existence of music is justified solely by its ability to disseminate the gospel message. It's seldom so clearly defined.

With this in mind I want to speak to the issue of how strongly we emphasize and repeat our various positions concerning what we believe to be the highest and best uses of music. Historically, the CCM community has not been very good at speaking plainly, and unfortunately it's been to our detriment and to the kingdom's detriment as well.

When we use emphatic phrases such as "our first priority," we should do so knowing the kind of power and influence they wield, particularly over young minds who are just starting to think these issues through. When we state that God gave music only for such important purposes as praise and worship, evangelism, and discipleship, we must understand that we've taken serious steps toward inferring that Christian music's ultimate justification is found in doing only these particular things. Many people both inside and outside CCM take our comments seriously and literally. If this *is* what we mean to infer, then we are in error. Music needs no human justification. God saw fit to include music in the totality of his creation and as such it needs no further justification. This is the starting place for thinking about music, period, full stop, end of report.

Even a Good Story Cannot Justify

For many people in and around CCM, this bedrock truth is very difficult to accept. Because so much has been accomplished using music in the ways common to contemporary Christian music, the thought of freely using music in other ways seems to many people like unfaithfulness or willful disobedience. In reality, it's when we fail to think in other ways that we risk being found unfaithful. Our musical calling is for God's purposes, which are vast. Faithfulness equals God's people and their music everywhere and in everything. I strongly believe that until this idea is understood and owned, clear thinking on the enjoyment and use of music will continue to elude our community.

Let It Be

In the course of framing this argument I may have given the impression that I'm bent on advocating and encouraging CCM to let the music be and that's all. On the contrary, what I hope to have communicated is that God's people are called to do the beautiful thing in every sphere of life, and that looking for practical applications for any part of creation, including CCM, is not the place to start with our thinking about the stewardship of music. We are free to let it be and we are free to use it responsibly.

Chapter 10

Stewardship, Freedom and Responsibility

Even though music needs no justification for its existence, it is still a priceless gift from God that we can use for good and productive purposes. If I were to believe that "winning young people to Jesus and discipling them in their walk" (to borrow from the WAY-FM open letter) is in fact the highest and best use of music, I needn't apologize for it. If I contend that using music to win young people to Jesus and disciple them in their walk is *not* the highest and best use of music, I'm entitled to this conviction as well. The only qualification for a bias, conviction, or opinion is that I know and understand what compels me to hold it. In other words, my conviction or opinion starts to become good only when I know why I believe it. That knowledge begins with the Bible and the testimony of creation, not with my gut. If I lean toward my gut, a little too much pizza the night before might very well cause me to hold some very strange convictions. I must know and understand what it is that compels me to take the position I do, and be ready to wrestle with any possible contradictions regarding uses of music in my own personal life.

God's Good Work

Music is not transformed into something good when crafty humans discover some good use for it. This is a very important distinction which must be understood by every reader, from parents, to pastors, to pop stars. Creation is useful because it is good. It is not good just because it is useful. One idea represents a kingdom perspective, the other a pragmatic and worldly one.

The good mind of God has created things which are good, music included, because God is nothing less than good. This is the starting place for thinking Christianly about the use of everything God has created. If Christians fail to start their thinking at this point, they risk falling into the error of the pragmatist. A pragmatist is one who believes that something is good or true only because it works or is useful. Pragmatism is a worldview which mirrors the world's ways of thinking. We don't want it. It's poison.

The kingdom perspective is upside down, the total opposite. Christians set their minds on things and ideas which are first good and true. Then out of this goodness and truth comes good and true use of the creation. Because God's creations are good, they can be used for good; but there is no guarantee that we as fallen creatures will always use them for good. On the contrary, it's possible for sinful human beings to choose very poorly when using something very good. History makes this point painfully clear.

The Glorious Freedom of the Children of God

We make our musical choices in an environment of freedom. All of us involved with CCM, including the audience, need to know and understand the role freedom plays in the enjoyment and use of music. In grace we have the freedom to say no to every form of ungodliness, and the freedom to say yes to our growing and compelling desire to live for God everywhere and in everything. We can reject all ideas which claim that the enjoyment of creation and its pleasures leads Christians away from godliness and therefore should be avoided. These ideas are an affront to God's imaginative creativity

(1 Tim. 4:4) and a challenge to the truthfulness of his Word (Gen. 1 and 1 Tim. 4:1–5).

The freedom to use and enjoy all of creation is qualified by the higher freedom of love. Love compels us to keep a watch on our exercise of freedom so as not to cause weaker brothers and sisters to stumble (1 Cor. 8:7–13). Love compels us to remember that while everything is permissible, not everything is necessarily beneficial (1 Cor. 6:12–13). Scripture also reminds us that our freedom can be misused. History teaches us that we have the intrinsic potential to choose very poorly on behalf of something very good, music included. The themes of freedom and servanthood work together in a pact of strength, as reflected in Galatians 5:13, 14: "You my brothers, were called to be free. But do not use your freedom to indulge the sinful nature; rather serve one another in love. The entire law is summed up in a single command: Love your neighbor as yourself."

If our freedom in Christ is governed and defined by love and service, then our freedom to use and enjoy music in a variety of ways ought to be guided by them as well. Only the most wide-ranging view of what it means to love will work here though. Loving you might require me to write a song that reminds you of truths you've forgotten or neglected. Loving you might require writing an instrumental melody for you that is remarkably beautiful in order to remind you of your need for beauty.

Like Water, Like Music

Another way to think of music as being good on its own, even if it isn't "doing anything," is to compare it with another of God's creations: water. Because water is good, it's useful. Yet despite its many important uses, I'm still free to hike along a stream high in the Rocky Mountains of Colorado and enjoy the absolute beauty of the water without ever making any practical use of it. Because it's there does not mean that I must harness it for some use. On the contrary, I can find pleasure in the water alone. I can let it be, and in so doing, find pleasure in God's good creation. In the beauty of the stream I recognize God's handiwork and I give him thanks and praise for it.

Genesis 1:26–30 teaches me that I'm a caretaker and steward over the planet, including the planet's water. As image-bearers of God and as Christians, part of our work on the planet is to take care of what God has created—water, music, and everything else. No one gets off the hook in this regard.

Beware the Sin Bias

Now for the qualifications: While we're free to enjoy water and find pleasure in it apart from any practical use it may have, we're not free to use it for something unworthy of its inherent good. We've said that because water is good it contains the potential for good use. We've also considered the fact that Christians are free, but are commanded not to use our freedom as a cover-up for sin, or for indulging the sinful bias within us—a bias which urges us to live contrary to the integrity we possess as new creations in Christ.

We can use water sinfully. I remember when the phrase *wet T-shirt contest* became a part of the cultural lexicon. Personally, I've never attended such a contest, but any kid who's ever gone swimming with a T-shirt on knows what happens when a T-shirt gets wet—it clings to your skin and your skin shows through. As I understand it, these contests are centered around women wearing the wet T-shirts, not men. Regardless of gender, using water for the purpose of a wet T-shirt contest is totally unworthy of its inherent good.

If a person chooses to use water in this manner, he willfully involves himself and others in a chain of sin against God. By indulging his sinful nature and using created things for purposes totally unworthy of their inherent good, he demeans the good of water, the good of human sexuality, and the good image within each human. Neither water nor human beings are made for such foolishness. The freedom to enjoy creation, whether it be water or the beautiful form of a woman, is not the freedom to choose sin. It is the freedom to love and to serve. In the example played out above, there's no evidence of love or servanthood. There's only evidence of sinful self-interest, which is always the bias of sin. Indulging the sin bias within always involves violating the integrity of creation.

On Doing the Good You Know to Do

While I'm free to enjoy my mountain stream for its beauty, I'm not free to ignore the good uses the stream may have. One of those uses might be to feed a reservoir whose dam creates hydro-electric power for the towns and cities surrounding the mountains. Going backwards in time, had the person or persons with the foresight to imagine hydroelectric power balked at pursing it, knowing full well the good it could contribute to people's lives, they would be guilty of willfully choosing to ignore a good use for water.

Today, if I hike a stream in order to enjoy its beauty, yet pollute it with trash left over from lunch, I am guilty of ignoring one good use of the stream which is to keep trout alive. As an avid fisherman and a caretaker of the planet, I have a vested interest in keeping trout alive. I should know that trashing a stream will have an adverse effect on its ecosystem. When I fish, I enjoy catch-and-release. In other words I don't eat the fish; I put them back in the stream. At present I don't need trout for food. However, someday I may, and I won't be pleased to discover that my abuse of freedom has threatened a good, God-provided food source.

If I become thirsty after hours of hiking along my private Colorado trout stream (sorry, the hopeful dreamer in me came out), the stream can now meet a very legitimate need. God created my body to require water and without it I will not live. I'm now free to drink from the stream in order to satisfy this need. By drinking from the stream, water, which earlier was a means of visual pleasure and delight, becomes a means of sustaining life. Water moves from something of good enjoyment to something of good use, and in both God is thanked, praised, and glorified.

The Genius of God's Multifunctioning Creation

A cursory glance at creation reveals that this kind of multifunctioning is all around us and in us. Take a redwood tree for example. Redwood is great for building homes, outside furniture, and decks because it's resistant to wet weather. As stewards of what God imagined and created, we're free to cut these trees and use their lumber for countless purposes. Yet, we're also free to create parks for the sole purpose of delighting in the majesty and beauty of these trees. We are free to let them be and we are free to use them.

Consider human sexuality. Is its function procreation, pleasure, or both? Do you see God's genius in designing creation this way? Look at Scripture for a moment: "And the Lord God made all kinds of trees grow out of the ground—trees that were pleasing to the eye and good for food" (Gen. 2:9a). Are human beings both useful and pleasing to the eye? Certainly this is beyond dispute, but just in case, the Scripture reminds us that God used Rachel, who "was lovely in form, and beautiful" as a co-builder of the house of Israel (Gen. 29:17; Ruth 4:11).

Music Has Been Left in Our Care

Now let's turn our attention back to music. *Because music is good, it is useful.* Like water, it too is full of uses. Despite the fullness of its uses, I'm free to enjoy music without having to consider what use I'm making of it while I'm enjoying it. Because music is available, nearby, or present does not mean that I must of necessity, that very moment, harness it for some use, like "winning young people to Jesus and discipling them in their walk." On the contrary, I can find pleasure in music alone, and in so doing, find pleasure in God's good imagination. I can give him thanks and praise for the unmerited favor he has shown me by sustaining his creation, by allowing for music, and by giving me time to be saved and time to enjoy his good gift of music. No apology need ever be made for enjoying the good that God has made (1 Tim. 4:4). In music I see God's handiwork, his order, his design, and I give him thanks and praise for creating it and for giving me the skill to write and produce it.

Like all of creation, music has been left in our care. Our responsibility is to enjoy it and make good use of it. Again, as with water, we are not free to use music for something totally unworthy of its inherent good, such as background music in a film promoting hate crimes. While we're free to enjoy music for its beauty, we're not free to ignore the good uses it may have, such as "winning young people to Jesus and discipling them in their walk." Music, like water, can move from something of good enjoyment to something of good use. Its beauty can soothe the restless soul, and its melody can give flight to extraordinary words, words that tell of the living water which takes away the thirst of humankind. In both, God can be thanked, praised and glorified.

Set No Limits

Music can be the melody you whistle while you work, it can be the melody and lyric which frame a worshipful response to God's grace, and it can be the sound of a string quartet playing in the background as you walk your twenty-one year old daughter down the aisle. Do you see God's genius in designing music this way? Does it make you want to praise him? I hope it does. It should be evident by now that I'm hoping to encourage you to set no limits on music, except those set by the principles which compose love and servanthood.

As the appointed caretakers of creation, our job is to imagine and create music, think of places where music can be of good enjoyment and good use, and support good enjoyment and good use whenever the opportunity arises. We are to put creation to good use in the loving and serving of people. This emphasis on people does not mean that we fail to love and care for creation. It simply means that the good gifts of creation exist to serve God's good purposes for you and me, his image-bearers. In this way people take precedence over all the rest of creation. If we see and imagine some good which could potentially come of good music and do not alert others to it, and do not work toward accomplishing it (once counting the cost), then we have failed to do the caretaking work assigned to us.

Getting at the Truth

As I've already highlighted, various voices of criticism have recently brought to the forefront what many Christians in and around CCM have been saying for thirty years—that Christian music ought to be used for Christian ministry alone. If what these brothers and sisters believe is that the highest and best use of music is *ministry*, and that *music ministry* is defined as music imagined and created in love as a grateful servant's response to God's grace, I am in agreement with them. If their definition involves creating music either for the worship of God, or for the purpose of serving the church and the watching world as artful salt and light, goodness and truth, then again, I could not agree with them more. They have my full endorsement. This is what music should be.

However, if these voices are trying to communicate something else, I vigorously champion disagreement with them. If they are in fact saying that the only true and good use of music is to serve the direct needs of the church (either through worship or as a witnessing tool), then I must speak out against the narrowness of their vision. Christians who advocate and carry out such a narrow vision for music are making a willful choice to relinquish the bulk of the caretaking work of music to the world. To do this is to turn your back on the calling. We cannot retreat from the world of music any more than we can retreat from the world of politics, law, education, sports, or medicine. To retreat is to abandon the call to live for God everywhere and in everything.

By making this kind of willful choice, men and women who are called to be salt and light in the world are foolishly contributing to the world's dominant influence over music and culture. This is not a choice we should endorse or an influence that we should accept. The object is for Christians to influence the world, not the other way around. To willfully abandon any part of the Christian mission, and to encourage others to do so as well, is error and sin.

A Vision of the Christian Mission

The Christian mission in the world is to serve and transform community and culture, to be salt and light. We achieve this by communicating the gospel of grace to unbelievers (Matt. 28:19–20; Luke 24:46–48) and by living good lives among them (1 Pet. 2:12). Living good lives involves loving our neighbors and giving of ourselves through acts of mercy and kindness (Mark 12:31; Luke 6:36). And, as I've explained at some length, the Christian mission involves continued faithfulness to the biblical mandate to care for and manage God's creation, including that part of his creation called music (Gen. 1:28; Ps. 8:6–8).

In this chapter we've taken a good look at what music is and what our responsibilities and privileges are in relationship to it. We've addressed our freedom in Christ to enjoy music and we've looked at how loving servanthood defines our uses of it. Next we come to the crucible of the conflict: the role and importance of the lyric in contemporary Christian music.

Chapter II

Lyrics at the Crossroads

It was in 1991 that Amy Grant's *Heart in Motion* album provoked the most highly charged discussion of lyric content in CCM history. It's tempting to say that little has changed since the fuss over "Baby Baby." Christian lyric content continues to make the news and stir debate. However, the big difference today is that people are no longer just debating it. They're drawing lines in the sand. The development and implementation of "lyric criteria" by gatekeepers at youth ministries, radio stations, and retail stores has turned up the flame on an already heated and often divisive discussion.

The Burden of Proof

Contemporary Christian music is an unusual genre. Every other form of popular music is classified by its musical style: jazz, blues, classical, folk, rap and rock. Contemporary Christian music incorporates all these styles and more; therefore, it cannot possibly qualify as a genre using the standard means of classification. The only option CCM has is to tie its identification to the lyric, or to a profession of faith by the artists. Years ago a listener might have been able to tell the difference, stylistically, between Christian music and non-Christian music (think Southern gospel quartets vs. the Rolling Stones). Today the listener can no longer count on the music to reveal to him that he is indeed listening to Christian music.

This being so, one important function of the contemporary Christian music lyric is to communicate to the listener that they are indeed listening to music which is Christian in origin, and therefore can and should be named as such. The most efficient way to achieve this desired end is to incorporate specific names, words, and intrinsically Christian concepts into CCM songs; for example: Jesus, Holy Spirit, redemption, heaven, sin, and glory. Using exclusive language, or at least words common to Christianity, helps Christians and many non-Christians quickly to identify the music as Christian in origin.

We must realize, however, that getting listeners to recognize Christian music does not ensure that they will engage the music and lyric with the depth of interest they need to derive some spiritual, emotional, or intellectual benefit from them. Every Lord's Day, Christians all across the world sing psalms, hymns, and spiritual songs filled with glorious truths. Yet this does not mean that these various truths are penetrating the singers' wandering hearts and minds. Overtly Christian words work toward ensuring that most listeners will identify the music as Christian. As important as it is for a CCM lyric to achieve this particular goal, connecting with a listener's personal ideas about Christian identity and purpose has become equally important.

Dealing with Listener Bias

According to conventional marketing wisdom, if we want Christians to purchase Christian music, we must build into the music an identity which closely mirrors the prospective buyer's perception of his own subjective understanding of Christian identity and mission. If for instance a Christian sees himself primarily as a victor in Christ (his identity) empowered to overcome the enemy Satan (his mission), he will naturally identify as

"Christian" that music which most accurately reflects his ideas about Christian identity and mission. Drew Powell, of the band Common Children, confirms that listeners take their notions of Christian identity and mission very seriously. "One of the most frustrating things for us, and I think for bands who are really putting their heart into the art, is that you experience things like having a guy come up to your merchandise table saying, 'So where are all your songs of victory?' And here we've poured our souls into an album which may not outright say, 'This is a song of victory and conquering,' but at the same time it's a part of us and it's in there. He just wanted it fed to him."[1]

While a listener's bias will alert him to lyrics which do not meet his criteria concerning Christian identity and mission, it will also likely hinder him from identifying lyrics which may in fact be congruent with a true kingdom perspective of Christian identity and mission. The principle is this: *The smaller and less comprehensive a person's kingdom perspective or biblical worldview, the greater the potential for suspicion and intolerance of lyrics which express a larger, more comprehensive kingdom perspective.* As unfortunate as this scenario is, it is made doubly unfortunate when we acknowledge that the potential for suspicion and intolerance runs both ways. Those who are mature in Christ are sometimes prone to exhibit intolerance for the young, immature, or weak in conscience. This is why the teaching regarding the weaker brother and sister ought to undergird all that is written here.

A comprehensive kingdom perspective is large enough to hold smaller views, but the smaller will never hold the larger. For example, a comprehensive kingdom perspective takes into account that God's people are victorious conquerors in and through Jesus Christ (1 Cor. 15:57; Rom. 8:37). However, this is just one small part of the vision. It also takes into account everywhere and everything which God has dominion over—something which is incredibly huge—bigger than we can know or imagine. God has dominion over everything from human sexuality to human creativity to quarks and black holes. And he has dominion over things we haven't even begun to discover. Because his kingdom is huge, a kingdom perspective must be as well. Lyrics written from a kingdom perspective will naturally include a number of topics—in truth an inexhaustible number. On the other hand, a smaller, less comprehensive perspective will usually only include those topics which reflect its bias.

If songwriters fail to write lyrics which use words commonly associated with Christianity, if they fail to connect with the identity and mission of their listeners, then the average Christian cannot be certain that he or she is listening to Christian music. For Andrew Patton of Christian radio station WFRN-FM this is a very real problem: "I am concerned when we find listeners asking us what kind of music station we are."[2]

Lyric Criteria at the Crossroads

Our industry is at a profoundly critical crossroads concerning lyric content. There is now a distinct division between those Christians who believe that CCM ought to promote lyrics which reflect a comprehensive kingdom perspective, and those who believe CCM ought to return to its original perceived mission of worship and evangelism. Intent on effecting change, several ministries and businesses associated with the latter have implemented "lyric criteria" in order to begin steering the industry back to what they sincerely believe should be the mission of Christian music, specifically that of worship and evangelism targeted at the youth.

From the very beginning, contemporary Christian music has had to accomplish some task assigned to it. It could never just be music. It had to serve a religious function which produced a tangible result. The idea that music can also exist as something good, true, and beautiful without having to do something is a concept largely foreign to CCM. In truth, the idea that any element of God's creation—be it music or a tree—has to do something in order to justify its existence is an idea more connected to capitalism, consumerism, and marketing than the doctrine of creation. I don't mean for this to deride the Christian music business community. My desire is simply to draw a fair comparison between what Christian music is most often asked and expected to do and what any other product, whether it's a pair of shoes, a bicycle, or a boat, is expected to do in the marketplace.

Boats and Christian Music: Closer in Kind Than You Might Think

The majority of products and services marketed under capitalism are required to do something. For example, if I market something as a boat, yet my so-called boat does not float, it is likely I will soon be out of the boat business. Consumers hold fixed ideas about what they expect in a boat, and above all they expect it to float. If you decided to shop for a boat at my boat store, Charlie's Boat and Marine, you would likely ask me a number of questions concerning the various boats in my showroom. You might inquire about price, horsepower, the number of people each boat could safely carry, warranties, and service contracts. But it's unlikely that you would ask, "Does this boat float?" Life and circumstance, context, and enculturation have prepared you to expect that a brand new boat, sold by a legitimate boat dealer, will indeed float. You trust that it will float. You are so confident about it floating, so trusting, that you will purchase it without ever having actually confirmed that it floats, haul it to a lake, put your cherished family inside it and take off for a ride in sixty feet of water!

A similar kind of thinking exists within the Christian music community. From its inception, contemporary Christian music was positioned by its pioneers as (1) music ministry, as in a type of vocational ministry and (2) a powerful tool for the purposes of praise and worship, and evangelizing and discipling of young people. Many Christian artists, industry folk, and music consumers have grown up under these ideas and remain highly influenced by them. As a result, they're apt to view them as the benchmark criteria for judging the authenticity of music created by Christians. They perceive the slightest movement to the left or right of this core criteria as failure to advance the very thing that they're zealously committed to creating, supporting, marketing, and purchasing.

Now let's plug "CCM" into my boat story. If I market a recording as Christian music, yet my so-called Christian music does not appear "Christian," it is likely that I will soon be out of the Christian music business. Consumers hold fixed ideas about what they expect in music named as Christian, and above all, they expect it to be "Christian." If you shop for Christian music at my store, Charlie's Christian Music & Books, you might ask me a number of questions concerning the various CDs and tapes available. You might inquire about price, style, popularity, and the life and history of the artists represented. Even still, it's unlikely that you would pick up a CD and ask me, "Is this one Christian?" Life and circumstance, context, and enculturation have prepared you to expect that any recording sold by a legitimate Christian music and book store will indeed be "Christian." In truth, most of us are so confident about the music being "Christian," so trusting, that we will purchase it without actually confirming that it's Christian, take it home, put it in our CD player and play it for our cherished family, all the while representing it as a Christian recording without ever having actually heard it. We have learned to trust the context or environment in which our purchase is made to be our primary guarantee of Christian authenticity. The reason for this is the same reason why we do not doubt the authenticity of a set of tires when we purchase them at the tire store and let a perfect stranger install them. If we enter a legitimate tire store, we have reasonable expectation to be sold an authentic tire, one which will safely carry us down the road. When consumer expectations are not met, when trust is violated, confidence in a product or service is eroded. This is as true of CCM as it is of any other industry.

An Erosion of Trust

The presence of recordings in the Christian marketplace which Christian artists, consumers, and industry people do not perceive to be "Christian" has contributed to an erosion of trust within the CCM community. We no longer completely trust the environment in which our purchases are made (or where we first hear the music, as in the case of Christian radio). Though our trust is far from being destroyed, we've found enough suspicious lyrics to dramatically increase the volume on the voices of debate and criticism.

Let's return to the boat illustration for a moment. If you purchase a brand new boat from me, haul it to the lake, put your cherished family in it, and it sinks like a stone, you're not likely to characterize yourself as a satisfied customer. On the contrary, since you have fixed ideas about what a boat should do, it's more likely that you'd be frustrated and angry at me. You might forcefully remind me that there are certain requirements integral to the creation of a boat, ones which must be met in order to name something a boat—specifically, the requirement that it float! Being the gracious person that you are, you might give me the opportunity to make amends by replacing your boat. But if boat number two also sinks like a stone, you will most assuredly suspect I have failed to grasp the most basic concept behind the creation of a boat. Having twice failed to provide you with a product composed of ideas integral to a boat, any confidence you may have had in me will have been replaced by *suspicion*. You will suspect that I haven't the slightest idea how to make an authentic boat. And you'll wonder aloud, if I don't know how to make a real boat, what in the world am I doing in the boat business?

Listen to the voice of one member of the band, the Supertones, and you'll see how all this relates to contemporary Christian music:

"In the secular stores we have the parental advisory stuff all over certain records. Are we going to have to get a 'Not Christian Enough for a

Christian Bookstore' sticker? What I'm saying is that mothers should be able to have the faith that their kid can go into a Christian bookstore and get any album and it bears the name of Christ. If a band just wants to be a band and not a ministry, then I think they should not use the name of Christ. Even if they are just Christians making art and they don't want to be a ministry at all, why would they want to be sold in church, if they are not claiming to want to be in church?"[3]

Here is a clear representative example of the voices of people in the CCM community who wonder out loud why people are trying to make boats that don't float. Or, why are Christian musicians trying to sell CDs to Christians when their music does not bear the name of Christ—when it is plainly not "Christian"?

Some artists, such as the band Plumb, are raising suspicion from several corners—including fellow artists, parents, and influential ministries. "We've had kids come back to us and say, 'My parents won't let me keep this CD because you don't mention Jesus Christ in your lyrics.'"[4]

These examples show how Christian artists, consumers, and industry people are taking issue with various Christian artists and recordings now being promoted to the Christian market. They sincerely believe that certain artists and their recordings fail to grasp the most basic idea behind the creation of Christian music, that it be "Christian" and that it be for "ministry." If it's not "Christian," and not for "ministry," it cannot do for them what they think it should do. They think it is a misrepresentation to sell it as "Christian." As a result, they become frustrated, angry, disappointed, and suspicious. This may in fact characterize you.

Jennifer Hendrix, a vocalist with the group Sierra, explains her frustration this way: "If I could change anything about CCM, it would be that everybody who pursues Christian music would have the heart for ministry."

"We have seen many artists," observes Jennifer, "who come into the Christian market. Maybe it's an easy way in, but they just want to be an entertainer. For us, it's like, why do you just want to entertain people in the Christian marketplace when there are so many people hungry, so many people, even Christians, who need encouragement and to be reminded of God's unconditional love? If you just want to entertain, why not go into the secular market and try to make more money, you know?"[5]

What Is a Christian Lyric?

If Christian artists, consumers, and industry people expect Christian music to be "Christian" and see the lyric as the only means by which the song can be identified as being "Christian," then what is a Christian lyric? For much of the CCM industry and audience it is easily defined—and it does not allow for the complexity of a kingdom perspective, does not allow for everything under God's dominion. This is the core issue which drives the debate concerning contemporary Christian music lyrics.

One person hoping to make his easily defined position known is music buyer Rick Anderson, whom you may recall had this to say about Amy Grant's album, *Behind the Eyes:* "It's not a Christian album. A Christian album should be clear on the person of Christ and these lyrics are not." Remember, too, my earlier mention of the two radio networks which declined to play Grant's single, "Takes a Little Time." One cited a lack of "lyrical relevance" and the other a failure to meet "lyrical criteria." Relevant to whom you might ask, or to what lyrical criteria? For Amy Grant, the relevance of her work is not connected to its ability to meet lyrical criteria. "I don't know if *Behind the Eyes* is a Christian record," Amy says. "Being able to label it Christian or non-Christian is not the point for me. The point was to make available the songs I wrote between 1995 and 1997, and to let them find their own audience."[6]

Here, Amy is at odds with an entire industry and much of its audience—ironically, an industry she helped build and an audience she helped to attract. While Amy may not define relevance in terms of meeting lyric criteria, many of her brothers and sisters in CCM do. When a lyric like that of "Takes a Little Time" comes along, which in fact does not clearly communicate Christ (the criteria), it makes sense that many who listen to CCM and work within its community would label such a lyric as irrelevant. However, in the case of "Takes a Little Time," it is the context or environment in which the song is heard which contributes most to its being labeled as irrelevant.

Not everyone within the Christian music environment believes "Takes a Little Time" is irrelevant; thus the debate. Brian Nelson of WJQK-FM, a station which did play "Takes a Little Time," reported that his station "received many listener calls, saying those lyrics offered them hope and challenged them to trust God in the midst of trial."[7]

Oddly enough, in the big picture of real life, a lyric like "Takes a Little Time" might have a high degree of relevance, if it could be experienced by both Christians and non-Christians in a different context other than that of Christian radio and retail. On the whole, both Christian radio and Christian retail have a very low tolerance for lyrics which deviate from common subject matter they deem relevant to their own biased mission. Lyrics which do not meet their criteria or perpetuate their mission, as they see it, are of little or no use to them. Yet a song like "Takes a Little Time" did garner some Christian radio airplay, partly because of Amy Grant's past reputation for lyrical relevance, and partly because there are Christian stations that do believe in airing the occasional song addressing social issues or love between two people. In spite of the occasional exception, the voices of criticism and debate would roar like never before if a station's shipment of singles from the record companies contained *nothing of use to them*. Here again we land on the question of use, a defining issue in contemporary Christian music.

How Donors and Consumers Help to Define What Is Christian

While many radio and retail gatekeepers hold strong convictions regarding the highest and best use of music, we cannot forget that the success of their own labor is directly tied to consumer and listener support. Their own survival requires them to listen and react to the voices of those Christians who support their businesses and ministries. This reality cannot help but shape their notions of what a Christian lyric is or isn't. Consumers of Christian music, whether they're tuning into the radio, watching a video show, or purchasing a concert ticket or CD, are voting on both the music and its lyrical content. By refusing to vote at the cash register (or with the dial or remote) for a particular song or artist when the lyric content fails to meet their criteria, they contribute to an industry-wide understanding of how Christian music is to be defined. Consumers hold fixed ideas about what they expect in music named as Christian. For the most part, those within the CCM community expect it to be "Christian" (as they define the term in relationship to lyrics) and they expect it to be useful to the religious dimension of their lives. If it is not useful to what they perceive to be the religious dimension of life, they find it difficult to identify its relationship to Christianity in any form.

Readers who are audience members take note—you have a great deal of power, and with power comes responsibility. How well equipped are you as a disciple of Jesus Christ to discern whether or not lyrics are congruent with a comprehensive kingdom perspective? Everyone involved with Christian music, including the audience, are called to live under God's rule. What God rules over is his kingdom and his kingdom is huge. Remember, God's kingdom is everything he has dominion over. Certainly such a kingdom encompasses more than a set of easily identifiable terms common to Christianity.

Chapter 12

The Ocean Too Big for the Glass

As long as I have been involved with contemporary Christian music, there have been those in leadership who have gently prodded artists and songwriters to focus their lyric writing on Jesus, and on topics which are easily discerned by even the most immature Christians as being related specifically to Christianity. This approach has two sides to it, both of which must be taken into consideration. On one hand, it seems to demonstrate a genuine godly desire to communicate simply and clearly to the youngest and weakest of our brothers and sisters. It makes allowances for immature believers, or for those who are simply very young in the faith. This approach does not require that all brothers and sisters listen, think, and discern with the maturity which comes from having walked with Christ for many years. If this view is born out of genuinely wanting to love and serve people, and if at the same time there is also music for more mature, growing Christians, this is a good thing. On the other hand, intentions are not always so pure, and biblically informed thinking is not always the motivation.

Entering the Hot Zone of Consumerism

A major portion of the work we do in CCM is aimed directly at the felt needs of the Christian consumer. This is one of the hot zones in our industry which has compromised both our music and our ministry. Through the power of our positions and authority, many of us can influence lyrics in such a way that they mirror the felt needs and product expectations of Christian consumers. When we mirror these felt needs and product expectations without godly concern for whether or not they are healthy, legitimate, theologically sound, or complete, we cross a line into the shadows of worldliness. Any movement away from the light of scripturally informed, godly intent is a movement in the wrong direction.

Qualifications

Focusing the style or lyric content of music toward your listeners is not wrong in and of itself. As I mentioned before, there are genuine reasons to do so—worship chief among them. Consider another example: Christians need songs of celebration which mark important moments in their lives. In the context of a marriage ceremony, there is often a need for a beautiful song which speaks of marital love. If I write this type of song out of a love for the church, which is a natural extension of my love for God, then I am bearing fruit in keeping with one dimension or one aspect of my calling as a musician and songwriter. In this scenario, I've done no harm in focusing both form and content in the direction of the consumers' need. However, if I create and promote music which seeks only to meet the Christian consumer's felt needs, to the exclusion of other needs equally important to the enrichment of their lives, I fall headlong into harm's way. If my method for meeting the needs of God's people is to satisfy the need with the loudest voice, I can be assured that many important needs will go unmet. If I concentrate solely on one voice rather than the whole, if I concentrate only on the voices of humankind, I'll never have a kingdom vision for music. It will forever elude me. It is one thing to possess a comprehensive, kingdom vision for music and have a genuine calling to a particular emphasis or focus. It is another thing altogether to believe your emphasis or focus is the end-all statement for what it means to create lyric and music in service of God, the church, your community, and the watching world. More often than not this is how we think and, as a result, how we falter.

Lyrics and Single Issue Politics

The focused, topical narrowness of CCM lyrics has its equivalent in the political arena, where the religious right is often accused of single-issue politics. Christians for the most part have not been encouraged or trained to think Christianly about all of life, nor have many seen a comprehensive kingdom perspective. As a result, they have only learned to identify a few key issues with the cause of Christ on earth. Overall, modernity has so fragmented our culture, including the Christian subculture, that it has become increasingly difficult to gather a sizable consensus on anything. It reminds me of someone running for public office. If a Christian wants to win an election, for example, he has to ensure that the maximum numbers of Christian voters go to the polls. He achieves this by focusing on the minimum number of issues which the maximum number of Christians will agree are most important. In the political arena a comprehensive kingdom perspective is of little use in winning elections. It's too big, too vast, and too glorious.

The very same scenario exists in CCM, the difference being that in the place of a cause, platform, or social issue, there is this lyrical emphasis. Like political issues, lyric ideas that produce a Christian consensus are also very few. It seems that Christians gravitate toward subject matter out of an intuitive feeling that Christian music is at its most relevant when it's illuminating, propagating, and defending subject matter easily associated with the most basic Christian fundamentals.

Looking again to the political model, it should be clear that Christianity is relevant to the abortion issue, and that the Christian mind ought to be brought to bear upon this important subject. Likewise, the connection between being a Christian and being pro-family is hard to miss. Thinking again of CCM, there is no problem with the conviction that Jesus is relevant to Christian music. On the contrary, his relevance to Christian music could not be clearer. Yet, a rub remains. If for you faithfulness to God means attending a school board meeting instead of joining members of your church in picketing an abortion clinic, it's likely that they'll think of you as someone who doesn't understand how serious the abortion issue is. Similarly, if you write a song about DNA, how lovely your girlfriend is, or the call to care for the environment, it's likely you'll be thought of as someone who's failed to grasp the most basic concept behind the creation of a Christian lyric. This is the rub.

Sometimes the rub turns into a jab. And it's not just your creative choices that are challenged; it's your overall commitment to Christ. Nashville's March for Jesus on May 30, 1998, produced a relatively small turnout (5,000 to 10,000) compared to the year before when 50,000 people marched. Writing for Nashville's daily paper, *The Tennessean,* religion editor Ray Waddle reported, "Some blamed the devil, others pointed to a lack of proper promotion." One marcher, a teacher with the Teen Challenge ministry, was quoted as blaming the devil for keeping people away, and added, "The people here are the ones who are serious about the Lord."[1]

Guess who isn't serious about the Lord?

This same type of thinking comes into play in the Christian music community regarding lyrics. They think writers and artists who meet core consumer expectations for lyrics are "the ones who are serious about the Lord." Writers or artists called to a different mission and focus are apt to have their Christian commitment repeatedly called into question. Without what Brian McSweeney of Seven Day Jesus calls contemporary Christian music's "permanent Jesus stamp of approval,"[2] artists experience a difficult time of it—not only emotionally but financially as well. There are only so many spots for songs on the radio and there are only so many people promoting concerts. Those without the stamp of approval are ushered to the back of the line or placed at the bottom of the list.

As for the March for Jesus parade in 1998, I didn't march in it because I was attending my son's high school graduation. Faithfulness to the Lord, my son, my family, and the Middle Tennessee Home Education Association required that I *not* march in the March for Jesus parade.

Though having your commitment to Christ called into question does sting, accusations like these go dangerously astray in their gross disregard for the sovereign purposes of God. They fail to take into account the doctrine of the body of Christ and the diversity and complexity of gifts, talents, callings, and responsibilities given to Christians by God for his countless and sovereign purposes.

The Argument

From contemporary Christian music's position as an industry, the greatest argument for writing lyrics which improve a listener's ability to identify the music as Christian is that if they like it, they can find it again and support it in the marketplace. For example: they would know the music is "Christian" because they recognized words fundamental to Christianity. They would know whether the singer is male or female. They might even remember the song title or the lyrics from the chorus. All they would need to do is look for the music at a Christian bookstore, or in the Christian music section of a mainstream music retailer. The bottom line is this: music that quickly and unmistakably categorizes itself as Christian gets the consumer into the stores and in front of the product in the most cost-effective way. The benefits are real and substantial, both spiritually and economically. Sales activity in the stores produces revenue which pays for the cost of doing business. This translates into God's provision for many families, mine included. Profits are distributed to owners, investors, and shareholders. These monies are used to continue the capitalization and growth of all kinds of endeavors, including contemporary Christian music and local church ministries such as evangelism and missions.

The spiritual benefits of steering the Christian to the musical product ought to be humbling and satisfying to those of us who create it, since God so often allows our music and lyrics to touch lives in the simplest and grandest of ways. If we can do that with a few guaranteed Christian music buzzwords, it's hard to imagine there being any downside to it. Christians and non-Christians alike will surely be blessed by an ability to identify Christian music as "Christian." But let's dig a little deeper.

The Making of a Genre

CCM is but one in a line of a thousand choices competing for the attention and resources of today's Christian music listener. This multitude of options contributes to the perception that the CCM industry needs to shape Christian music into an easily recognizable genre. When you hear blues music, there are unique characteristics that tell you you're listening to the blues and not classical music. Blues has its own creational integrity and ideological bias. You use *blues* ideas to create a blues song. If you use *reggae* ideas, your song will never turn out to be the blues. Contemporary Christian music, as I've pointed out, depends on the lyric to give the listener sufficient clues that they are indeed listening to Christian music and not the blues, or any other genre of music.

Listeners must be able to recognize something in the lyric—words, phrases, names for God—which will alert them that the music they are hearing is Christian in origin. As soon as it cements that identification, the lyric has done its work. It has acted as the necessary proof to make CCM a separate category of music. It has justified itself: it can be categorized. The music alone—melody, harmony, and rhythm—doesn't carry any specific category clues. The fact that the lyric defines the category is both inevitable and problematic.

Genre: Another Idea with Consequences

The decision to define and market Christian music as a genre based on the lyric has led to problems with serious consequences which Christians—called to live for God under his rule, everywhere and in everything—cannot ignore.

It's convenient for the CCM industry that their efforts to stimulate near-immediate product identification also serve traditional and legitimate ministry purposes, emphasizing devotional, confessional, and worship themes. The fact that CCM uses the lyric and not the music to define its genre, and because there are legitimate ministry purposes for lyrics which lend themselves to categorization (such as lyrics of a confessional, devotional and worshipful nature), potential exists for the illegitimate use of legitimate lyrics.

Anyone who writes songs of a worshipful, confessional, or devotional nature, or songs which directly proclaim the gospel, uses language fundamental to Christianity. If the use of music is praise and worship, then naturally the music will incorporate language which articulates praise and worship of God. A lyric such as Charles Wesley's "O for a Thousand Tongues to Sing" is a good example of this, while my own "Monkeys at the Zoo" is not. Compare the two.

Wesley:
O for a thousand tongues to sing
My great Redeemer's praise,
The glories of my God and King,
The triumphs of his grace!

Peacock:
I have got to clean house, got to make my bed, got to clear my head
It's getting kind of stuffy in here, smells sort of funky too like monkeys at the zoo
I have been a whoring after things 'cause I want to feel safe inside, that's a big fat lie
No amount of green, gold or silver will ever take the place of the peace of God.

Consider the language in each of these examples. Both of us were faithful to our intent, but look at the words Wesley used to articulate his intent: Redeemer, praise, glories, God, King, grace—all words commonly associated with Christianity. Now look at my lyric. You'll see that with the exception of "peace of God" at the end of the last line, I haven't used any language commonly associated with Christianity. Why? Is it because I don't know the first thing about writing a Christian lyric? I hope not. My intent in writing the song was completely different from that of Wesley's. His lyric was directed at God in praise of God. My lyric was directed at humankind in light of the reality of God. The intent gives shape to the outcome.

Since Wesley's commonly used "Christian" word count is so much higher than mine, his music naturally has a much greater chance of being accurately identified as Christian music. People will recognize this lyric as using language common to the Bible and will likely identify it as Christian in origin.

If Wesley wrote his lyric as a praise response to God's grace, which I believe he did, then it's good that he thought to choose language which simply, accurately, and poetically expressed his gratitude to God. We should all aspire to such a faithful response. For a moment, though, let's pretend that Wesley's intent was one different from what history has recorded.

Reimagining Wesley for the Worse

Let's imagine that his use of words and names such as Redeemer, praise, glories, God, King, and grace were in fact intentional, but that his motive for using the words was something entirely different from framing a worshipful response to the gospel. Let's imagine Wesley understood the church well enough to know that if he used words common to Christianity in his songs he could insure a predictable outcome: (1) Even young, immature Christians would recognize and name "O for a Thousand Tongues" as Christian in origin, and (2) because of this recognition his song would be

accepted as relevant and useful to the Christian community. And let's imagine Wesley understood that by creating the opportunity for this first predictable outcome, he would in turn create the possibility of the second outcome which might result in the sale of a copy of the music to "O for a Thousand Tongues."

Had Christian radio been around at the time of Charles Wesley, the version of Wesley I've conjured up in my imagination would have also had to make these kinds of lyric choices in order to insure that his song would meet the lyric criteria and expectations of Christian radio and its listeners. He would have also made these choices in order to insure that youth pastors and various parachurch organizations would easily give his song their endorsement. He would have been compelled to pander to any keeper of a gate to which he desired entrance.

Because there are significant spiritual and economic benefits in steering listeners toward Christian music, it is often difficult for Christians to see the various problems which have surfaced as a result of artists, industry, and audience working overtime to shape Christian music into a recognizable genre. The most significant problem is that it works to make the gospel and the kingdom of God appear demonstrably different and tragically smaller than what they actually are. We can get at the reason for this very quickly by analyzing the idea of genre and the bias it produces.

Getting at the Truth of Genre

The idea of genre is to take a category and break it down into smaller categories. Its built-in bias is that it assumes everything needs categorization. If the bigger category were books, then the bias of genre would want to break it down into smaller categories—mystery, romance, and science fiction. With music it's blues, Latin, jazz, country, and others. Though seldom desirable, we tend to accept the notion of musical genre as long as the defining characteristics rest primarily with the music and not the lyric. As soon as the music is labeled as Christian, the proof of genre immediately shifts from the music to the lyric and what was once marginally acceptable becomes altogether unacceptable. This shift sets in motion an incompatibility which no amount of rhetoric can overcome.

Two opposing forces are at work. While the idea of genre attempts to make the range of lyrical subject matter *smaller and less comprehensive* (and as a result more easily categorized and recognizable as "Christian"), the idea of what is truly Christian, which encompasses all creation, attempts to make lyrical content *bigger and more comprehensive.* In the latter, wider view, the content becomes more difficult to recognize as truly Christian, since most Christians are likely to overlook indirect spiritual references, even when they are congruent with the all-encompassing narrative of Scripture or a general perspective of God's kingdom.

When we start talking about what it is that defines lyric images and ideas as Christian, we have to recognize that Christian ideas are first kingdom ideas. Christians and Christianity sit inside something larger—the kingdom of God. The kingdom is a bigger idea than the church even though the church is an incredibly important idea. The kingdom idea is far too big and important to fit within a genre. It's like trying to put the world's oceans in an eight-ounce glass. It can't be done—it's impossible. An eight-ounce glass could hold a drop or two from each ocean, but with its limited capacity it could never pretend to contain the oceans of the world. No genre is big enough to hold a comprehensive kingdom perspective—it does not have the capacity. Genre is about reducing content. The kingdom is about expanding it. These two are incompatible. They just don't go together. They can't go together.

Reviewing the Kingdom Perspective

A comprehensive kingdom perspective sees the world as God sees it—as much as is humanly possible. At the heart of this perspective are two important truths:

(1) Everything created by God is good. His dominion is everything and everywhere. He has called his people to be stewards of the good he created and to be his representatives in the kingdom at hand, everywhere and in everything. Therefore, everywhere and everything should be the subject matter of lyrics written by Christians. Christians should speak to what they know, and what they know should represent every aspect of creation.

(2) God has spoken in history, giving his people a narrative that not only frames our view of the gospel, the church, and the kingdom, but reminds us that God acts in history on behalf of his people and that these acts are stories worthy of being told again and again. He is still acting on behalf of his people today, and we should be telling today's stories. All God's actions in history represent good and worthy subjects for lyrics written by Christians.

Genre and the Church Music Continuum

You may have figured out by now that the historical idea of church music, from the Psalms of the temple to Gregorian chants, to Handel's *Messiah,* to the Fisk Jubilee Singers, could easily qualify as a distinct musical genre. Many people do in fact see these as a part of a continuum and identify them as Christian music. However, anyone trying to fit contemporary Christian music on the whole into this continuum will have a very difficult time making a case for their position.

Granted there are artists within CCM who serve the church in ways similar to the traditional historical role of church musicians, and there are modern congregational songs which were birthed within contemporary Christian music—the songs of Michael W. Smith, Twila Paris, and The Maranatha Singers, for example. But this is where similarities end. While contemporary Christian music as an industry has its pockets of people who create music in service of the church, specifically for the congregational worship setting, the majority of CCM mirrors the larger industry of which it's a part—the mainstream music business.

On the whole, contemporary Christian music is really just pop music that attempts to satisfy the musical and lyrical needs of its original community while reaching outward to new listeners. Latin music does the same thing. Jazz does the same thing. Folk does the same thing. Gay and lesbian music does the same thing. Christian companies were purchased by the large mainstream entertainment corporations in order to give them a presence in the Christian marketplace—in other words, in order to have one more musical genre covered. A corporation does not have to like jazz to purchase a jazz label and thereby increase their gross revenue. Nor do they have to profess Jesus Christ as their personal Savior in order to purchase a Christian label. (Jimmy Bowen, the record executive who arranged the purchase of Sparrow and StarSong by the London-based music conglomerate EMI, and who essentially started the whole mainstream label acquisition spree, was so impacted by his involvement with contemporary Christian music that he allotted barely a sentence to it in his biography.)

There's solid justification for the position that the church can and should have music which has been composed for the church alone—with the intent that it be used for its confession of faith and its worship of God when the church gathers as a worshiping body. I think it's appropriate to set out to serve the church in this way. Some portion of God's songwriters and composers obviously have this intent—as well they should.

A Job Well Done: The People Get It

When it comes to the phenomenon known as contemporary Christian music, people in the church and outside the church mostly treat it as one category of music—one genre—among many. The leadership of CCM has done a remarkable job in selling their music as a genre. People get it now. Television gets it—both late night and the morning shows. Magazines get it—even the ultraliberal ones like *Spin* and *Details. Time-Life* gets it. They're selling it on TV just like they sell all the other genres. Everyone gets it. Unfortunately, what they get is usually a further reduction of our already reduced and marginalized version of Christianity and the kingdom of God. And it comes out so incredibly small that the result is like that eight-ounce glass trying to hold the oceans of the world—only a few drops fit.

Here's an example of how one very well-known sitcom got it: The March 19, 1998, episode of *Seinfeld* began with Elaine driving off in her boyfriend Putty's car. After pulling into traffic she turned on the radio and began to bop along to the music. Suddenly she looked down at the radio with a perplexed look on her face. She'd caught herself bopping to the following lyric:

> Jesus is one, Jesus is all
> Jesus, pick me up when I fall

Elaine quickly chose another preset on the radio, only to find that her boyfriend had programmed every preset to a Christian radio station. Completely befuddled, Elaine muttered the word *Jesus,* only she wasn't recognizing the second person of the Trinity; she was taking the Lord's name in vain. Later back at the restaurant Elaine discussed the incident with George.

Elaine: "Here's one. I borrowed Putty's car and all the presets on his radio were Christian rock stations."

George: "I like Christian rock. It's very positive. It's not like those real musicians who think they're so cool and hip."

Thank you, George, you had to rub it in, didn't you? And "positive," where have I heard that? Didn't CCM have a try at Positive Country with not too positive results? Susie Luchsinger, a singer who was marketed as Positive Country, never did agree with the tag. "What bothered me the

most," says Susie, "is that when you say 'positive country' well then what's all the rest of it? . . . it's not all negative."[3] According to former EMI Music president/CEO Jim Fifield, EMI got into the Christian music market because they "felt that the positive message that Christian artists convey would appeal to a much larger segment of the population."[4] Phil Quartararo, former president/CEO of Virgin Records America, told *CCM Magazine* that "there's no reason why we can't sell this to the mass appeal pop consumer, and it wouldn't hurt 'em to get a dose of a nice message."[5]

Positive and nice. Helpful and friendly. Hmm, sounds more like a description of the Ace Hardware man than music informed by a story so huge that it's still being written today—a story so real that it involves every action, emotion, and thought under the sun—a complex, bloody, beautiful, redemptive, truthful story. Positive and nice? Helpful and friendly? Certainly the martyr Stephen found his complete trust in Jesus helpful while he was being stoned to death by those who opposed his message. And I suppose you could say that he was nice or friendly to those who opposed him, since he did cry out these words to Jesus right before he died: "Lord, do not hold this sin against them" (Acts 7:60).

It's Positively True

Many sincere Christians (and you may find yourself among them) believe Christianity is true because it works. They represent Christianity as if it were the best among today's glut of self-help programs and religions—a kind of higher form of self-help in which Jesus partners with the believer toward the abundant life. For us to think of Christianity and to represent the kingdom of God in this way is to totally misunderstand and misrepresent the mind of God. The gospel is not a self-help program that really works; it is the truth. And because it is true, it possesses the power to change lives. Changed lives go on to change the world, and in this sense it does work, but not in the grossly limited ways in which people sometimes perceive it to work. Stephen, with his changed life, contributed to the kingdom story by telling the truth and dying a violent death for it.

When we attempt to prove the truth of the gospel by evidence of its being cool or positive, or by its ability to render unto us our version of the beautiful Christian life, we set the gospel—and Christianity on the whole—up for failure. This version of the gospel and the kingdom of God will eventually fail because in reality it is no gospel and no kingdom at all. What many naive western Christians do not understand is that there are places in the world where belief in Jesus Christ and his teaching can lead to torture and death. Should you or I ever experience this kind of persecution, I don't think our lives will be demanded of us for believing that Christianity is positive, or nice, or true on the grounds that it gave us everything our consumer-oriented hearts could ever hope for. No, I think that under the thumb of persecution, we would experience prison, torture, and death only if we persisted in openly declaring the truthfulness of the gospel, the magnitude of the kingdom story, and the falsehood of any religion or system of thought that contradicted it.

Contrary to what some earnest believers have stated, the problem with Christian lyrics isn't that not enough songs mention Jesus any more, or that the "J" word has become non-hip. The problem is much bigger than the absence of Jesus' name in songs. The problem is that we've failed to hear and act on the calling to be God's people under his rule, everywhere and in everything. The problem is that we've failed to accurately represent the reality of his grace and his kingdom. *This is the CCM problem.*

Our calling in the industry is to do the good we know to do by composing true and beautiful music for the needs and purposes common to the gathering of the called ones—the church. Having shared in this privilege, we move outward into the "everywhere and everything." We move out into the rest of God's dominion. Here we bring the comprehensive kingdom perspective to bear upon all of life. We ask a question such as, "What does God think about pain and suffering?" then we study to know his thoughts and we put those thoughts into the narrative of a song. We tell a story—an earthbound, kingdom-at-hand story, informed by the eternal God who possesses all knowledge and all truth. We keep alert and remain inquisitive. Then we ask another question and write another song. We do it again and again and again and we never stop. And that is why God's people, making God's music under his rule, legitimately touch on every aspect of God's dominion, and why this music will never fit within a narrowly defined genre.

On Becoming the Ocean Too Big for the Glass

Contemporary Christian music is a drop or two in the eight-ounce glass. There's a whole ocean of possibilities awaiting the musical children of God, the men and women who equip them, all the people who listen now, and those who might listen in the future.

The Scripture tells us that through Jesus "all things were made" and that "without him nothing was made that has been made" (John 1:3).

How big is the kingdom? It's as big as Jesus imagined it to be. It is everywhere and it is everything.

In the Gospel of John the author tells his readers he transcribed not the whole story, but rather a true and sufficient story. According to John, "Jesus did many other things as well. If every one of them were written down, I suppose that even the whole world would not have room for the books that would be written" (John 21:25).

If there's not enough room in the Gospel of John to tell the whole story of Jesus, there certainly isn't room within a rigidly defined musical genre to do the job. Before the contemporary Christian community can create, market, and support music that reflects the full impact and power of God's message to the church and the watching world, we have to stop making man-centered rules and guidelines for that message to follow. We're in no position to define God's boundaries. We can't put the ocean in a glass. We can't stuff Christian music into a genre.

As John noted in his Gospel, Jesus' interests and concerns touched on every facet of human experience. If Jesus were to appear to you in the quiet of your home, have a seat at your table, and explain to you in scientific, new-physics detail how he's the glue that holds all things together in the universe, would you wonder to yourself, "What's 'Christian' about what he's telling me?"

It's a silly question, but no sillier than challenging the "Christian" content of songs because they lack the approved buzzwords that officially place them in the CCM category. Not only must music industry professionals resist this misguided attempt to box in the Christian message, but music consumers must stand against it as well. In fact it's the audience, not the music makers, who ultimately determine how freely music can express the gospel and the kingdom. The more any enterprise is controlled by the sound of the cash register and the applause of people, the more the audience response matters. But what matters most?

Look at the ocean of God's music all around you. Imagine with me and throw away that glass.

Chapter 13

Stopping to Think

In some corners of the CCM community, the tension regarding the role of the lyric has melted into apathy. People have grown weary of the lyric debate. There is a sense that continuing to pursue a reasonable consensus on the subject is, well, unreasonable. Many of us, artists, industry folk, and audience, have long since gone on to construct various rationalizations to explain our own choices and to deal with the tension and confusion that surround the subject.

Dazed and Confused

The daily mass of random word and image disseminated by the media into our already crowded lives leaves most of us dazed and confused. Artists, songwriters, and industry leaders bring these feelings of "enough already" to our roles as creators and marketers. We understand that consumers won't take the time to read, or to think things through, because we ourselves don't have the time or inclination to do so. The result is that the contemporary use of language in all its forms, from lyrics to advertising copy, is limited to the superficial. Everything is made small. We know that the Christian music audience does not often stop to think whether a lyric is harmonious with a biblical worldview or comprehensive kingdom perspective, because we ourselves often do not. Instead, we all tend to listen to lyrics through a mental grid the size of chicken wire, rather than listening through a more discerning grid the size of window screen. As a result, information deserving our attention, both contrary to and congruent with Scripture, slips through unnoticed. This information flows through without recognition, not because it is less important, but because it is made to seem less important or irrelevant in relationship to the things Christian culture does view as important and relevant. It is not necessarily biblically less important or irrelevant either, but again it is culturally less important or irrelevant since only a small number of Christians in Christian culture are thought to relate to its importance or relevance.

Following the Wrong Leader

More often than not, the contemporary Christian music industry shapes its lyric content to follow the lead of those in the Christian music audience (the church) with the least inclination to think Christianly about broader life issues. Songwriters and artists admit doing it, and publishers and record company leaders admit encouraging it. Most of the industry understand this to be one of the limitations of writing for the church, and accept it as such. Though there are notable exceptions, most of the time the industry considers this state of affairs to be rigidly unchangeable, and this is where it errs.

It is wrong for leaders in the contemporary Christian music industry to give in to the churches' general unwillingness to think on or cultivate a kingdom perspective when writing lyrics for the Christian marketplace. What is most disturbing is that rather than seeing the churches' inability to discern spiritually and think Christianly as a cause for tears, we view these enormously important issues as everyday problems for which we must find pragmatic solutions. We diligently work toward answers that will help us carry out the day-to-day business of Christian music, and succeed at it as the world and the forces of capitalism view success. We often appear to be more concerned with this particular mission than with the mission of tending to the overall spiritual health of the body of Christ—of doing good to everyone, especially believers (Gal. 6:10).

Rather than living in response to grace and in knowledge of the kingdom of God, we react to the consumer alone and let the marketplace define how we think, create, perform, and subsequently live. This is incongruent with our primary calling to live as God's people under his rule. We are not to be defined or ruled by anything other than God. It is his lead we are to follow.

The churches' general inability to discern spiritually, think Christianly, and demonstrate a comprehensive kingdom perspective are serious health problems in the body of Christ. They ought to inspire our imaginations to create music that addresses them—music that models a comprehensive perspective and initiates good thinking, good imagining, prayer, praise, repentance, and healing. Shouldn't love for God and his church inspire us to this kind of faithfulness? Isn't this the good we know to do?

Music, Language, and God's Will

Music is not a neutral container for the dissemination of ideas. Nor is it something which God created as a kind of sleight of hand to get otherwise disinterested humans interested in important ideas expressed through human language. On the contrary, music, like language, is an integral part of God's creation. He has built into both music and language an intrinsic power and benefit that we must respect. When the two are brought together in the form of vocal music, there are consequences. If the creator of the vocal music has respected both the music and the language, there is great potential for both music and language to shine brighter together than if heard separately. In order to achieve this, the two must become one in such a way as to yield to one another, without becoming less than what they were created to be. The marriage of music and lyric is very much like a human marriage in this respect. To the degree that the composer errs in this regard, vocal music will suffer. For this reason, I maintain that unless the listener can appreciate the music on some level, be it the melody, rhythm, style, production, or emotional response, they will receive little perceivable benefit from an easily recognizable Christian lyric. Unless the listener likes something about the music, apart from the lyric, it is unlikely that he or she will engage with the lyric on any level other than the superficial. Please understand that I believe God can do anything he wants with human effort, be it extraordinary or ridiculous. Yet just because God is in control does not mean that his people are exempt from thinking these things through. Nevertheless, I understand this to be an arguable point since many Christians believe that one of the strongest reasons to advocate lyrics which are easily recognizable as Christian in origin, is that they disseminate the Word of God, and the Word of God shall not return void.

Getting at the Word That Will Not Return Void

The idea that God's Word does not return void appears in Isaiah:

For as the rain comes down, and the snow from heaven,
And do not return there,
But water the earth,
And make it bring forth and bud,
That it may give seed to the sower
And bread for the eater,
So shall My word be that goes forth from My mouth;
It will not return to Me void,
But it shall accomplish what I please,
And it shall prosper in the thing for which I sent it.
(Isa. 55:10–11 NKJV)

In context, these thirteen verses frame an invitation to the nation of Israel to take hold of the life which is truly life. The chapter begins with a call for Israel to come to the One who alone can meet Israel's truest needs. Next comes the promise of an everlasting covenant (one eventually fulfilled in Christ and his church). Then a call to repentance. And finally, renewal, the lifting of the curse and the forgiveness of sin.

According to scholar Alec Motyer, who has devoted most of his life to the study of this book, the central preoccupation of this chapter "is with the Word of the Lord"[1] and that the "Word" in question is "directly the Word of the Lord."[2] As the Scripture emphatically states, it is God's Word going forth from God's mouth which makes good the guarantee that God's Word will not return to him void. The emphasis here is on God and the power of His direct Word to create and effect change. Belief in the power of God's direct word as Creator and Redeemer, one who can create and effect change, is a belief absolutely central to Christianity. However, if we emphatically state that a four-minute "Christian" pop song carries this same identical weight and effectiveness every time it's heard, we make a serious error. Verses eight and nine of Chapter 55 speak directly to this kind of presumption: "For

My thoughts are not your thoughts, nor are your ways My ways," says the Lord. "For as the heavens are higher than the earth, so are My ways higher than your ways, and My thoughts than your thoughts." The emphasis of this chapter is God's divine and perfect purposes, not man's well intended but nevertheless human and fallible thoughts and purposes.

In his commentary on the Book of Isaiah, Alec Motyer writes: "The Word of God is the unfailing agent of the will of God."[3] Motyer reminds us of the deep connection between God's Word and God's will. Behind the Word of God is the will of God. We cannot divorce the Word of God from his will. His Word accomplishes what he has willed it to accomplish. This is why his Word does not return to him void. Motyer continues: "As the rain furnishes both seed and bread, so the word of God plants the seed of repentance in the heart and feeds the returning sinner with the blessed consequences repentance produces."[4] It is by the power of his Word that God "wills and effectuates the repentance which brings sinners home to himself."[5]

With the best of intentions and worst of methods, artists, industry people, and CCM fans have distorted the meaning of these Scriptures, perpetuating a false view of them year after year. We have been, to borrow from noted author Richard Weaver, "hysterically optimistic" regarding the power of CCM. In theory, we may believe that the emphasis of verse eleven is on God and the power of his direct word to create and effect change. But in practice we turn it around. We act as if it is God's word, going forth from humanity's mouth, which makes good the guarantee that God's word will not return to humanity void. In acting this way, we place the emphasis on humanity and our ability to use the power of God's word, and various lyrical derivations of it, to create and effect change for the desire and will of humankind in God's name. This is not what these Scriptures teach. We must be careful not to turn the good word of God into a kind of lucky charm which we rub into our songs in order to justify having created them.

Does God ever use four-minute "Christian" pop songs laced with Scripture and spiritual principles as an example of his word not returning void? I imagine so, but only if it's his will. Remember, Satan quoted Scripture to Jesus. But it didn't inspire Jesus to change his mind.

I believe that one of the reasons our community has embraced this idea and perpetuated it for so long is that it provides a seemingly criticism-proof justification for many of our choices regarding music and lyric. How can we possibly find anything wrong with music that carries the power of the direct word of God?

The Necessity of Worship and the Ups and Down of Comfort

When the church gathers to worship God in his majesty, the language of the lyric must reflect the intent and purposes of worship. It must of necessity use words common to its purpose, common to Scripture, the history of the saints, and to contemporary believers.

There are many benefits to creating lyrics that are clearly Christian. Christian listeners will respond to the music sooner and may enjoy it more. Once they realize the lyric is Christian, they can confidently enter into the music. Serving the listeners' comfort level is a benefit as well. Some listeners are uncomfortable with anything other than Christian music. They listen exclusively to Christian music out of obedience to God as a matter of conscience. These brothers and sisters are only comfortable to the degree they can listen to music with the assurance that they're not violating their conscience. Familiar words common to Christianity help to assure this type of listener that they're giving their hearts and minds to something they believe to be appropriate and safe.

The Possible Reactions of a Non-Christian Listener

When non-Christian listeners hear Christian music, the fact that they are able to easily recognize the music as "Christian" improves the possibility of a reaction to the content. The reaction may be:

1. Positive, in that the listener is open, and remains open to easily recognizable Christian content as long as he or she perceives the music as good. For example: "I really liked the song and wasn't too far into it when I realized, hey this is a Christian song. At first I was like, wait, I don't listen to Christian music, I'm not even a Christian. But then I honestly had to say that the song was really good. It helped me to see that there's some Christian music worth listening to. I went out and bought the CD."

This example helps us to see how creating songs which are easily recognizable as Christian in origin might in fact be a good thing.

2. Negative, in that the listener is closed, and remains closed to easily recognizable Christian content regardless of whether he or she perceives the music as good. For example: "I really liked the song and wasn't too far into it when I realized, hey this is a Christian song, which really bummed me out because I was really liking the song a lot. The music was cool, but the lyrics

just don't relate to my life. It's not what I'm into spiritually at all and especially not politically. There's so much politically about the Christian Right that I just can't hang with, and truthfully it just turns me off to the whole thing."

This example helps us to see how creating songs which are easily recognizable as Christian in origin might in fact be counterproductive, especially when common words, phrases, or clichés trigger negative comparisons and associations. Here, common words, phrases, and clichés actually distract from the very truths they seek to communicate. The listener doesn't think about what the artist is saying in the lyrics. The listener believes he knows what a Christian is, knows what Christians are about, and wants nothing to do with them or their music. Scott and Chris Denté from Out of the Grey anticipated this kind of reaction when they first started writing songs. "Our initial approach to songwriting was based on the idea that you don't hit people with a sledgehammer, because they put their religious God-filters up when they hear certain phrases and words."[6]

3. Indifferent, in that the listener remains largely indifferent to easily recognizable Christian content, regardless of whether he or she perceives the music as good, bad, or somewhere in between. This kind of reaction is common to listeners who are committed relativists and/or pluralists. For example: "I really liked the song and wasn't too far into it when I realized, hey this is a Christian song. So what, though, everybody's entitled to their own spirituality as long as it's positive. It's a good song—not so incredibly good that I have to run right out and buy it, but if somebody gave me a copy I'd probably listen to it."

This example helps us to see how our pluralistic culture has allowed Christianity to occupy a spot on the menu of spiritualities available to the religious consumer. In this case, the use of cliché and common Christian terms so easily identifies the work as being "Christian" that even though it's recognized as Christian in origin, it is not engaged intellectually on any level. It is acknowledged and tolerated, but not necessarily taken seriously, especially as a declaration of objective truth.

Wait Till You See the Side Effects

Serving the Christian listener's comfort level has an unfortunate side effect. It often works against the spiritual maturity and growth of the church. This is because many immature Christians live radically compartmentalized lives and, as a result, arrange their music purchasing and listening into compartments as well—compartments which correspond to their felt needs.

If they need to feel romantic, they might listen to the love songs of Babyface or Luther Vandross on their local adult contemporary radio station. Or they purchase romantic music at their local mainstream music retailer. On the other hand, if they need to feel "Christian," they will listen to Christian music on their local Christian radio station. Or they will purchase Christian music at their local Christian music retailer. They do not turn to mainstream love songs to feel hopeful and heaven bound. Nor do they turn to Christian music to feel romantic or to have God's thoughts about love and romance enter into their own. This type of Christian listener comes to Christian music as a consumer who finds comfort in knowing that there is a Christian product available which matches his or her very narrow felt need.

"The most we seem to be able to do," notes David Wells, "is to take daily inventories of personal needs and then try to match up people, products, and opportunities with them." The irony according to Wells, "is that this psychological hedonism, in which self is the arbiter of life, is self-destructive."[7]

These consumers know what they want and are uncomfortable and disappointed with music which declares itself to be Christian (either directly or indirectly), yet does not meet their personal religious needs. For them the ability to easily identify the music as "Christian," or to have record companies or retailers give it their "permanent Jesus stamp of approval" takes the guesswork out of shopping and insures that they will indeed purchase only the kind of product they want.

A retail advisor to my record label's parent company posed the question, "What is a Christian album?" The answer, he suggested, is up to the consumer. "Why do people shop Christian music and bookstores?" he continued. "I believe it is summed up in the orthodoxy. In today's economy, Christians will buy their Kenny G, Garth Brooks, Frank Sinatra, and Counting Crows at just about anyplace, fully expecting that it will possibly/probably not be an album of Christian values. But when it comes time to buy an album for their friend/relative/selves, they want quality control of sorts. What will this album say? Will it have the substance that I am shopping for? Most Christian albums are sold through Christian retail establishments for that very reason."

"When it comes to lyrical content," he concluded, "most music buyers . . . rely on the record companies to police the content of their albums until somebody complains at the consumer level."[8]

Most record companies understand their role in policing the content. In my survey of Christian artists, 37% of those polled answered yes to the question: "Has a Christian publisher or record label executive ever asked or required you to change a lyric, because in his or her opinion, the lyric was theologically or biblically incorrect?"

Twenty-five percent (25%) answered yes to the question: "Has a Christian publisher or record label representative ever asked or required you to add a name for God, such as Jesus, Father, Spirit, or Lord to the lyric of a song?" One artist who answered no also added, "They roll out the red carpet when you do."

Rather than seeing the psychological hedonism Wells described as a problem to grieve over and pray about, many of us in the CCM industry see this kind of thinking and behavior as indicative of consumer trends which must of course be followed and served in order to stay profitable. Even Christians, it seems, must live by the motto "The customer is always right." It sounds charitable enough and superficially smart from a business standpoint, but it's really more Dale Carnegie than Jesus in origin. Since Christians belong to Jesus, we've got other issues to factor in—especially those of us involved in books and music.

In an e-mail sent to the EMI Christian Music Group, the retail advisor mentioned above proposed this question to a colleague of mine: "As a Christian concerned about content, isn't it my responsibility to honor my customer's trust?"

To this question I would reply, "Don't we have a responsibility to God, his church, and his kingdom to create, to manufacture and to stock on our shelves books and music which tell the whole kingdom story to date—a unified, yet diversified story? Aren't Christians called to see things as God sees them, that is, as much as humanly possible? Isn't this the Christian maturity Paul advocates?"

The Christian music audience deserves artists, songwriters, and business people who prayerfully seek inspiration and wisdom to create and market music that is truly good—music that meets a great number of legitimate needs. But to get this, consumers must be diligent, and they must not allow the industry to treat them merely as retail sales targets. Because consumers are brothers and sisters in Christ first, and consumers second, those of us who are creators, marketers, and retailers must first want what is good for the CCM audience, over and above what we know we can sell them. The responsibility goes both ways.

This is a Christian approach to creativity, marketing, and retailing. It exhibits a kingdom perspective. This approach is distinctively different from the approach used by most of the world. It's distinctive because it starts with that which is good. And good is its starting place. Always the starting place.

Chapter 14

Defining and Naming: Truth and Consequences

In September of 1997 I was asked by the Awards and Criteria Committee of the Gospel Music Association board of directors to join an advisory group formed to help the GMA produce "a succinct, working definition of what constitutes 'Gospel Music.'"[1] At that time the committee was in the process of revisiting the "criteria upon which recorded product is eligible to be nominated for, and receive, a Dove Award.™"[2] According to the letter they sent me, this revisiting of the criteria had come about because some Christian Booksellers Association member stores were stocking recorded music not "Christian" in nature.

After three days of trying hard to contribute something, I concluded that coming up with a definition was both too simple and too complex. To say that "gospel music" is music which communicates the good news of Jesus Christ's atonement for our sin is simple and true, and this in fact might be one definition. But sticking to this kind of succinct definition left me troubled. Under a definition this narrow, the majority of songs I had contributed to contemporary Christian and pop music over the last sixteen years could not be categorized as gospel music. This kept me searching for answers.

What I now know for certain is this: Jesus Christ and the good news of the gospel is indeed my life and my music. For sixteen years the gospel has inspired and informed my life. Everything I believe about anything is either informed by or checked by the Scriptures. I received the Bible as God's word to me after having believed the gospel. In short, my life and my work move outward from a kingdom-based gospel center or core. This however is where the complexity really begins. From this point outward, trying to define gospel music is a bit like trying to lasso DNA. It is simple to say that gospel music is either music about the gospel of Jesus Christ or music in praise of Jesus, the source of the gospel. It is another thing altogether to attempt to extract a soundbite definition of gospel music from what it means to live in light of the gospel and the kingdom of God.

Stumped, I wrote back to the GMA stating that "I regret that I cannot provide you with a definition that honors both the simplicity and complexity of the gospel, takes into account the seriousness of the gospel, and gives you and your committee a definition for the purpose of identifying music which does or does not qualify for a Dove award."

Many questions remained. Among them: What does it mean for a created thing to be Christian in nature? Can a created thing actually and truly be Christian in nature? And what are the ramifications of naming created things "Christian"?

What's in a Name?

The act of naming is an essential part of our stewardship role in creation. Names are derived from the distinctiveness of the thing being named. Though human beings are distinct in that we alone know the privilege of bearing God's image, we were not created as distinctly "Christian" in the sense that we understand this term to mean a disciple of Jesus Christ. We must become a disciple of Jesus Christ in order to be called a Christian. Even then our distinctiveness is extrinsic, in that it's imparted to us by Christ at our new birth. Christians are named after Christ, to whom we belong.

Furthermore, this Christian distinctiveness is at first an inward reality, which over time (hours, days, and years) manifests itself outwardly, in ways of thinking and doing unique to those who are the called-out-ones, God's people.

Every healthy Christian longs to become incrementally more like Jesus. To the degree that we succeed, to that degree the church becomes more like Jesus, and so, a much healthier entity. Each individual believer has the power to contribute to the overall well-being or ill health of the body of Christ. It ought to follow from the testimony of Scripture that only human beings can be "Christian." Only human beings are offered God's plan of salvation by grace through faith in Jesus Christ. Only human beings can mirror God's image. Only human beings can follow Christ as his disciples, carrying out the image-bearing activity of being God's direct representatives on earth in the kingdom at hand in the name of Jesus, under the guidance of the Holy Spirit, for God's purposes, and to his Glory, everywhere and in everything.

If this is all true, then it would appear that all the things we so easily name as "Christian," such as Christian music, Christian coffee houses, Christian motorcycle clubs, and Christian radio, do not possess the creational integrity to be called Christian in a scriptural sense.

A Case for Naming

We can make a case for naming things Christian because they have a Christian beginning, in that Christians provide the economic support for them to exist, with an end goal in mind somehow connected to ideas fundamental to Christianity, such as contemporary Christian music.

Or we can make a case for calling things "gospel" in order to indicate that it is for the purposes, wants, and needs of Christians who believe in the gospel that these types of things exist, such as the Gospel Music Association. There is no crime in having organizations, events, and various other entities named to directly reflect the thinking or identity of their participants, such as the Democratic National Convention or Alcoholics Anonymous. One is for Democrats, the other for alcoholics. If the Democrats are planning their national convention and hope to have Democrats attend, it would be prudent to refer to the event as the Democratic National Convention. Likewise, if you are a recovering alcoholic traveling through a city on business and would like to attend an AA meeting, it's helpful to be able to open the phone book and look up Alcoholics

Anonymous. If you are creating, marketing, and selling products you believe only Christians will be interested in for the most part, then it's prudent to put the word "Christian" in the name of your business: EMI Christian Music Group. This is really just common sense. But it is not a neutral choice. All ideas have consequences, including the idea of naming things Christian.

The Reality of Kingdom Life

There are at least two problems associated with naming things Christian. The first we looked at in a previous chapter, "The Ocean Too Big for the Glass." We said when we start talking about what defines anything as being Christian, we first have to recognize that Christian ideas and things are kingdom ideas and things before they are Christian. Christians and Christianity sit inside something larger—the kingdom of God. We are certainly free to speak of something which Jesus taught his disciples as a "Christian" idea. But truthfully if it is a Christian idea, it is a part of a much larger gathering of ideas—kingdom ideas.

For example, Christians would consider the Lord's Supper as a Christian idea or concept, and if you were to write a song about it, naturally people would say that the song was a Christian song. But look at the Scripture. It teaches that the cup is representative of Jesus' shed blood and the bread is representative of his broken body. His blood was shed to bring forgiveness of sin in order to bring about the fulfillment of the kingdom. The king makes kingdom choices on behalf of his subjects. The kingdom is always about God's purposes in history whether it's creation or redemption. Kingdom life is life that is abundant and full to overflowing. This is what we want to be about. You can't reduce this. It's too big to wrap your arms around it. Too big for any label.

Small privatized ideas about Jesus as the personal Savior can be reduced small enough to fit inside a half-hour sitcom. What we want to be about is something which is so enormous, so life-penetrating that it cannot be contained in all the sitcoms in the world. Songs informed by a comprehensive kingdom perspective will not be small. They will include all of history as well as visions for the future.

When the reality of kingdom life is defined in restrictive, exclusive terms, Christians begin to think that those terms represent the kingdom. As we rub shoulders with people who do not profess Christ, they in turn assume that what we're saying in our lyrics is what we think covers the whole story. And it's out of this small and insufficient picture of the reality of kingdom life that our music gets categorized, the gospel gets trivialized, and our faith in Jesus gets caricatured.

The contemporary Christian music community must begin to write music and lyric from a kingdom perspective regardless of the pulse of the consumer or the official definitions of gospel or Christian music. Psalm 19:1 says, "The heavens declare the glory of God; the skies proclaim the work of his hands." Granted, it wouldn't represent the most commercially viable of topics, and I understand that it might render me ineligible for a Dove Award, but I'd be willing to write, record, and market a song about the relationship between quantum mechanics and the glory of God.

When naming media, vocational pursuits, inanimate objects and all our various activities as "Christian," we must remember that the thing we're naming was not empty of meaning and purpose prior to our naming of it. It was not a neutral entity waiting to be christianized. Not only does whatever we name have its own unique design or creational integrity; it also has its own ideological bias.

If we could name things "Christian" and allow them to keep their creational integrity, there would be little reason to examine the issue. Unfortunately, we can't. For example, consider a Christian coffee house. Before a coffee house ever becomes "Christian," it is first a place where, we hope, excellent coffee is served at a fair market price to people who find pleasure in drinking coffee. A coffee house may do other things like serve food and provide a forum for musical performers and poets, but a coffee house is only a coffee house to the degree that it possesses the creational integrity of one. A little storytelling will cement this point.

A Cup of Good Coffee

In college Tom Watson had been a strong student leader active in the Fellowship of Christian Athletes. Upon graduation, Tom and two close friends, Jake and Eric, decided to pool their life savings into opening a Christian coffee house on the main street of Blakeford, their little college town. They rented a storefront and set about the task of turning it into what Jake referred to as "a place cool enough for non-believers to hang out at." Jake wasn't joking with this comment. All three were in it for the ministry, not out of a burning love for coffee. They were on fire for Jesus, and more than anything, they wanted people to become Christians as a result of their

efforts. Not that they didn't want to do good business—they did. In fact, together they had pledged to always pay their bills on time and to be extra courteous to all their customers since they wouldn't necessarily know if a customer was a Christian or not, and they wouldn't want to miss the chance to make a good impression for Christ. They all believed that doing good business was doing good pre-evangelism, and evangelism was very important to their coffee house vision.

Dr. Robert Kahane had been a philosophy prof at State for twenty years. Coming from Berkeley, California, he had fond memories of late night discussions in the coffee houses along Telegraph Avenue. Therefore, it was with some interest that he read the flyer he'd plucked from beneath the left windshield wiper of his Volvo announcing, "Killer coffee and killer sounds!/All in a cool Christian atmosphere."

"So, the Christians have opened themselves a coffee house," he mumbled under his breath.

He smiled and grunted, "I wonder if an old Jew can breathe in a Christian atmosphere?"

It was just before five o'clock on Friday when Professor Kahane walked through the door of Mars Hill Coffee. He found a seat on a comfortable couch across from two students he recognized from State.

"Good afternoon," he said to them in his best professorial voice as he reached out to retrieve a large book from the coffee table. It was entitled *Jack,* a biography of C. S. Lewis. The professor had always appreciated Lewis. Of course he didn't agree with Lewis's theological conclusions, but he admired him as a writer and as a thinker. He placed the book down and took a sip of his coffee. Lukewarm.

"What is this?" He wondered. "It's definitely not the dark roast of my experience." Disappointed, the professor put down the cup. He had so wanted it to be good. He really had hoped to recommend the place to friends and faculty members. Blakeford needed a coffee house and he'd hoped this would be it. He pledged to himself to come back; they deserved the chance to improve. On the way out he caught the eye of a young man folding and counting T-shirts—shirts presumably for sale. The young man was modeling his fare. Emblazoned on the front of the shirt: "This Blood's for You."

"Not for me," thought the prof. "How do they take any of this seriously—something trivialized to this degree and handled with so little reverence?"

Six weeks later, Tom, Jake and Eric received a kind letter from Professor Kahane on his personal letterhead which together they read out loud with great anticipation.

> Dear friends at Mars Hill,
>
> Six weeks ago I was delighted to hear of the news of your opening. I've thought for a long time that we've needed a good coffee house in Blakeford. Unfortunately, after trying your establishment several times it is my opinion that you've shot a bit wide of good, and need improvement in several areas. The first and most important area that needs improvement is the basic cup of coffee you serve. Frankly, it is not good coffee. Have you folks been to very many coffee houses? Something tells me you haven't. Who is your coffee vendor? Are they reputable?
>
> It may or may not matter to you in the big picture, but I won't be coming back for awhile. After some time has passed, if you are still open for business, I will return to try your coffee again. Please tell the thin blond girl with the nose ring that, no, I still do not want to receive Jesus Christ as my personal savior. All I want right now is a good cup of coffee.
>
> Respectfully,
> Professor Kahane

Tom put down the letter and sunk into the nearest chair. Jake did as well. Eric was not so passive. "Man, I told you guys we should have never bought those cheap beans."

The Naming and the Damage Done

I've led you on this fictional journey in hopes of making a point: when we take it upon ourselves to name something "Christian," we compromise its creational integrity. And we hold the image of Christianity up to microscopic examination by a cynical world that is only too eager to see it fail. If a coffee shop uses cheap beans, it reflects badly on the owners of the coffee shop. If a Christian coffee shop uses cheap beans, it reflects badly on Christianity. Which ultimately reflects badly on God. Rather than extending

the message of the gospel, this well-meaning but misguided effort sets extremely difficult obstacles in the path of Christianity's advance.

Naming something "Christian" is not a neutral choice. It's a choice that must be carefully and prayerfully thought out. We must count the cost of its possible effect on people's perception of Jesus Christ, the church, and Christianity, as well as its effect on whatever we're naming. Our fictional coffee house entrepreneurs sought to create a "Christian" business and a coffee house. The way they combined the two violated the integrity of both.

A coffee house with integrity will serve good coffee for a fair price. Christians who own a coffee house should be known for serving the best coffee in town at a great price, not for having "Christian" on their sign in the parking lot. In this way, the Christians' vocation honors the call to live godly lives in the sight of their brothers and sisters in the community. You can own a coffee house without justifying its existence by naming it a "Christian" coffee house, while at the same time ministering to others in the name of Christ.

The "Christian" name tag becomes an easy target when things go wrong. When a "Christian" business fails to honor its commitments, it drags the honor of Christ down with it in the eyes of an unbelieving world. Our Professor Kahane was a fictional example, but I have seen far too many real ones among the recording studio managers, musicians, and engineers in Nashville. As a record producer I work closely with these people, and for years I've heard their horror stories of not being paid on time by "Christian" music businesses, being nickeled and dimed to death by them for lower fees, and so on. Because of the "Christian" identification, violating the integrity of the music business (bad enough) is transformed into a violation of the integrity of their witness before the world (far worse). Better that our colleagues and customers know us as Christians by our love and good deeds rather than by our letterhead.

When my son Sam was a little boy, he asked me to take him to the store to buy some Coke. In his estimation our family needed to start drinking a whole lot more of it. When we asked why this was, Sam replied with a perfectly straight face, "So we can recycle."

Any time we set something up as a front for something else, things get silly. And more often than not people can see right through the facade.

Perhaps the single greatest problem with the naming of anything as Christian (apart from the church and things directly related to it) is that in doing so we always seem to end up misrepresenting God. God cannot be contained in things made by the hands of fallen humanity. The church is the only thing he has given his name to and perhaps it should remain that way.

"Christian" Confusion

The recording company I've been affiliated with most, Sparrow, is a part of the EMI Christian Music Group. Since the principal mission of the company is to create and market music for and to the Christian church, "Christian" in the name makes perfect sense. EMI has invested in the various companies of the Christian Music Group in order to capture a share of the $500-million-plus Christian music market.

The name becomes a problem when artists affiliated with the EMI Christian Music Group want their music marketed to Christian and pop markets at the same time. The fact that they come from a company with "Christian" in the name can be very confusing to people in the pop marketplace. Their position is, "If you're a 'Christian' act, what are you doing trying to make a go of it in the pop arena? You have your own genre to work in."

The issue seldom gets down to resistance based on the truth claims of Jesus Christ. If this were the case we could give God praise. It is unfortunate that our successful efforts at establishing CCM as a competitive genre now work against us when we try to place artists from our community in the mainstream. We have taught the world that the music is Christian without teaching them what Christian actually means. As a result they've come to believe that Christian music is a genre like jazz or latin music. When we take an artist from our community (who wears the tag "Christian artist") and equip him or her to be salt and light in the culture at large (rather than the church), this is very confusing to the pop music infrastructure and its gatekeepers. Under this scenario, naming obscures our message and undermines our mission rather than clarifying and supporting it.

The Consequences of Ceasing to Name

There are at least three excellent reasons why we Christians should stop naming everything Christian:

(1) Christians could no longer choose to purchase things simply because they were "Christian." They would be forced to decide on their own whether or not the ideas embedded within created things were congruent with a comprehensive kingdom perspective. In short, Christians would mature.

(2) Christians could no longer hide from the world inside comfortable subculture surroundings. They would be forced out into the everywhere and everything of the kingdom at hand. They would be more faithful to the Christian mission as a result, and God's people would come closer to the idea of being God's people, in God's place, under God's rule.

(3) Non-Christians could no longer write off Christians and their work without encountering them directly. This would force non-Christians to deal honestly with Christians, their work, and their ideas.

When I imagine such things as this, I start to see more ocean than drops in the glass.

Guarding Against Misunderstanding

When people start to imagine, talk, and write in the way I've been doing for the last little bit, there is great potential to be misunderstood. Please understand that I have a high view of the calling to create good and truthful music for the church in a number of settings for a number of purposes. Don't interpret my willingness to write songs about quantum mechanics as promoting a new lyric direction for contemporary Christian music. All I'm concerned with promoting is Jesus Christ, his kingdom, and faithfulness to what he's called his people to. Since I'm a musician, I'm concerned with how this plays out for musicians.

Also, please don't hear in my "three excellent reasons" to stop naming everything Christian a rant against Christian record companies, media, and retail, or a demand that they cease and desist immediately with calling themselves Christian. What I'm concerned with here at the crossroads is doing the difficult work of carefully thinking these issues through in order to discern which way is forward. Each of us will have to decide for ourselves which direction that is. For myself, I'm praying to remain a teachable sinner—someone more afraid of not knowing the truth than having been found in error. And so I'm fearfully wrestling, looking for truth.

Two Views

The debate over lyric content is between two main groups. The first group represents those who believe Christian music should be "Christian." They think that, with few exceptions, Christian music should exist to represent lyrical themes related to CCM's original mission of worship and evangelism. Some in this group have imitated and championed the "lyric criteria" we discussed earlier. Some in this group endorse a sacred/secular split. Still others maintain that lyrics should adhere to common Christian lyrical themes in order to be named and marketed as "Christian." Absent the "Christian" nametag, they would not oppose a greater diversity of subject matter for lyrics written by Christians.

The second group represents those Christians who believe music created by Christians ought to promote lyrics that reflect a comprehensive Christian worldview, which is nearly the same as what I've been calling a comprehensive kingdom perspective. In short, this group believes that everything under God's dominion is worthy subject matter for songwriting.

On Making the Two, One

As heated as the debate has become at times, I still maintain that these two groups are not as polarized as they might think. For example, to promote lyrics that reflect a comprehensive Christian worldview or kingdom perspective *is* to promote worship and evangelism. In this way the kingdom perspective group does support the agenda of the worship and evangelism group. Where the second group does differ from the first group is in their promotion of thinking Christianly about all of life, and the belief that all of life can and should become the content of Christian lyrics.

To think Christianly about all of life—from romantic love to new physics, from ambition to Jesus—and to write lyrics based on such topics, is to dramatically increase the depth and breadth of Christian music. The Christian worldview/kingdom perspective (second) group takes its cues from Scripture, which is comprised of stories, sermons, genealogies, prayers, letters, songs, poems, and proverbs of every conceivable style, incorporating every imaginable literary device from hyperbole to alliteration, to acrostic, to stream of consciousness. The subject matter is all of life, both the hellish and the heavenly. The same Scripture that brings us the good news of Jesus Christ also tells the story of a fat king named Eglon, who was murdered by a left-handed man named Ehud. When Ehud stabbed the fat king the Scripture says that, "Ehud did not pull the sword out, and the fat closed in over it" (Judg. 3:22). The Scripture is chock-full of this kind of truthful, descriptive narrative.

The same Scripture that describes the ministry of the Holy Spirit also includes these words: "Let him kiss me with the kisses of his mouth—for your love is more delightful than wine" (Song of Songs 1:2).

These remarkable passages were included in God's Word for a reason. Yet, if stories or phrases like these were shaped into songs and recorded by Christian artists, it's likely that many well-meaning people would insist that there is simply no place in Christian music for songs about the murder of portly kings and lovemaking "more delightful than wine." The Christian worldview/kingdom perspective group is asking for the freedom to shine the light of Christ and his Word on a myriad of subjects (though we hope not portly kings).

The first, or "lyric criteria," group is calling for faithfulness in singing about our Lord, faithfulness in honoring him in worship, and faithfulness in spreading the message of the gospel. If you are a Christian, you must share this group's concern. If you fall more in the category of the second group, I appeal to you to communicate to those in the first group that you believe Christians ought to be about communicating the gospel, living lives of worship, *and* bringing the truth of Scripture to bear on a multitude of topics. Tell them you want to make the invisible kingdom visible.

Bolstering the Big Idea

It's hard for me to imagine that the group championing lyric criteria really believes that Christians ought to abandon commentary on culture, or avoid addressing the most basic of human concerns in lyrics. To believe in such a way would be especially difficult for parents. While you might teach your child about the lordship of Christ over all of life, the child would soon learn that Christian music has very little to do with the lordship of Christ over all of life, and that for music having to do with love and romance or a host of other topics, they would have to turn to some place other than Christian music. This doesn't square.

Raise the Bar, Don't Lower It

I understand the zeal of the worship and evangelism group to promote our Savior and the gospel. I hope all involved in this often fiery debate do. But to these brothers and sisters in Christ, I must give a firm but gentle warning: You are lowering the bar, not raising it. You're making it far too easy to enter your gates. You are unknowingly creating a climate where it is fast becoming more admirable and profitable for artists to *appear* Christian, in the most simple and superficial sense, than to *be* Christian, in the most biblically comprehensive sense. As a result, striking a rock-star pose and hoarsely commanding the audience to spell out J-E-S-U-S is often interpreted as an unwavering commitment to Christ, whereas lyrically addressing all of life through a comprehensive kingdom perspective is often misinterpreted as lacking in commitment to Christ. This should not be.

God has called his people to something profoundly greater than human ideas about genre and lyric criteria can contain. The kingdom is at hand and the kingdom is coming. And in the kingdom there are no small dreams for music. We must accept that God is doing a different yet complementary work in each of us. Artist, industry, and audience must commit to making the total subject matter and narrative of the lyrics we write and endorse into the ocean too big for the glass. And we've got to do it soon, before we thoroughly confuse not only our own children, but the talented and gifted artists coming up who want nothing more than to live out the reality of kingdom life everywhere and in everything.

To the Listeners

To my readers who represent CCM's listeners and supporters, I ask that you contribute your part in raising the bar of the CCM industry. Consider whether you yourself have played a role in creating a climate where it's more admirable and financially profitable for Christian artists to *appear* Christian in a superficial sense than to *be* Christian in the most biblically comprehensive sense. Are you looking for easily recognizable words common to Christians in the lyrics of Christian artists? Or are you looking and listening for great music written from a comprehensive kingdom perspective—music which might touch you, challenge you, and bring you pleasure in a multitude of ways, including reminding you of the gospel of grace and initiating a response in you toward Jesus? Don't miss God, his truth, and his kingdom while looking for how many times the name of Jesus is mentioned in a Christian song. Know the issue and learn to discern. If all it takes to convince you that a song is "Christian" is to see that it mentions Jesus, the CCM audience and the industry which feeds it is at an all-time low.

Raise the bar. Anyone can put the name of Jesus in a song. Only a Christian can possess a comprehensive kingdom perspective. Only a Christian can see what God sees (as much as is humanly possible). Only a Christian can think, imagine, and create music and lyric in a way which faithfully represents Christ and his kingdom. And only a Christian can listen to such music and discern its truthfulness and faithfulness. With ears to hear, listen.

Chapter 15

Contemporary Christian Music and the World

From its beginnings almost thirty years ago until the present moment, CCM has increasingly embraced the ways of the world in its business practices, and increasingly looked to the world for inspiration and acceptance. From songwriting to production, from marketing and promotion to artist management, there is no corner of CCM untouched by the world's ways of thinking about the creation and business of music. Many of these ways show us healthy stewardship principles that make good sense and that are in sync with God's Word. Others are bankrupt, with no connection to biblical imperatives—they are worldly. Love for God and his kingdom requires that we accurately identify our worldliness, repent of it, and have nothing more to do with it.

However, accomplishing this with any degree of faithfulness will be next to impossible as long as the men and women of CCM see worldliness only as *acting* wrong, rather than *thinking* wrong.

The Bible speaks of worldliness as thinking wrong. It teaches that the fruit of thinking wrong is acting wrong. As long as Christians view worldliness first as acting wrong, wherein acting wrong is tied to a short list of infractions such as adultery, drinking, smoking, and swearing, CCM's worldliness will go undetected. By focusing on a short list of sinful behaviors, we miss the most important idea of all—that worldliness is essentially sinful, futile thinking in the form of dependence on the world rather than on God. Worldliness, to draw a familiar biblical parallel, is about trusting in Egypt's horses, horsemen, and chariots, instead of the Holy One of Israel. It's about trusting in the world for your provision and your meaning.

The World in the Word

Scripture defines the world in three ways: (1) the earth as a place created by God the Creator, (2) all the people groups of creation, and (3) all the ways of thinking and doing which are contrary to God's ways of thinking and doing. The first two definitions refer to our Father's world, a world which is ours to enjoy, care for, and transform. The last refers to the world of sin and Satan—a world of thought and deed that the Bible instructs us to avoid at all cost. By examining this world we will discover whether there's any degree of truth in Steve Camp's charge that CCM "has gone too far down the wide road of worldliness."[1]

Modernity: The Values and Meaning Systems of the World

If you don't spend a lot of time in academia, or reading books of a theological or sociological nature, it's likely that the word *modernity* is not in your day-to-day vocabulary. It is, however, a word which all Christians in our time should know and understand. Its meaning has powerful consequences for all of us in CCM. Modernity is a word that describes the values and meaning systems of the world which shape modern life.

The ideas and thought systems of modernity dramatically effect everyone, including Christians—perhaps Christians most of all. According to author John Seel, "Long before modernity changes the doctrinal content of belief, it alters one's assumptions about how life is to be organized day to day."[2] Once our assumptions about life are altered by what is valuable and meaningful to the world, and society is transformed by all that is modern, modernity chisels away at our core values and beliefs. It seeks to undermine them by telling us they're unnecessary, outdated, illogical, irrelevant, inefficient, and unproductive. Unfortunately, it often succeeds in its mission. When modernity succeeds in this regard, worldliness moves in to take the place of the good that modernity has chipped away. It's in this way that modernity and worldliness also work together to subtly undermine our belief and trust in God. A page from the life of the young band Reality Check illustrates how modernity sneaks up on sincere people attempting to do good things in the name of Jesus.

Reality Check

Prior to signing a major record contract with StarSong, the band Reality Check had established itself as a potent and viable youth-oriented music ministry. On their own, with very little help from the CCM system, they were able to acquire a tour bus, a sound system, stage lighting, and eventually develop a sizable audience for their music—something most groups are incapable of doing without the help of a major label. Most importantly, on their own apart from the CCM system, they were able to spend a good deal of quality time with their audience developing important and lasting relationships.

In Reality Check's 1998 press kit, the band voiced clear and definitive ideas about the importance of their relationship with the audience and what it meant to minister to them:

"We don't want to come in and do an intense show, get everyone pumped up and then leave them hanging. We want to see kids saved, but then we want to make sure they have Bibles and other materials, and that they get plugged in somewhere where they can grow. We like the Billy Graham model of ministry where people get saved, get counseled, have follow-up, and get planted in local churches."

In April of 1998 I asked the band if signing with a major label, a manager, and a booking agent had altered their ministry at all. What you will hear in their responses reflects the influence and fruit of modernity. Listen closely.

Chris Blaney: "Before we were signed we were able to spend an hour or two after a concert playing basketball with all the guys. It used to

be we would sit and hang out, and meet friends, and be able to spend what I would consider more quality time with people we've just met at the concert."[3]

Rod Sheller: "It's harder now to connect with the people. In the past we would have a day or two to hang out and really build some relationships, but now it's like we do a show and we're on the bus and headed to the next city. That's been very hard for me personally."

I asked Rod why the change in ministry philosophy. "It's happening," Rod said, "because we're doing so many dates now because we're trying to broaden our ministry. The thing is, you don't want to have to sacrifice, but you almost have to in order to meet a wider audience."

According to band member Nathan Barlowe, "the advantage of being with a label is that they are going to get you to more people so your ministry is able to grow."

Now let's analyze what we've heard, but first some questions. What is most valuable and meaningful to the world, the concept of more or the concept of less? More of course. How is growth defined? Is it the quantity of growth or the quality? With few exceptions, it's quantity. The more of any product consumers buy, whether it's a ticket to a concert or a new deodorant, the more successful the product is considered to be by the world's standards.

Before the days of mass communication and worldwide travel, our definition of *more* was generally kept in check by practical limitations. People broadened their ministry by getting to know their neighbor down the road. Success in ministry might have been defined by making a single friend and lovingly leading them to Christ through word and deed.

Today, the ideas and systems behind modernity have dramatically altered our expectations for a successful and effective ministry. We go where we please, we get there fast, and we move on quickly in order to maximize our influence. The fact that we are largely unrestricted in our travel takes over our thinking and redefines the way we choose to live out our callings. When we finally stop to think and pray, we find that the values and meaning systems of modern life have chiseled away at our own core values and beliefs. We usually find out the hard way that just because we have the ability to do something doesn't mean we should.

Have you ever wondered why people living in a society filled to the brim with time-saving devices and systems have absolutely no time for one another? The reason is fairly simple. To a man with a fax machine or an e-mail account, everything looks like important and urgent correspondence.

But it's not. The same holds true for the good but biased support structure surrounding today's performing artists. To a booking agent everything looks like a potential concert date. To a manager everything looks like a strategy or a career opportunity. And to a publicist everything looks like an opportunity to publicize or maximize an artist's appearances. Yet in the economy of God everything is not a potential concert date, a career opportunity, or an opportunity for publicity.

There is no Christian enterprise, including that of an eight-member modern-rock band with an evangelism emphasis, which is beyond the power and corruption of modernity's touch. Good people who love God start out with a kingdom perspective that recognizes the value of spending "quality time with people" and end up finding it hard to "connect with the people" because modernity has reshaped their kingdom thinking into its own image under the guise of broadening their ministries. Os Guinness stated it well. "Under the influence of modernity, we modern Christians are literally capable of winning the world while losing our own souls."[4]

To borrow from author/teacher Dick Keyes, "The goal in life isn't to just accomplish many things." Nor is it to just accomplish many things for the Lord. "Life," says Keyes, "is first to be a certain kind of person before God."[5] The kingdom perspective of growth certainly allows for and encourages quantity, but it does so without ever defining growth strictly in terms of quantity. God's Word emphasizes quality growth. The size of the tree is far less important than the fruit the tree bears. This is why the "more" of ministry is always connected to a greater quality of fruit and not just a greater quantity of people. Broadening one's ministry will always be about faithfully loving and serving those within arm's reach, long before it's about casting bigger nets.

What all artists (not just Reality Check) find out sooner or later is that signing with a major label and taking on a booking agent, a manager, and a publicist are not neutral choices. Each of these businesses or services is a legitimate calling, but we must never forget that they each have ideologies deeply influenced and shaped by modernity. When overseen by a comprehensive kingdom perspective, they can be used for tremendous good, and often are. Yet by forgetting modernity's power and ignoring the core ideologies present within created things, we risk becoming something entirely different from what we faithfully set out to be. Even more frustrating is that we often become something we don't want to be, and do things we don't want to do, all in the name of ministry. You can search the Scripture through and through for examples of more ministry as defined by quantity alone, but you will be hard pressed to find them. Look for Scriptures encouraging us to a greater quality of ministry and you will be up for days.

While Jesus lived and walked among us, he could have had it all and done it all. He could have been king. He could have healed everyone and fixed every problem, but he didn't. He was on a mission and He stayed his course. You see, we have a Savior who knows firsthand that the pace and pressures of modern life, "constantly threaten to diffuse our concentration and dissipate our energy."[6]

Jesus' disciples were often as sold out to contemporary ideas of success and wider influence as any of us today. For example, they thought they were about to take up residence in a palace with their king. They tried to get Jesus to start acting like a king and quit talking with women and children—quit connecting with people. He would have nothing of it. The kingdom He came to establish was and is a kingdom upside-down from the values and meaning systems of the world.

"Modern life," says Os Guinness, "assaults us with an infinite range of things we could do, we would love to do, or some people tell us we should do. But we are not God and we are neither infinite nor eternal. We are quite simply finite."[7]

"Yet," offers Guinness, "as we make our contribution along the line of our gifts and callings, and others do the same, there is both a fruitfulness and a rest in the outcome. Our gifts are used for the purpose for which they were given us. *And we can rest in doing what we can without ever pretending we are more than the little people we plainly are*" (emphasis mine).[8]

As wonderfully informed as Os Guinness is on this topic, we can do no better than to turn again to Jesus, recognizing that the same Lord who gave the commandment to his disciples to "go" (Matt. 28:19) is the same Lord who told his disciples to "stay" (Matt. 26:38). In God's kingdom there is time enough for everything. In the world, under its ways of thinking and doing, there is never time enough.

Who's in Charge Here?

"The citizens of Our Time," charges David Wells, "actually believe so little in God because they believe so much in what is modern."[9] It may be difficult at first glance to see how a statement like this could even apply to the artists, industry, and audience of CCM. After all, we openly profess that we believe in God a great deal, not a little, and that our main purpose in using what is modern (technology, corporations, etc.) is to disseminate an important combination of music and message. We would never say that we believe in what is modern. Modern techniques, methods, systems, and technologies are only tools to us—or are they?

It's long been obvious that contemporary Christian music believes in the powerful tool of celebrity, but never more obvious than at the 1998 Gospel Music Association Dove Awards telecast. Six months prior to the April 23 broadcast, Frank Breeden, president of the Gospel Music Association, announced the GMA's intention to "follow the example of other highly-rated awards shows and get a great host."[10]

"Viewers will see our artists at their best," Breeden explained, "but when it comes to presenters, and hopefully sponsors, they will be looking at known quantities."[11] Those known quantities turned out to be John Tesh and Naomi Judd. To sweeten the pot, Whitney Houston was added to the bill as the evening's star performer. Tesh's profession of faith in Christ and his experience as a co-host of *Entertainment Tonight* made him an obvious celebrity choice, not to mention that he had recently begun to promote his own music in the CCM arena. While Tesh showed himself to be a more than capable host, Judd's actions and comments caused some GMA members concern. In addition to little things such as mispronouncing the name of the 1997 New Artist of the Year, Jaci Velasquez, Judd's theology of gospel music worked its way into the event, and its media coverage as well. According to Judd, "We've got to get people to realize gospel music is not about this uptight religiosity stuff. It's fun and it's cool. Jars of Clay opened for Sting last year."[12]

Without coming off as someone uptight and religious, is our motive in creating and promoting gospel music to show the unbelieving world that gospel music is fun and cool? I know it can be fun, and I suppose it could be cool, but is this why we do what we do? Does this articulate our calling? Did Naomi Judd as the host of the GMA Dove Awards faithfully represent the truest and best motives and intentions of our community? And if Sting's cool rubbed off somewhat on Jars of Clay, making them a little cooler for opening a few concert dates for him, does their increased cool trickle down to Jesus, making him a little bit cooler?

Brad Schmitt of *The Tennessean* reported in his May 1 column that "Whitney Houston's participation in the TNN-televised Dove Awards show cost show producers more than $50,000." What did the investment in the tool of Tesh's, Judd's, and Houston's celebrity yield? According to Schmitt,

"the show only drew about half the audience it got last year [1997]. The Dove Awards got a 0.5 rating this year; last year: a 0.9 rating." In other words, following "the example of other highly-rated awards shows" did not produce the results the GMA wanted—which was and is to increase the exposure of gospel music. They're trying to broaden the ministry to include more people, which is not a bad thing in and of itself. How, why, and when they (or any of us) do it is another matter altogether.

What concerns me greatly is how quickly we (and I include myself) can bet on the power of a person's celebrity without giving more than a passing prayer and acknowledgment to the power of God. And not just the power he demonstrated in creating our world, or in feeding the five thousand, but in the power and wisdom of the cross.

The Wisdom of the Cross

The wisdom of the cross is foolishness to the world. Sadly, its grand significance is often lost on Christians as well. Without the wisdom of the cross, the spiritual vision to see what we need to see will constantly elude us. We will see celebrity as the answer and we will see more quantity as somehow more profitable than less quantity but greater quality. The wisdom of the cross is paradoxical and is upside-down from the wisdom of the world. For example, the first shall be last and the last shall be first . . . whoever wants to save his life must lose it . . . while we were enemies of God he saved us . . . God rejects the prideful success but receives the humbled failure.

On the cross Christ looks like a loser, not the Almighty, and certainly not a king. He looks like a crazy fool, not the Son of God. He looks like a man who needs a celebrity to get him off the hook. Like any crucified man, he is incapable of saving himself. He is vulnerable to the point of death. But things are not as they seem. There is a secret wisdom to Christ's cross. Out of the apparent defeat of the cross comes an amazing victory. Three days later he's alive, sin and death are forever defeated, and the gospel of grace and the kingdom at hand are a tangible reality. Who knew? God knew—that's who! God still knows in our time, and he is still at work in an upside-down manner.

The wisdom of the cross is the wisdom to see its connection to reality—to real life. On the cross Christ looks abandoned by the Father. Three days later he is vindicated. What if the greatest thing the Dove Awards could do for the kingdom of God was to appear to fail by the world's standards of success? Would we be willing? I would like to propose that we do just that.

Let's give it up. Let's rethink the whole affair. Perhaps if the CCM community were to face this kind of Good Friday reality (the appearance of failure), we would then taste of "Easter-morning possibilities that few have dared to hope for (true success)."[13]

In his book *The Mystery of the Cross,* Alister McGrath writes, "As Good Friday gave way to Easter Day, the experience of the absence of God began to assume new significance. Where was God? And as those bystanders watching Christ gazed proud, looking up to the heavens for deliverance, they saw no sign of God and assumed he was absent . . . The presence of God was missed, was overlooked, was ignored, because God chose to be present where none expected him—in the suffering, shame, humility, powerlessness and folly of the cross of Jesus Christ."[14]

What if the GMA/CCM community were to produce a half-hour television show with the sole purpose of humbling ourselves before God and the world? What if we were to confess on national television that by following "the example of other highly-rated awards shows" we had lost all distinctiveness; that instead of being salt and light we simply added to the world another television variety show it obviously didn't need? What if we were to ask the forgiveness of God and the church and take a moment to outline a new and better way to communicate what our community is doing with the call to music? Rather than trying to show the world we can be cool, what if we were to show them we can be fools for things worth being foolish for? Perhaps God would be present in our shame, our humility, our powerlessness, and our folly. Perhaps in this way we would broaden our ministry.

As Mark Shaw has wisely pointed out, "God's way of working in the lives of those he loves as his children . . . is to bring them low in order to raise them high. The pattern of Christ's life, spelled out in the Gospels and summarized in Philippians 2:1–11, is the pattern of humiliation and exaltation. This is God's pattern for us as well."[15] The reality of this pattern is why our theology must be undergirded and deeply informed by a theology of the cross.

The people of contemporary Christian music should neither lose hope nor allow themselves to be deceived. Remember: "The crucified and risen Christ is at work in the weakness of the church, preparing to show his strength. Likewise, the crucified and risen Christ passes judgment upon the church where she has become proud and triumphant, or secure and smug, and recalls her to the foot of the cross, there to remind her of the mysterious and hidden way in which God is at work in the world."[16] In order to possess the vision necessary to see where God is at work, many of us will have to rethink our ideas about what constitutes God's blessing—or God's movement.

A blessing is anything that frees us from the grip of pride and self-sufficiency and drives us into the arms of Jesus. God's work and movement can look as much like failure as it does immediate success. This being so, we must be careful not to err by saying anything that looks like failure must not have God in it, and anything that looks like success surely has God in it. This is a false view of life in the kingdom at hand.

Worldliness: What Is It?

The term *worldliness* represents thinking and doing in ways contrary to God's ways. Worldliness is connected to what the Bible refers to as "the basic principles of the world" (Gal. 4:3), or "the pattern of the world" (Rom. 12:2). In its purest and deadliest form, worldliness is the thoughts of man and devil, void of the influence of the thoughts of God.

Any serious search for worldliness within CCM must consider the possibility that the ideas and systems of the world may have succeeded in transforming us more than we've transformed the world. Even more serious is the possibility that what Titus 1:16 says about unbelievers applies to many of us in CCM as well: "They claim to know God, but by their actions they deny him." Love for God requires that we seek the truth in these matters.

Worldliness exhibits self-centeredness. Unlike godliness, which acknowledges that only God can be at the center of his creation, worldliness places the human at the center of the universe. Whereas godliness recognizes that all human thoughts are to be judged against the thoughts of God, worldliness encourages the thoughts of humankind to be judged against fallable human standards. Worldliness is the way that seems right to a man, but in the end leads to death. Worldliness is "life characterized by self-righteousness, self-centeredness, self-satisfaction, self-aggrandizement, and self-promotion."[17] Even when the worldly are weak, they don't seek God; they seek self-help.

Worldliness is all about shortcuts. But there are no shortcuts in the kingdom life of grace. There are no sneaky roads. In the desert Satan tempted Christ with shortcuts, and he does the same with us as well. Imagine how different history would be if Jesus had traded the hard way (the cross) for the easy way (an earthly crown). This is the temptation the people of CCM face daily. Recognize this reality and be prepared for it. We must live by the management principles of Jesus and not those of Satan. The management principles of Satan are the same ones Jesus declined in the desert. They are, as Dorothy Sayers wrote in the play *The Man Born to Be King,* "fear, greed, and the promise of security."[18] Just as Jesus rejected these, so should we.

In his book *The Jesus I Never Knew,* Philip Yancey writes: "To its shame, Christian history reveals unrelieved attempts to improve on the way of Christ. Sometimes the church joins hands with a government that offers a shortcut path to power. 'The worship of success is generally *the* form of idol worship which the devil cultivates most assiduously,' wrote Helmut Thielicke about the German church's early infatuation with Adolf Hitler. 'We could observe in the first years after 1933 the almost suggestive compulsion that emanates from great successes and how, under the influence of these successes, men, even Christians, stopped asking in whose name and at what price.'"[19]

This is not to take a cheap shot at CCM by playing the Hitler card. It is simply a reminder that we can never afford to stop asking "in whose name and at what price?" To succumb to worldliness is to make this error. That's why the people of CCM should take Steve Camp's charge of worldliness very seriously.

Getting at the Ideas Behind Worldliness

Since so much of the CCM industry is directly copied from the ideas, systems, philosophies, and methods of the world, I believe that worldliness is present in CCM. Maybe we've yet to go "too far down the wide road of worldliness" as Steve has charged. Nevertheless, let's presuppose that worldliness within CCM is to some degree a problem, then consider what the cause of our worldliness might be. The most obvious cause is that Christians are still yet sinners. But let's get at the ideas behind the sin.

The systems, philosophies, and methods of the world are not inherently bad, and involving ourselves with them does not necessarily have to lead to worldly thinking and action. It's only when we allow these ideas to reign free, unchecked by biblical ways of thinking and doing, that they contribute to our worldliness. As we interact with the world's systems and ideas, there will be times when their ideological biases will be at odds with biblical views. When they are, we should identify them as such, showing they are the world's ways of thinking and doing, not God's. If we fail to do so, we irresponsibly acquiesce to ideas and positions totally incongruent with who and what we are as Christians. To do this is to succumb to worldliness. This is how the world contributes to our darkness. It is sin to allow these incongruent ideas to set the agenda, but I believe that with very few exceptions we have done just that. This is why I believe worldliness is indeed present within CCM.

Remember, every idea and system we use in CCM comes with a creational integrity and an ideological bias. Artistry has one, the corporation has one, marketing has one, radio has one. Everything has one, and they're all predisposed "to construct the world as one thing rather than another, to value one thing over another, to amplify one sense or skill or attitude more loudly than another."[20]

Handle with Care

Is it possible that those of us in positions of leadership in CCM have been on too easy terms with the world's ways of thinking and doing? Have we mistakenly handled the world's ways as if they were neutral and void of ideology—as if they possessed no creational integrity of their own, no ideological bias? Have we viewed the world's systems, techniques, and methods as simple, neutral tools to spread the good news? Have we missed the idea that even the simplest of tools, a hammer, for example, comes with an ideological bias? Have we forgotten to bring the fullness of the Christian mind to bear on artistry, industry, and audience? A yes to any of these questions insures us that CCM is polluted by worldliness. Whether it's a toehold or a journey "too far down the wide road of worldliness," I cannot say, nor do I think it matters. As I understand Scripture to teach, any amount of worldliness is too much.

The Audience at Risk

The values and meaning systems of the world work toward convincing the Christian consumer that any music and lyric which is not easily recognizable as "Christian" is unnecessary, irrelevant, inefficient, and unproductive. These notions move in to replace a larger biblical definition of that which is good or that which serves by way of ministry. Contemporary trends perpetuate the value of "star power" and promote the idea that more in quantity is better or more admirable than more in quality. As a result, Christian music consumers are influenced by sales trends—what's hot and what's not—as much as any other audience. Like all modern consumers they move toward the sound of applause. They're more apt to label a ministry successful and effective based on size, efficiency, and productivity rather than on the value of the message. Even Christians have arrived at the point where they have little respect or use for small but quality ministries.

Being Aware of the Danger

To be involved with Christian music, yet uninvolved with thinking Christianly about the ideas, systems, philosophies, and methods used to disseminate it, is antithetical and dangerous. If I fail to stop and think about what untruths I may have assented to, I will never stop to dissent. As a result, I will continue to be incrementally captured and imprisoned by those particular untruths, and possibly others. If I'm accommodating to all of CCM's ideas, systems, philosophies, and methods without the slightest critical reflection and questioning, I'm likely to find myself more a servant of the world's ways of thinking and doing than those of Jesus. Honestly though, these are not just errors likely to happen to me. They have happened. I am guilty of failing to assess, and call by name, the untruths I've so easily assented to. I'm also guilty of failing to think with a biblically informed, critical, reflective, and questioning mind. I have often been more a servant of the world's ways of thinking and doing, rather than a servant of King Jesus. I confess this; I repent of it; and I ask God's forgiveness and the forgiveness of my community. And, by his grace, I receive his forgiveness.

Chapter 16

Capitalism, the Corporation, and the Record Company

After a concert or speaking engagement, I enjoy the fellowship of talking with members of the audience. Without fail, there is one question in particular which always seems to surface: "Charlie, are there people who are into contemporary Christian music for the ministry, or is everybody in it for the money?"

Yes, there are people who are into CCM for the ministry, and no, not everybody is in it for the money. But it's also truthful to say, yes, everybody's into CCM for the ministry, and yes, everybody is in it for the money.

It all depends on what you mean by "in it for the money." The phrase can mean that you have no other reason for doing it than to get rich, or it can mean that you are a steward over good products which you sell to your community in exchange for money which you then reinvest in the community.

There's also more than one way to interpret "into CCM for the ministry." It doesn't necessarily mean you do it without expecting to get paid. Does ministry place anyone beyond the constraints and conventions of the culture in which they are attempting to minister? No, it doesn't. We are called to ministry wherever God's people are—including Fortune 500 companies, the grocery store, or a coliseum full of ticket-buying music lovers.

The issue is not a struggle between money and ministry. It's whether we will choose to serve ourselves, or serve God and others wherever God puts us, with however much money he puts in our pocket. The question is not, "Charlie, are there people who are into contemporary Christian music for the ministry, or is everybody in it for the money?" The question is: To what or to whom have we given our trust, our allegiance, our affections, and our worship?

Many CCM critics and loyal listeners have oversimplified the issue of money and business to an unrealistic degree, creating in their minds an unholy alliance between ministry and money. Friends, there is no unholy alliance here, just sinners. When money and business challenge us not to do the good we know we ought to do, and we fail to do God's will, it's because we are sinful people who let worldliness get the best of us.

Profit and the Health of the Economy

The Scripture has much to say about profit and wealth. Jesus emphasized productivity. The more extra uncommitted resources present in a community, the healthier the economy of the community is. Extra uncommitted resources allow for the funding of important new ideas which are beneficial to society. They are often ideas whose core values ride outside any consideration of profit and wealth; for example: caring for those who cannot care for themselves, the funding of churches, crisis pregnancy centers, and academic scholarships. It's profit that ensures the presence of extra uncommitted resources, which in turn ensures that money is available for worthwhile endeavors that don't pay their own way. The bottom line is that capitalism encourages profit, and profit, when used properly, creates and supports many good things, including the spread of the gospel.

The Knot of Contradiction

Capitalism is an economic system fueled by supply and demand. When fans rush to the stores to buy a new CD, we take it as a cue to manufacture more. This being so, it is impossible for contemporary Christian music to avoid involvement in capitalism. Nor is it necessary for CCM to attempt to do so, as Keith Green did in 1980 when he began experimenting with giving his recordings away. Though Keith's decision was born out of what he perceived to be a directive from God, his decision left his ministry no less dependent on capitalism.

In her book *No Compromise,* Melody Green Sievright explained that "Keith figured most people knew the going price of recordings in the bookstores and understood that making records was very expensive. What he actually set up was an honor system of payment—trusting that if someone could afford to buy one they would."[1]

In spite of his good intentions, Keith found himself wrestling with the apparent contradiction inherent in this approach:

"My whole reason for giving the album away is that I love people! Of course I don't want to see 50,000 people send in nothing. At the same time I don't want people to feel that I'm doing this to get a donation, or that they have to send in a donation."[2]

Keith didn't want anyone to feel that he was giving the album away in order to get a donation. Yet, he willingly admitted he wanted them to send in something. The knot of contradiction Keith tied himself up in is one very common to people who wrestle with issues of ministry and commerce. A ministry that begins with the admirable intention of living out a genuine love for people and an utter dependence on God quickly becomes caught up in the contradiction of: *no one has to send money/someone has to send money.* Getting trapped in this impasse is completely unnecessary. God in his wisdom has given us sufficient guidance to understand the relationship between our labor and the provision it provides—it is his gift to us. Solomon spoke to this in Ecclesiastes 5:18—19:

"It is good and proper for a man to eat and drink, and to find satisfaction in his toilsome labor under the sun during the few days of life God has given him—for this is his lot. Moreover, when God gives any man wealth and possessions, and enables him to enjoy them, to accept his lot and be happy in his work—this is a gift from God."

Avoiding the Pseudospiritual Reaction

Because many of us fear that money and success will become our bottom line, we often try to arrange our lives so as to keep money and success from ever tempting us to sin. This pseudospiritual reaction to money and business will never produce lasting fruit.

Instead of living in response to the grace of God, we often make fear-based assumptions that leave us tangled up in semantic knots similar to the one Keith Green experienced. This kind of thinking also leads to very unproductive compartmentalization. If we fail to bring the whole of Scripture and the history of the saints to bear upon our thinking about money and ministry, we will never find sufficient truth to free ourselves.

"Those that don't have anything can get an album for nothing," Keith Green declared from the concert stage. "And those that have little can get it for little. We believe the gospel's been getting a little too commercial. So, we wanted to uncommercialize our part of it."[3]

Keith's word reveals a common error we can all learn from. By stating that "we wanted to uncommercialize our part of it," Keith tried to remove himself and his ministry's monetary needs from the cultural sphere—a sphere God has clearly allowed for and uses for his kingdom purposes.

What is especially naive here is the failure to see that the freedom to "uncommercialize" under the economic system of capitalism is only made possible by some number of people in society agreeing *to commercialize.*

Later, Keith adopted a different posture, starting with a letter of amends to bookstore owners across America, saying, "I hope you can understand that I am a man of principle, and yet, like a pendulum, I have a tendency to go too far to make a point. I fear that in the past I have done just that."[4] According to Melody Green Sievright, "Keith wanted the bookstores to go ahead and sell his albums, but he wanted to have a sticker on each one that said, 'If you cannot afford the retail price of this album, write to Last Days Ministries and we'll send you information on how you can get it for whatever you can afford.'"[5]

Wrestling with Freedom

There are going to be people in every generation who struggle with these issues. The struggle is good—as long as you really are seeking the truth and the will of God, as Keith Green sincerely was. It honors the Lord far more to struggle and agonize over these things, missing the mark here and there, than to float through life with your conscience, your emotions, and your mind on cruise control. There is absolutely nothing inherently wrong with Christian capitalism, even in the context of what you perceive to be your ministry. In truth, we must participate in it, both out of necessity, and in response to our calling to be God's people everywhere and in everything. Where we go wrong in our association with capitalism is in our tendency to "evaluate life solely in terms of products and services, to assume that everything in life is amenable to capitalistic techniques, to grant efficiency the value of an ultimate criterion."[6] To err in this way, asserts David Wells, is "to become so anthropocentric, so 'this-worldly' in spirit, as to be worldly in the biblical sense."[7] It's this we want to avoid.

Wells believes that "those who slide into worldliness this way are not likely to be conscious of the fact that they are doing so; the ways in which capitalism works are so much second nature to them that they will barely ever think about it. And since capitalism has been so extraordinarily successful, a person who prizes efficiency as an ultimate criterion will scarcely have any grounds on which to question its techniques."[8]

A look at the relationship between capitalism and technology will clarify Well's point.

Capitalism and Technology

Capitalism is one layer in the soil of modernity where worldly values often blossom. They are perennial, returning over and over again. The soil of capitalism is made rich by technology. Technology lives to offer the "new" and to reinterpret the "existing." It lives to increase efficiency and productivity. Where technology achieves these goals, profits also increase. This is why capitalism has so much admiration for technology. Profits produce capital to fund new technologies, and the cycle continues. This is why technology has so much admiration for capitalism. They love to work together whenever possible.

As with capitalism, technology is not inherently bad, and Christians should not be afraid to take advantage of it for the benefit of all humankind—including the spread of the gospel. Even still, like capitalism, technologies come with ideologies which cannot be ignored.

One of the greatest downsides to living in a capitalistic, technological society is not the automatic teller, mass transit, cable TV, or the Internet, but something far more insidious: technology's ability to shape our thinking in subtle, incremental ways over time, until we think differently about something than we previously thought. It is a kind of worldly counterfeit *metanoia.*

Technology can shape our thinking in ways incongruent with Christianity. If technology's efficiency and productivity help us to achieve a desired end, such as a ministry goal we perceive to be good, we will naturally call that particular technology good. After all, it was the means to a good end. Once we perceive one efficient, productive technology to be good, we're inclined to give other technologies the opportunity to show that they too are efficient and productive. If and when they prove themselves, it's likely we will call them good as well.

Now we're at the precipice, the point of real danger. If we stop to think Christianly, we'll be safe. If we don't, we will teeter or fall headlong into pragmatism.

It's About the Starting Place

The problem has to do with our starting place. The crucial point is to realize where good comes from. Is it God or technology? The point is this: Expediency, efficiency, and productivity are too weak to be the foundation for something as weighty as goodness or holiness. This is the real problem, and this is exactly how modernity or worldliness gets us so turned around in our thinking. Just because it works does not make it good.

Here's a rule of thumb: expediency, efficiency, and productivity can be named as good when and only when the good you think they've accomplished is tested against biblical ideas of good and proven to be true. This principle applies to everything in business and industry. All of business and industry must submit to the truth requirement.

Front Load the Scripture

Capitalism is only good if it passes the test of Scripture, the test of thinking Christianly. Most important, the tests of Scripture should be front-loaded, not back-loaded. We should be so biblically minded that we are always in the process of accepting and rejecting ideas and systems that come into our sphere of influence. We should never accept any of these ideas and systems outright, no matter how much potential we think they have for good, without a front-end examination and understanding of their intrinsic ideologies. This principle holds for artists, radio, retail, television, print, record companies, new media, marketing, corporations, artist management, concert promotion, legal affairs, talent agencies—everything that has anything to do with contemporary Christian music.

The Corporation and the Record Company

A corporation is a legal entity capable of owning assets such as record and publishing companies, incurring liabilities and engaging in specific activities such as producing, marketing, and distributing CDs and tapes. It exists to serve its community through products and/or services and to serve its shareholders by delivering a return on invested capital that exceeds viable alternative investments. A record company exists to produce, market, manufacture, and distribute the recorded performances of musical artists. Today, all the major Christian record companies are owned by corporations. Whereas the goal of a record company is to produce a quality, competitive, profitable music product, the goal of the corporately owned record company is this and more. Its goal is to produce a quality, competitive, profitable music product, and a competitive return on the shareholders' investment.

A corporately owned record company is actually involved in the creation of two products, their music and the increased stock price of their parent corporation. This is a reality which many Christians do not understand. The more successful and profitable their music, the more marketable and valuable the corporation's stock. The more people who purchase a corporation's stock, the more capital is available for acquisitions and growth. Rising stock value, acquisitions, and growth all increase the competitive worth of the corporation.

Most record company employees are a very special combination of passion and precision. Their passion for music and its place in the culture creates a great deal of tension when it clashes with corporate culture. For example, at the heart of the record business is the idea of nurturing and developing musical artists in order for them to make long-term contributions to popular music. The pop history books are filled with examples of important artists, such as Bruce Springsteen and U2, who required time to develop before delivering on the promise people first saw in them.

But corporately owned record companies have less and less time to develop and nurture talent. The focus shifts from long-term potential to short-term profit. It's all about meeting and exceeding corporate projections. According to Don Weir of Huntleigh Securities in St. Louis, "U.S. Corporations have developed a myopic preoccupation with short-term results, with corporate policy shifts in many instances dictated by whether or not the next quarterly earnings report will be up and, if so, up as much as the shareholders and the general investing community expects."[9]

Falling short of financial projections is a serious matter for corporations, as this excerpt from the Money section of the March 27, 1998, edition of *USA Today* illustrates:

"PolyGram, the world's largest music publisher, said Thursday that its first-quarter earning will be sharply lower than a year ago because of poor record sales and higher promotional costs. PaineWebber slashed its earnings estimate for PolyGram from $100 million to $20 million. Polygram shares dropped 3 5/16 to close at $48 3/4."

When your sales are tied to the stock market and the earnings estimates of prestigious market analysts, the pressure to produce results is intense. While it's essential for a corporation to serve its shareholders, Don Weir believes the drive to impress shareholders with ever increasing profit "has come dangerously close to supplanting not only the mission to serve their consumer-base, but their employees as well." Every savvy employee who's ever been "down-sized" knows that the quickest way for a corporation to increase revenue is to eliminate overhead. When Christian men and women are called upon to let good employees go in order to meet corporate and shareholder expectations, it is a difficult and unrewarding assignment.

While independent record companies may keep the passion for music alive, it's the corporately owned companies who define the record industry, and who ultimately acquire the most successful of the independents. Once acquired, the independent *may* incrementally morph into the image of the parent corporation until they are one and the same.

The Bottom Line

Christians must be cautious and vigilant when dealing with capitalism, the corporation, and the record company. It is our sinfulness and the propensity of these three entities to shape life in ways out of sync with a kingdom perspective that cause us so much trouble. Contemporary Christian music does not have to make money and success the bottom line in order to move within the business world and minister to the musical and spiritual needs of the church and the kingdom. The question does not have to be "Are there people in CCM for the ministry or is everyone just in it for the money?" Ministry, compensation, and profit are not incompatible ideas.

However, their compatibility depends on how ready and well-prepared God's people are to take on the challenge of living in a complex and fallen world with the kingdom at hand.

When CCM's sole purpose becomes economic success, without regard for God and his creation, the wants of a few will have eclipsed the needs of many. This is what the corporately owned Christian record company must guard against most of all. Christians are about—should be about—the needs of many, and it's this mission alone that should define CCM in relation to money and the business of music.

Chapter 17

Music and the Christian Mission

Often when young musically talented Christians come in contact with CCM, they become, as one voice of criticism has suggested, "confused, disillusioned and wounded." Some of these young people come to CCM as artists committed to a comprehensive mission of evangelism, acts of mercy, and musical stewardship, only to find that CCM as an industry is not necessarily set up to serve or equip them in this regard. If this is true, it should baffle and disturb everyone involved with CCM, audience included. Evangelism, loving our neighbors, acts of mercy, and the stewardship of creation absolutely define the Christian mission to the world. Christians are called by God, to God, and for God, everywhere and in everything. This being so, if CCM is unable to help young artists remain faithful to this calling, it's no wonder young people are confused and disillusioned with CCM.

Evidence of the Presence

Evangelism, acts of mercy, and the stewardship of creation are all present within CCM artists, industry, and audience. Artists past and present, from Rez Band, Keith Green and Mylon LeFevre to Carman, Geoff Moore, and NewSong have maintained an evangelism focus.

Sparrow Records staff, Amy Grant, and Margaret Becker are just a few CCM folks who, by working with the ministry of Habitat for Humanity, have helped disadvantaged people receive safe and affordable housing. Michael W. Smith, the late Rich Mullins, and many others have faithfully supported the work of Compassion International in caring for the poor and needy children of the world. Steven Curtis Chapman's and Kathy Troccoli's work with Prison Fellowship is further evidence that the people of CCM are filled with mercy and kindness.

Jars of Clay, Susan Ashton, BeBe & CeCe Winans, Ashley Cleveland, Amy Grant, Kirk Franklin, Sixpence None the Richer and others, each in their own way, have shown that the faithful stewardship of musical talent can go beyond the confines of the church. As salt and light in the culture, they have reminded us that there are many good uses for good music.

Defining Presence and Priority

For all these examples, the voices of debate and criticism continue over the presence of evangelism, acts of mercy, and broader ideas regarding musical stewardship within CCM. The problem is failure to distinguish the difference between *presence* and *priority,* and to understand what the dominant bias of CCM actually is. While there is the indisputable *presence* of evangelism, acts of mercy, and broader musical stewardship within CCM, these are not CCM's *priorities.* As a complex organizational system, the industry's main priorities are to:

1. Identify those in the body of Christ whose extraordinary talent in music uniquely equips them to create, record, and perform music for the enjoyment, edification, and general use of the Christian church, or at the very least, with the wants of Christian consumers in mind.
2. Seek mutually beneficial relationships with these artists in order to further equip them for the above stated vocation, and to fund the

recording, promotion, marketing, and distribution of their music, their artistry, and their ministry to the Christian community.

3. Support all the components and players within the infrastructure of the CCM system, including producers, songwriters, musicians, recording studios, engineers, graphic artists, photographers, publishers, parachurch ministries, talent agencies, attorneys, managers, concert promoters, writers, critics, retail, youth pastors, and all forms of media including print, television, radio, and the internet, to the end that the ministry, recorded product, and live performances of Christian artists reach Christian consumers in numbers significant enough to sustain industry.

Are Criticisms Fair?

I believe these accurately represent the core priorities of the industry and organizational system that is contemporary Christian music. There are exceptions to this emphasis, but not nearly enough to establish true diversity or flesh out the full kingdom perspective of calling with respect to music. It's this lack of diversity and overall failure to live for God everywhere and in everything that brings many of God's people to raise their voices in concern.

Still, should CCM be forced to make evangelism a core priority? Isn't that the work of evangelists? Isn't personal evangelism played out against the backdrop of everyday life anyway? Businesses and individuals within CCM give generously of their time and resources to all sorts of outreach and charitable causes. Isn't that enough?

Moreover, is it fair to require CCM to embrace a comprehensive view of musical stewardship over and above its emphasis on Christian pop and worship music for the Christian consumer? Perhaps providing music for the church of Jesus Christ is important enough. Perhaps it isn't fair to ask the industry to risk exchanging the known benefit of its impact in one area for the unknown potential in another, especially when God seems to have equipped and blessed the work of CCM as it is.

These issues deserve our careful consideration.

If I Had a Nickel . . .

When I was a little boy I noticed something peculiar about my father. If something happened to him often enough, like having the same question asked of him again and again, he'd say, "If I had a nickel for every

time you've asked me that question, son, I'd be rich as Rockefeller." Though I hadn't a clue who Rockefeller was, imagining a million nickels helped me catch the drift of what he was trying to communicate.

In the course of my career as a recording and touring artist for both mainstream and Christian record labels, a record producer, a record company head, and a teacher on Christianity and the arts, I've come in contact with my share of aspiring Christian recording artists. And, if I had a nickel (make that a dollar) for every time one of them told me he was writing with unbelievers in mind, or that he was called to take his music to unbelievers, I'd be rich as Bill Gates!

Time and time again, artists have shared with me their dreams and desires to contribute gospel-inspired, relevant music of excellence to the culture at large, to take their music to those who do not know Jesus as their Savior, and to those (saved and unsaved) in need of mercy, love, help, encouragement, the good, the true, and the beautiful. I've come to see that there are three core missions in the dreams and desires of these artists: the mission of evangelism, the mission of service, and the mission of transformation. Artists who embrace these three missions can be broken down into four general types:

Type One: The music evangelist.

Type Two: The musical artist whose music is potentially relevant and appealing to both mainstream and contemporary Christian audiences.

Type Three: The musical artist whose primary appeal is to mainstream audiences, and whose relevance and appeal to the contemporary Christian audience is limited at best.

Type Four: The musician whose mission is absolutely relevant to the Christian mission on earth but considered largely irrelevant to CCM, because the industry doesn't trust this particular mission to accomplish the priority goals of CCM.

Type One Artistry: In Search of Lost Sheep

Artists in the Type One category describe their music as an excellent tool for use in communicating the gospel. They clearly believe that their ministry is to the lost and may emphasize the message over the music. Many speak of themselves as evangelists in the same way that an evangelist speaks of his own calling. They are looking for someone to help them take their music, but particularly their message, to where the lost are. They are looking for Christians who can help them gain access to the mainstream record-buying public. *Their question is always the same: Can CCM as an industry help me accomplish this good mission? No, I have to answer, not at this time.*

David Pierce from the band No Longer Music is a Type One artist. In writing about his calling to reach the lost, David makes his mission position very clear. "It is important," he asserts, "to understand a vital principle about lost sheep. Lost sheep are lost!"[1]

"We often don't take that into consideration when we try to reach them," observes David. "Instead, we hold Lost Sheep Rallies. We advertise and we say that all lost sheep are welcome. We may reach a few, but usually ninety-five percent of the crowd are 'found' sheep. Why? Because lost sheep are lost and we have to go out and find them."

According to David, if Jesus were with us today he would frequent the clubs, the discos, and the bars. "He would know the names of all the bartenders and he would be friends with all the prostitutes."

"Jesus was a friend of sinners," says David, "and I've come to realize that, unless I am too, I am not like Jesus."

Consider, if you will, a day in the life of this music evangelist in Amsterdam:

"As we were about to finish our last song, 'I Love God,' a group of Satan punks . . . came into view. They stopped beside us and started to scream about how much they hated God and loved Satan.

"One of them . . . spat in my face. Another took a bottle and broke it over the drum kit, and with his hand bleeding, held it menacingly up to my face.

"'How many of you believe that Satan is in Amsterdam?' I shouted, my face covered in spit and the angry punk holding the bottle inches from my face.

"'We do!' the group of Satan punks shouted back.

"'How many of you love Satan?' I responded.

"'Yes, we love Satan,' they said in unison.

"'Well, I have another message,' I said. 'God is in Amsterdam, too. He loves this city. He didn't just talk about his love, but he proved it by sending his son to die for us. Jesus took our place and died. But he didn't stay dead. He rose again from the dead and he's alive tonight in Amsterdam.'

"The guy next to me moved the jagged bottle from my face and smashed it to the ground. A group of them rushed forward and began to slash the tires of our van with knives, while others broke the headlight and windshield. Still others tried to throw us and the equipment into a canal nearby.

"Two Dutch policemen arrived on the scene but it was such a flammable situation they had to call for reinforcements before they would even try to intervene."

Floyd McClung, executive director of international operations for Youth with a Mission, sees in David Pierce "the gift of an evangelist." McClung concludes that "when God looks around to find someone to fulfill a tough assignment and there's nobody radical enough to do it, he calls on David Pierce."

Type Two Artistry: Serving and Transforming

Type Two artists are those who do not consider themselves to be evangelists (as the Scripture delineates evangelists; see Eph. 4:11), but instead think of themselves as musicians called to create music which serves and transforms. Their definition of music which serves and transforms is a broad one. If the need is for music which tells the truth, then they want to serve by telling the truth. If the need is for music which is beautiful, then they want to serve by creating music of beauty. Their definition of music which transforms is akin to the biblical teaching regarding salt and light. They understand that good and truthful music has the ability to transform its environment as light does darkness. They believe in the transformative power of good art. They know that good and truthful music created and performed by teachable sinners has the ability to push back the effects of the fall—of preserving the good. Knowing all this, their primary desire is to be salt and light in the culture at large. Though their music and lyrics would certainly make sense to much of CCM's industry and audience, what these artists are really hoping for is a way to contribute music to the ongoing cultural conversation outside of CCM. Though they recognize the value of creating music for the church, and are often ready and willing to do so, what many of these artists are looking for is a way to make an impact on the culture by leaving the comfort of the ninety-nine to reach the one who is lost. More than anything they're ready and willing to contribute Spirit-inspired ways of thinking and doing to whatever sphere of existence God would call them to. They are prepared to answer the call to live for Him everywhere and in everything. *Their question is always the same: Can the CCM industry help me accomplish this good mission? No, not exactly, I have to answer. Perhaps in time, but not immediately.*

The duo Out of the Grey were Type Two artists at their inception. Scott and Christine Denté, who comprise Out of the Grey, met at the prestigious Berklee School of Music in Boston. Christine, already a Christian, befriended the unbelieving Scott one day by telling him to "turn the TV off and do your homework." Soon she had him listening to Amy Grant's *Unguarded* album and actually enjoying it. After Scott's conversion to Christianity and their subsequent marriage, the young couple dreamed of one day seeing their own music connect with unbelievers the way Amy's music had connected with Scott.

Not knowing the best way to achieve their goal, but seeing Amy Grant as a healthy model, the duo signed with the Christian music label, Sparrow Records. Scott remembers their naiveté: "We didn't know anything about the [CCM] industry when we first came into it and we knew a lot right away after we jumped in."[2]

According to Scott, Sparrow Records was very forthright about the nature of their own mission. "When we signed with Sparrow, [EMI Christian Music Group president] Bill Hearn pretty much told us, 'We know how to sell records over here in the CCM market. If you want to mess with the mainstream you may be talking to the wrong people. If the door opens for that, we might help you walk through it, but CCM is what we know how to do.'"

Out of the Grey, whose music has connected with the Christian audience to a large degree, quickly made the adjustment toward accommodating the mission and core priorities of CCM. "The adjustment," Scott explains, "gets made as soon as you start getting booked, getting out there and playing all over the country. You're playing in churches and you're playing at youth events. We've been playing to the church for seven years, so you make the adjustment, you learn the language. It's not false, we are the church, we're part of the church. So you make the adjustment."

Even though Out of the Grey has been playing for the church and not the lost as they had initially hoped to do, the dream to see their music reach non-Christians hasn't been completely dashed. "We've gotten many comments," Christine reports, "saying yours is the only Christian music that I'm able to share with my unbelieving friends."

Sixpence None the Richer is another band that has made the adjustment, but unlike Out of the Grey, they confess to being on uneasy terms with it. "Our top priority right now," says band member Matt Slocum, "is to go over into the mainstream and just try to make it there."[3] One of the main reasons for their uneasiness has to do with the expectations of Christian concert promoters. "It seems that all of the promoters you run into think they're having you for something completely different from what you're coming in to do." Noted author and columnist John Fischer confirms that the youth pastors and concert promoters who book bands like Sixpence "want music that will provide a strong witness for Christian kids and an opportunity to preach the gospel to any non-Christians who might come under the influence of the youth group."[4] According to Fischer, these youth pastors and promoters are "not as concerned with the artistic aspects of the music as they are about providing a safe, alternative cultural experience for Christian teenagers, and they assume all Christian [music] groups have this same goal."

Matt Slocum, on the other hand, is concerned with the artistic aspects of the music because he believes that his secondary calling is to music and not vocational ministry. "I'm a musician," declares Matt. "That's what I do and it's how I make my living. I think it boils down to this: I don't get paid for giving my testimony or witnessing. It's because of my faith and what I'm called to do that I do those things."

While there are many artists like Out of the Grey who do make the adjustment, and others like Sixpence None the Richer who try but eventually decide its not what they're called to do, there are an increasing number of artists who do not fit within CCM and do not believe that they are called to serve its core priorities.

Type Three Artistry: Made for One Thing Only

Type Three artists are those with the desire to reach out to the largely unbelieving mainstream record business and its millions of pop music listeners. Though they often have much in common with Type Two artists, these performers are usually so confident of their specific calling to the mainstream that they seldom even consider the option of making the adjustment to CCM. For the most part, CCM rarely offers opportunities to these artists—the exception being small, independent Christian labels.

Type Three artists want to live out a good story in front of the music industry and its audience. They recognize that the "everywhere" aspect of God's calling includes living as a committed musician, vocalist, and composer/songwriter in the culture at large. Their mission is to make authentic, honest relationships with people who don't know Christ, love them with tenderness and mercy, and faithfully transform the culture with music shaped by image-bearing excellence and a comprehensive kingdom perspective. They are just as comfortable with the ability of art to entertain as they are with its ability to transform. They are not apt to think that the two must be separated. They are musicians and storytellers who tell the truth; but like the poets, writers, and musicians they usually claim as influences, the way in which these artists tell the truth is unique. It may be the poetic language they use, or the fact that their version of sin and redemption is one that aches, bleeds, and isn't all that pretty. Whatever the case, their uniqueness makes it difficult for the CCM industry and audience to connect with the underlying sub-text of biblical truth which so often informs their music. When artists such as these interact directly with CCM, they usually face a good deal of opposition to their creative choices.

Characteristically, these artists work hard at their craft so that their musical and lyrical choices connect with a musically discerning culture. As a result, they are usually less concerned with appeasing the church than capturing the attention of music listeners everywhere. These artists love music and unashamedly call it their work, and to the surprise of many skeptical Christians, they are (for the most part) just as unashamedly prepared to share their testimony with anyone who asks. Yet, they make it very clear that they are not Spirit-gifted evangelists. They are musicians, vocalists, and songwriters looking for someone, including Christian brothers and sisters, to help them gain access to the mainstream music-buying public. Not only do they want to go to where the lost live; they sincerely believe that for them to do anything else would be to miss their calling. *Their question is always the same: Can CCM help me accomplish this good mission? No, I have to answer, not at this time.*

Those Type Three artists who immediately come to mind are the iconoclastic troubadours Bill Mallonee of Vigilantes of Love, David Wilcox, and Bruce Cockburn, as well as the bands Over The Rhine, and Burlap To Cashmere. Certainly Bono of U2, Peter Garrett of Midnight Oil, and Michael Been of The Call fit in here to a certain degree as well. Sarah Masen, and the group Plumb, both of whom had their debut records released to the mainstream and Christian markets, are two more artists who seem to fit the model.

Though she considers herself a musician and not an evangelist, Tiffany Arbuckle of Plumb speaks as if she's been reading evangelist David Pierce's mail. "I would like to see us take the What Would Jesus Do trend for a reality instead of a trend. What would he do? He wouldn't hang out in a church all day, and he wouldn't talk about himself and his father all day, he actually would love people and go to the prostitutes, tax collectors, and the drunkards."[5]

Bono of U2 couldn't agree more. In 1987 he offered the opinion that if Jesus Christ was still on earth "you'd probably find him in a gay bar in San Francisco. He'd be working with people suffering from AIDS."[6]

"Obviously," Tiffany explains, "Jesus was in the temple and he was preaching, but he also got outside of that and went into the street. As a band, that's where our calling is. Our motive is pure. When we play at a club or at a festival sponsored by a mainstream radio station, it's not because we are condoning and supporting what they condone and support; it's because we are trying to be a light in the midst of the darkness. I think people truly confuse our mission with seeking fame and fortune and selling out."

These types of artists often find themselves at odds with the CCM and evangelical communities, usually because their critics misunderstand or misinterpret their unique ways of discussing Christianity, or for their idiosyncratic behavior in general. In addition, many of these artists are unwilling to speak or write lyrics that align them with the Christian subculture status quo, or to respond to questions about their faith in the predictable ways many Christians have come to expect from their contemporary Christian artists.

Peter Garrett from the Australian band Midnight Oil speaks eloquently of Jesus as a "transforming figure," noting that "this capacity for transforming is something that is offered freely as a gift."[7] Yet, when an interviewer asked Garrett to describe the role the church plays in his life, Garrett's eloquence seemed to disappear. "Language is hard in these areas, isn't it? I just can't find the right sentence for it without people misinterpreting me." Ironically, this is exactly the kind of response that usually results in artists like Garrett being misinterpreted and misunderstood, especially by the contemporary Christian music audience.

Later, during this same interview Garrett proffered a description of a church as a "particular type of two or more gathering. It has to do with less self, more other, more giving and less taking, more openness, less closedness . . . And, if you like, there is a bearable lightness of being around the place." Though Garrett's response is true, again it is just vague enough and poetic enough to keep most CCM listeners and gatekeepers from giving Garrett the cherished "permanent Jesus stamp of approval."

According to singer/songwriter David Wilcox, "A beautiful part of retelling the story is to start with something people haven't heard and to say it fresh so that it's striking. Yet, whenever you do that, it's going to anger all those people who are clinging to their own metaphors."[8] And it does. It especially angers and confuses Christians. The avoidance of tried and true metaphors is one of the key reasons why the CCM audience has such a difficult time relating to this particular type of artistry. The street runs both ways, though. The Type Three artist has an equally difficult time adjusting to the narrow lyrical expectations of CCM. They're more interested in portraying the hugeness of the kingdom story in its diversity and complexity than the smallness of the American contemporary Christian music story in its oversimplification and conformity. For example, when David Wilcox says that "it's amazing to have a faith that always resists being captured," he opens himself up to the criticism of Christians who most certainly believe that it can be captured completely by the human mind. The artist who proclaims the mystery of God and the strangeness of the kingdom at hand faces tension and frustration trying to communicate with an industry and audience that clamors for easy or pat answers.

Bono of U2 probably understands this tension better than any musically talented Christian of the last two decades. "People expect you, as a believer, to have all the answers," says Bono, "when really all you get is a whole new set of questions."[9] Bono's quote exemplifies the type of statement that is simultaneously thought-provoking to some while deeply disturbing to others—particularly Christians who know Jesus is the answer, but are not really sure what the questions are.

Type Four Artistry: Tuning into the Right Channel

Type Four artists enjoy making music in a setting which is neither CCM nor the pop mainstream. What sets these artists apart from Types Two and Three is that they passionately want to accomplish something with music that is outside the norm of both CCM and pop. The music itself might be completely compatible with CCM, and hugely relevant to the church audience. Likewise for the pop audience. But it's the context these artists have chosen which makes working with record labels difficult. They want to go where they are needed, whether it's to the lost, the poor, the dying, the young, or the old. And these people don't buy many CDs and tapes.

Type Four artists are not necessarily opposed to having mainstream or CCM recording contracts, and in many cases feel it might be useful to their mission; for this reason they do seek them out. Still, the pursuit of a record deal is not their primary objective. They want to serve and transform. They are often called to various combinations of artistry, songwriting, youth

ministry, preaching, teaching, and ministries of mercy that seldom find a comfortable fit within the contemporary Christian or mainstream music industries. *Like the others, their question is always the same: Can CCM help me accomplish this good mission? No, I have to answer, it cannot, except in rare instances.*

Two well-known artists come to mind who fit the Type Four artistry model, Rich Mullins and Chris Rice. The late Rich Mullins, a popular singer/songwriter, had a desire to serve the Native American Nation with his gifts and talents. Rich and his friend Mitch McVicker moved into a hogan at the Navajo Indian Nation reservation in Window Rock, Arizona, in 1995. Don Donahue, Rich's A&R representative at Reunion Records, remembers that Rich had alerted the label several years before that this was his plan. "Rich wanted to stop touring. He wanted to get a teaching degree in order to teach music to Native American children on the reservation. The tension we had with all this at Reunion was that he was our number two artist at the time. His manager would call us up and tell us, 'Rich isn't available to tour.' Rich held us up from marketing him. He didn't care about that. The old school marketing approach was about exploitation—getting the artist out there as much as possible, doing in-stores, interviews and appearances. Rich wasn't about exploitation; he was about tuning into the right channel."[10]

Before his hit record and six Dove nominations in 1997, Chris Rice spent eleven faithful years as a teacher/singer/songwriter/worship leader at retreats and youth camps around the country. Ironically, Don Donahue, now Chris Rice's A&R representative at Rocketown Records, finds himself in a similar situation to the one he experienced with Rich Mullins years before. CCM doesn't consider youth camps and retreats to be the kinds of events that make the most cost-effective use of a popular artist's time. Nevertheless, in spite of his well-received CCM debut, Chris Rice will return to the camps and retreats he loves doing. And, breaking the mold of old school marketing, Rocketown will be right there with him. "We not only support what he does, it drives what he does," Donahue confirms. "To separate him from what he has invested his life in would hurt his art. It would hurt what God is doing in his life. Doing these camps and being with these kids is what makes him tick."

Making the Adjustment

These are the four types of artists who so often become confused and disillusioned by CCM. If they can make the "adjustment" as Out of the

Grey did, find a willing partner as Chris Rice did with Rocketown, or record for a mainstream pop label and license their recordings back to a Christian record label as Burlap to Cashmere did, then the relationship with CCM can be healthy and mutually beneficial. If they cannot adjust, and if their mission and music remain misunderstood, denigrated, or deemed unmarketable, then confusion and disillusionment are usually inevitable. It is difficult for these types of artists to understand why professing Christians, involved with the production and marketing of music, seem to be far more interested in taking their music and mission and conforming it to the CCM model than equipping men and women to be the type of artist they've been called to be. If the mission is for Christians to live for God everywhere and in everything, it is confusing to find out that the largest group of Christians in the world involved with music appears not to live by this same mission as it applies to music.

A few pages back I gave evidence to support the idea that evangelism, acts of mercy, and broader ideas regarding musical stewardship are undeniably present within CCM. However, none of us involved with CCM, especially artists, should misinterpret the mere presence of these ideas as evidence that they are a priority for CCM. When artists mistake presence for priority, they become confused and disillusioned. It's time for them to move beyond these honest but counterproductive responses to honest and well-informed dialogue with CCM. Artists such as these have the potential to make enormously positive contributions to rethinking the Christian interaction with music, here and now, in the kingdom at hand. But they must invest in the community. Their artful, thoughtful contributions will have little impact unless they are wrapped in the forbearance, charity, and sensitivity that comes from investing in an understanding of the CCM community, how its core priorities came to be, and what concerned, committed people within the ranks are presently doing to bring CCM into faithful alignment with the Christian mission.

While the artists have a responsibility to communicate with the Christian music industry, the industry has a responsibility as well. It's time for contemporary Christian music to take these artists seriously. It's time for CCM to tune into the right channels. *It's time to make the Christian mission our priority.* We cannot continue to present ourselves as taking the whole of the Christian mission seriously if, in fact, we have not. We cannot confuse the mere presence of an idea with having made the idea a priority.

Of the thirty-five popular CCM artists and groups I polled for this book, nearly 86% said that they entered CCM thinking they would be making music for Christians and non-Christians alike. Like Out of the Grey, they've had to adjust to the truth that the overwhelming majority of their audience is Christian. When asked to estimate the total number of letters received from non-Christians over the span of their careers/ministries, over 50% gave ten or fewer letters as their answer. Carman's extraordinary numbers aside, we must give serious consideration to the possibility that we're producing very little evangelism and cultural penetration for the cause of Christ.

The Fruit of the Fusion: Rhetoric or Reality?

William Romanowski is correct in his observation that when CCM began, "it justified its existence and activities on the assumption that contemporary popular music was an effective vehicle for bringing the evangelical message of personal salvation through Christ to the modern youth culture and promoting 'traditional' beliefs and values."[11] Romanowski is also correct when he writes that CCM's pioneers believed a "fusion of marketing and ministry would simultaneously save souls and generate profits." However, the fruit of the fusion has been that "evangelism became the industrial rhetoric, not the spiritual reality." This has never been more true than today. It's time to lower the volume on the rhetoric and truthfully define not only the present relationship between CCM and evangelism, but CCM and a comprehensive kingdom perspective of the Christian mission altogether.

Chapter 18

The Truth Is Out There

Artists committed to comprehensive missions of evangelism, mercy, neighbor love, and musical stewardship quickly realize that major Christian record labels will support almost any of these, provided they reach the Christian consumer base in the process. Certainly, creating music for the church is vitally important, and the impetus to do so is driven by such powerful ideas as love and stewardship. Even so, the question remains as to what, if anything, reaching a Christian consumer base has to do with evangelism, acts of mercy toward unbelievers, or broader ideas regarding the stewardship of music in the culture at large.

This question gives us some insight into why it's difficult for the contemporary Christian music industry to make a priority of supporting an artist like music evangelist David Pierce. An audience of one hundred Satan punks and ten Christians does not constitute a CCM consumer base. An audience of ninety-five Christians and five Satan punks does. If you're thinking something doesn't add up here, you're right. Whether it adds up or not all depends on whose math you're using. The economy of God, which allows for resisting the comfort of the ninety-nine sheep to invest in the one who's lost, runs counter to the economy of the world. God's math is upside down, yet he has called us to live in an equally upside-down world where the economy of the world simply cannot be ignored. He knows our dilemma and has given it to us to sort it out with the help of the Spirit and the Scripture. As is said, the truth is out there.

Evangelism: Behind the Rhetoric

If CCM artists like Russ Lee of NewSong or Steve Wiggins of Big Tent Revival show themselves to be evangelizing artists out of sincere and faithful hearts, this will in no way stop born-again Christians from attending their concerts. On the contrary, it's likely that more Christians will attend. The CCM community understands this phenomenon and uses it to its benefit. Christian music and evangelism have a long history of coexistence, and many churches, pastors, artists, industry folks, and fans in the audience like it that way—even though it is, effectively speaking, more rhetoric than spiritual reality. Many churches, youth pastors, and promoters have come to expect evangelism at a Christian concert, even one primarily attended by Christians. If this seemingly contradictory expectation goes unfulfilled, it stirs up voices of criticism. Remember these words from the WAY-FM open letter? "In our opinion, the gospel also has been diluted to some degree in live concerts. We have been disappointed in the last few years with some of the concerts our stations have promoted. In some instances, there has been little or no ministry throughout the entire event." These comments represent the thoughts of a great many Christians on the importance of a gospel appeal in a Christian concert.

Because of this, a Christian record company faces neither difficulty nor risk in supporting artists who evangelize. It makes perfect sense for them to. It perpetuates the founding idea that the primary purpose of CCM is the discipling and evangelization of youth. By helping to perpetuate the idea that CCM is seriously about the business of music and evangelism, it deftly maneuvers through the maze of contradiction that the evangelism issue has become. In good conscience, the record companies can tell pastors, artists, parents, and fans that nothing has changed, and that they continue to be, as they have historically been, strong advocates of music and evangelism. And here's why:

1. CCM record companies know that Christians attend Christian concerts even when evangelism is emphasized. Some come especially because it is. This fulfills the record companies' priority of getting the music to their core consumers.
2. CCM record companies know that some portion of the Christian audience will bring unsaved friends, neighbors, and relatives to hear a gospel appeal. This fulfills, in part, the need of Christian men and women inside the record companies to get involved in evangelism. It affirms to them that they are doing something which has eternal value.
3. CCM record companies know that some portion of the audience will be composed of children and teenagers who attend church with their Christian parents, but have yet to come to a saving faith in Jesus Christ. A Christian concert where the gospel is proclaimed is yet one more opportunity for these children and teenagers to acknowledge Christ as their Savior. As in point two, this helps fulfill the need of Christian men and women inside the record companies to involve themselves in evangelism, if only indirectly. And again, they feel an affirmation that their labor has eternal value.

The Christian Concert: Tricks or Truth?

From CCM's inception, concerts have been used as a tool to draw unbelievers to an event where the gospel will be preached—something I've long referred to as the music-as-magnet method. Peter Furler of the Newsboys understands this reality, but makes it quite clear that such methodology does not represent his own thinking. "You might find someone," Peter confirms, "who totally believes with all their heart that our music is meant to draw kids along so we can preach to them. To be honest, I have never ever thought that in my life, in my whole fifteen years of being on the road with a band playing music. I've heard preachers tell us that, when we've done a crusade or a tent revival, saying, 'I'm glad you're here, the music, bringing the young people along.'"[1]

Unlike Peter Furler, Nate Sjogren of the Insyderz stresses it's been instilled in him "that music is a viable way to get people to listen to what you have to say."[2] Emphasizing the music-as-magnet method, Nate explains, "There's a draw with a band. I grew up in the Salvation Army and William Booth said that if he had to stand on a street corner and play a tambourine standing on his head, he would do that, if it meant that one person would listen to him talk about Christ."

I agree with Nate. Standing on your head on a street corner playing a tambourine will draw attention to yourself. However, an unbeliever will seldom be drawn in to CCM-styled evangelistic concerts without an invitation from a believing friend or relative. The believer who invites the unbeliever to a Christian music concert bets on the entertainment value of music to entice an unbeliever to attend. The fact that the gospel will be preached at the event is more often than not left as a surprise, something Phil Joel of the Newsboys takes exception to. "I think there is a little bit of dishonesty in the old Christian concert model. In that sort of situation, kids definitely need to let kids know what's going to happen. In those old-fashioned sort of tactics, and I think that's what they are, they don't understand you're going to have power in integrity, power in honesty. That's where God hangs out. He hangs out in truth, he doesn't hang out in tricks."[3]

The Billy Graham Approach

The approach of inviting unsaved friends and relatives to a Christian concert is similar in many ways to that taken by people who attend a Billy Graham Crusade. There are some distinct differences though. With Dr. Graham, music is not necessarily the draw, and the gospel appeal is *featured* rather than downplayed, hidden, or relegated to five minutes in a ninety-minute event. Most unbelievers who attend a Graham crusade know ahead of time that a preacher, albeit the world's most famous, is going to preach to them about salvation in Christ alone. Due in no small part to Graham's sterling reputation, unsaved people willingly come to his crusades, and by God's grace they walk out new men and women. My wife's mother came to faith in Jesus this way.

Most artists who evangelize in the Christian concert setting do so with full knowledge that the audience before them is largely composed of people who already know and love Christ. This being so, artists who evangelize within CCM will often announce ahead of time that their concert tour will have an evangelism emphasis (Geoff Moore and Carman for example). This alerts the saved to bring along the unsaved. Armed with the assurance that unsaved children and adults are present in the audience, the artist faithfully makes an appeal for the gospel. This is the attitude and approach which best characterizes the popular group NewSong.

"Evangelism is our goal," states Russ Lee of NewSong. "Music is a vehicle that we use to share the gospel of Jesus Christ."[4]

"The bad news," continues NewSong member Eddie Carswell, "is that our ministry is more of an inreach. We're about a bunch of different things. We're encouraging the guy out in row eight, we're about getting people to support kids through World Vision, and we're in prisons. As far as the evangelistic side, if that's all we're about, we should be down at Wal-Mart on a flatbed, probably."

The Altar Call

My own experience with evangelism in a Christian concert setting is similar. I have given appeals for the gospel at Christian concerts and have seen people come to a saving knowledge of Christ—never in large numbers, but I've never had the privilege of sharing the gospel before a large crowd of unsaved people. In the settings where I've spoken, it would not have made sense for large numbers of people to come forward, unless of course the Christians in the audience had decided to get up from their seats. Even still, there are well-meaning pastors, churches, and promoters intently involved with the Christian music community who've yet to realize that Christian concerts are primarily the domain of Christians. And that CCM artists and bands face promoters with wholly unreasonable expectations regarding evangelism, especially surrounding the nature and fruit of the "altar call." The band Small Town Poets relates a story surrounding this issue which epitomizes the "altar call" experience for many Christian musicians:

"Our ire was raised a little bit when a concert promoter sent back our manager's concert follow-up evaluation sheet and it said, 'The altar call was weak resulting in few decisions.' At the end of the show Miguel took about five minutes to explain the gospel in layman's terms, just as simple as he could. He told them, 'that's the gospel, that's what Christ did for you, if you'd like to respond to it, please walk down.' Our take on the promoter's comments was this: The gospel can't be weak. It's the good news of Christ. It's salvation to all that believe. All Miguel did was speak it, and if the Holy

Spirit moved on people's hearts, it's their responsibility to react. I guess we could have played some piano music, I guess we could have cried, but all we did was present the gospel and that's not weak. And the fact that he said it resulted in few decisions, well, there were decisions."[5]

These kinds of stories regarding evangelism are not uncommon. And they exist in no small part due to confusion over the nature and outworking of our secondary callings.

Faithful or Fooled?

I've shown you how Christian record companies and artists make sense of a seeming contradiction. Now let me make clear how it doesn't make sense. First a question. How do you carry out music evangelism when the overwhelming majority of people you're evangelizing are born-again Christians? The answer is you don't, except in the way described above. Is there anything wrong with this approach? Nothing at all, as long as it's not accepted as sufficient or comprehensive. As long as we're not fooled into thinking it represents living for God everywhere and in everything. It misses that particular mark by a long shot.

What this approach does do is model something that occurs in churches across America every single Lord's day. Come Sunday our churches fill up with true believers who share the pews with people who feel they are believers but aren't, the occasional curious spiritual seeker doing a taste test, and the unsaved relatives, friends, neighbors and children who come, either as guests of Christians or, in the case of children, as required by their parents. Though the salvation message is often preached in church, and people do come to Christ in church, no Christian who has ever skimmed the Bible believes formal worship fulfills the Lord's directive to go into the world and make disciples of all men.

Given this, does it make sense for Christian record companies, staffed mostly with Christians, to choose willfully to limit their support of music and evangelism, or the pre-evangelism of being salt and light in the world, especially when CCM is without a doubt the world's largest representation of Christians involved in the stewardship of music? Remember these words from Billboard columnist Deborah Evans Price: "I can't tell you how many interviews I've asked about mainstream plans for a particular artist or song and get the response that the company is 'exploring options,' and nothing ever happens."

On the surface, it makes no sense that Christian record companies would fail to exhaust every opportunity for sending truth and goodness into a dark world. Launching God's message of hope into the darkest corners of creation should be a priority. But what if Christian record companies are simply being faithful to their particular calling, a calling which does not necessarily involve taking Christian music to the unsaved mainstream music lover? What if, like the apostle Paul before them, Christian record companies are faithfully doing the good they know to do in the CCM arena, and do not wish to duplicate or build upon the good work which Christian brothers and sisters are already doing in mainstream music (Rom. 15:20)? If this is justifiably the case, then many critics of CCM's narrow focus have no basis for criticism.

But it's *not* the case. Every artist, every songwriter, every producer, every record executive, every manager and booking agent, every magazine and radio station, every key player in the system and many in the audience know in their heart of hearts that this is not the case. Inwardly, many grieve that it isn't, all the while faithfully giving their best thinking to making the most of what they can do within the CCM system. They adjust and look for ways to contribute. Like Eddie Carswell from NewSong said, "We're about a bunch of different things. We're encouraging the guy out in row eight, we're about getting people to support kids through World Vision, and we're in prisons." Such servanthood is good and leads to good. Unfortunately, steering the ship of contemporary Christian music to other equally good ports of entry feels like an overwhelming and impossible task the majority of the time. Impossible for man. Not impossible for God.

A Wake-up Call

When young people committed to a comprehensive Christian mission of evangelism, acts of mercy, neighbor love, and musical stewardship come to CCM looking for help, they remind us of other good work we should be about. They remind us of callings unfulfilled. It's time for those of us in leadership to stop reacting to their presence and their insightful questioning of CCM's priorities as a threat to the good work we have accomplished. On the contrary, these artists and the missions, dreams, and visions they represent are a wake-up call, not a threat. They help to remind us that God's musical people are to be his musical representatives everywhere and in everything.

In the beginning, the CCM industry came alongside the artists, and the artists looked to the industry to equip them for their various missions and callings. Now CCM looks to the artists to adjust to the corporations' mission—their calling. The relationship between artist and equipper has become, as they say, a case of the tail wagging the dog.

When these artists sit with industry leaders and share their dreams of being used of the Lord in transforming the world, all of us in leadership know very well that we are ill-equipped to help them in this regard. And we know we are without excuse. We cannot say we have plenty of Christian counterparts in the mainstream record business. We cannot tell young Christian artists that though the CCM community does not make a priority of equipping their particular musical calling, there are plenty of major record companies stewarded by Christians who do. We cannot refer them to any other labels. They don't exist. We are it, and as a result of our narrow focus, these important brothers and sisters are without Christian community when it comes to music.

They can certainly go directly to the mainstream companies, and some artists do. This is entirely legitimate. But they cannot count on finding even one major Christian record company that makes a priority of funding and promoting artists with the purpose of taking their music to both the mainstream and Christian markets simultaneously. If there's any major record company who promotes themselves as doing this, under the pretense that together with certain artists they have a radical priority commitment to communicate the gospel or the reality of kingdom life to the lost through music, they are incredibly deceived. In sixteen years I've not seen any evidence to support such claims. You cannot have a radical, priority commitment to the lost on any front, from evangelism to impacting the culture with good music, unless you are willing to dwell among them or go to them. This is the mission CCM as an industry has refused to accept.

After having funded and managed an independent record company whose mission it was to take Christian artists to the mainstream and Christian markets simultaneously, I am not unsympathetic to the reasons why major Christian record companies do not make this mission a priority. It is incredibly difficult, uphill work especially in the beginning. For many veterans of CCM, it would seem like starting over to embrace this mission.

The Re:think Story

In 1995 I started a small record label called re:think, a solely owned, privately financed label with distribution to the mainstream through EMI Music Distribution (EMD) and to the Christian community through Chordant (EMI's Christian music distribution). I created the re:think label to record and promote a diverse though like-minded group of artists. Like every Christian record company, my vision for re:think was to identify those in the body of Christ with extraordinary talent in music. I was looking for Christian artists who through their lives and music demonstrated a unique equipping to speak to both the church and the watching world, without ever changing who God created them to be. They had to be unapologetically Christian in their beliefs and worldview, but also equally unapologetic in their commitment to creativity and the life of the imagination.

Like any other record company, re:think sought to form relationships with these types of artists with the purpose of recording and promoting them to the marketplace. What made re:think distinctive was its mission to simultaneously market and promote these artists to the Christian community and to the mainstream. My hope was that re:think artists would refresh the hearts of the saints, challenge the minds of the saints, replicate good, truth and beauty, salt the culture with truth and musical excellence, glorify God, and enjoy what he himself had imagined and created through the gift of music.

No Names to Name

The mission I've described isn't much different from that of any other Christian record company, with the exception of the use of the word *simultaneously* and the phrase *salt the culture.* By adding these, a whole other world comes into view—the world where those who do not listen to contemporary Christian music, and where those who do not know Christ actually live. To simultaneously promote and market music to the mainstream and Christian markets, with the intent of salting the culture and refreshing the hearts of the saints, means something entirely different from what Christian companies are doing in the mainstream.

True, Christian record companies have followed up on the mainstream opportunities presented to their artists. They have pursued mainstream partnerships for their artists when the artists have requested it. They have distributed Christian product to mainstream retail through the distribution arm of their mainstream owner or partner. They have appropriated marketing funds for mainstream publicists and radio promoters in an attempt to make inroads for their artists with mainstream media. They have partnered with mainstream companies to market and promote some of their biggest artists, including Jars of Clay, Bob Carlisle, Amy Grant, Michael W. Smith, dc Talk, and Kathy Troccoli. Each of these acts has had significant pop hits in the mainstream.

Now, let's name the popular artists whom major Christian record companies have introduced and diligently promoted to both mainstream and Christian markets, spending relatively equivalent marketing dollars in each market from their debut release forward.

That's right, there are none.

Taking the Harvest to Market

Major Christian record companies take their product to market based on three existing scenarios:

1. The priority scenario, which is to promote, market, and distribute Christian music solely to Christians via CCM distribution, media, retail, and concert promotion. All promotion and marketing efforts are aimed at reaching the Christian consumer.
2. The priority-plus scenario, which is everything involved in the priority scenario, plus mainstream distribution of any product deemed salable in that market. With very few exceptions, all promotion and marketing monies are aimed at reaching the Christian consumer.
3. The crossover scenario, which is everything involved in the two scenarios outlined above, plus the addition of a mainstream label partner who commits to bring their own priority scenario to the marketing of the product. Promotion and marketing efforts toward the Christian consumer and the mainstream music consumer are relatively equivalent.

In the priority-plus scenario, don't confuse distribution to the mainstream with promoting and marketing to the mainstream pop music consumer. This is something altogether different. This distribution goes only as far as getting the product to the mainstream stores where Christians are also known to shop. Under this scenario, marketing and promotion budgets are spent on select Christian product sent to the mainstream, but the money committed for this purpose is almost always directed at the Christian consumer. Though the target buyer at mainstream retail is a Christian, CCM marketers hope that non-Christians will occasionally become curious enough to purchase one of their CDs. However, most of the time this requires non-Christians to browse a store's gospel or CCM section—a rather unlikely possibility. Except in rare instances, it's only the most successful of Christian artists who find themselves racked next to their pop equivalents.

Experimenting on the Clock

In June of 1996, re:think, using the *priority-plus scenario,* released the debut of Sarah Masen. In an attempt to fulfill re:think's stated mission, we adapted this scenario to fit our specific needs. With the "plus" portion of the scenario providing access to mainstream distribution, we set out to create a new, fourth scenario. Our hope was to position ourselves as a small, independent label taking advantage of the two different distribution systems to achieve the maximum amount of success for our artists. In our case this meant EMI Music Distribution on the pop side and Chordant on the Christian side. Our mission was to be a record company. Not a Christian record company that spent most of its money trying to reach the Christian consumer while dabbling in the mainstream. On the contrary, we were taking both sides very seriously, especially the mainstream, since the mainstream was where we had the most to learn. My small staff and I put together substantial marketing plans for both markets and set about the business of cutting a new trail, hoping to remain faithful to our mission of refreshing the hearts of the saints *and* salting the culture with truth and musical excellence.

On the pop/mainstream side we worked with several key people at EMI Music Distribution and Chordant. These knowledgeable people helped us to navigate the massive organizational system which makes up pop music. Working closely with EMD's artist development reps, we arranged for price and positioning, co-op ad buys, radio time buys, and listening posts—all with the purpose of encouraging mainstream retail stores to take Sarah Masen's music seriously. The reason some artists seem to have so much exposure at music retail while others have little to none has everything to do with whether these *marketing tools* are budgeted for and maximized.

We hired independent radio promoters to work her record at adult alternative radio. In addition, we retained a national publicity firm to solicit mainstream reviews of Sarah's record. As a new label looking to add value to our product, we were the first record company in America to contact and partner with America On-Line to include an AOL installer on the CD-ROM portion of Sarah's CD. We set up and executed an extensive U.S. promotional tour for Sarah through Borders Books and Music. In some cities Sarah performed as many as four times a day, all for the purpose of exposing the mainstream community to her music. She played at in-stores, at one-stop distributors, EMD branch offices, at showcase clubs, for *Radio & Records* and for *Billboard*. She attended the Gavin Radio convention in Boulder. In short, we attempted to do with Sarah what every pop label does with their new artists. We promoted her to the music-buying public the best we knew how with the resources given us. We believed in her and wanted her music and artistry to be taken seriously. And most importantly we made these choices in response to God's call to us to live for him everywhere and in everything—including the mainstream music business.

By getting a bird's eye look at the amount of money and human resources required to adequately introduce a new artist to both the pop and CCM markets, I understand in part why major Christian record companies do not go head to head with their mainstream counterparts, bypassing crossover altogether. Even still, it was my conviction in 1995 when I started re:think—and it remains my conviction today—that Christian record companies must develop mainstream strategies in addition to, and possibly as a replacement for, the crossover scenario. While the crossover scenario has produced some fruit, it is wholly insufficient as a comprehensive strategy for introducing and marketing Christian artists to the mainstream music consumer.

Overrated Crossover and the Christian Mission

At present, crossover is defined as a Christian artist crossing over from the smaller Christian marketplace to the larger mainstream marketplace. It is taking an artist whose primary audience is the church and seeking to expand it to the wider music-buying public—Christian or otherwise. Christian artists do this, in conjunction with their Christian record company, by capturing the interest of a mainstream record company and convincing them to market the music to the mainstream pop music consumer, while the Christian label retains the rights to the Christian market.

While this method of placing Christian artists in the mainstream has proved successful in a handful of cases, it has its drawbacks as well. First, crossover is dependent on an artist having started his or her musical career in

CCM and having had significant success in that market. This criteria eliminates the hope of ever simultaneously marketing debut artists in both markets.

Sales and artistry determine whether or not an artist is offered the opportunity to cross over. In both instances the power of veto belongs to the mainstream record company. They are given the role of the autonomous expert. The sales threshold required to be considered a candidate for the mainstream is a decision left up to the mainstream record companies. They also determine whether an artist would be competitive, musically viable, and marketable in the mainstream. This is perhaps the most disturbing thing about the present crossover model. It is also, I believe, the darkest of the downside to working with the mainstream entertainment corporations—the mainstream company is allowed the final say in determining whether or not Christians should fulfill their mission to be salt and light in the world and to be good stewards of our music, our gifts, and our talents.

There is a new version of crossover emerging. Unfortunately, it shows very little improvement over the present one. Its only twist on the old is that it begins with the Christian record companies, contacting a mainstream label who shares their same corporate owner (such as EMI companies Forefront and Virgin meeting together) to play them the music of new artists they've just signed, or veteran artists with new recordings. These meetings take place for two reasons: (1) the Christian label believes they have artists under contract who might, if given the opportunity, find an audience among mainstream music consumers, and/or (2) the artist or the artist's management requested that this be done.

Though this new version of crossover does involve debut and veteran artists, the power of veto still rests with the mainstream record company. If there's no interest on their part, there's no faithfulness on the part of the Christian record company beyond what they're already committed to in the Christian community.

Many people take positions and formulate arguments against my point of view. I'm not advocating doing away with everything the Christian record industry has put in place. Instead, I'm praying for and hoping to inspire some means of fulfilling a greater degree of faithfulness to the Christian mission and to the new artists emerging within our communities and churches. I have no other mission than to inspire God's people to works of service—to use their good gifts and talents—and to live in light of the reality of the kingdom of God.

In listening to the voices of the artists in the CCM community, you

can hear the inspiration and you can see the light of the reality of the kingdom of God.

Listen . . .

Sinners and the Gospel

Chris Blaney of Reality Check admits that he's experienced a bit of a reality check himself. "The more I've thought about it," says Chris, "I realize that the mainstream success of groups like Jars of Clay and dc Talk allows them to reach somebody like Budweiser because Budweiser is promoting their shows. Reality Check isn't going to reach anybody from Budweiser. They're not going to hear anything about what we have to say because we're in First Baptist Church."[6]

Shelley Breen of Point of Grace wishes that her group's music "could be just like any other music and it could all be out there together. If you're a Christian, I think you should want your music everywhere. You would want it to stick out and be a light. I would love to go on Jay Leno and sing a Christian song and cause somebody to think and to acknowledge that there is a God."[7]

Cindy Morgan would love to stick out and be a light given the opportunity. "I just wish I could sing to people who aren't Christians. I wish there were people who would feel comfortable coming to a concert of mine, even if they weren't Christians, just because they would enjoy the music."[8]

Cindy's not alone. There are plenty of artists who would love the opportunity to sing for people who aren't Christians. Jars of Clay lead singer Dan Haseltine seems to have a good handle on why it is that we've failed to answer the call to take our music and our message everywhere and in everything:

"There has been so much division between the church and the world that it really does seem out of place for Christians to be in the world. You become a Christian and in some senses you're fed the line, 'Now you're one of us, you're part of the elite group. You don't have to go back out there any more and you don't have to be a part of what is going on out there.' I think this idea has caused a lot of misguided direction in terms of what ministry is and what the impact of art can be on a world which is very much impacted by art, especially Christian art. I think I would encourage the church to blur the lines and recognize that there aren't two groups—the Christians and the non-Christians—there's sinners and the gospel."[9]

Perhaps some of the teachable sinners within CCM, sinners who know the gospel, might be hearing the call to rethink crossover altogether and simply start putting our tremendous resources and talents to work toward taking our music into the world and not having to ask permission from the world to do it.

Where do we start?

"It may start," suggests Matt Odmark of Jars of Clay, "with a group of people who firmly believe Christianity belongs right in the middle of rock-n-roll as much as Christianity belongs anywhere."[10]

Matt is correct. It is about God's people, everywhere and in everything—rock-n-roll included. But this group will have to be weak enough to know how much they need Jesus. If they start with such knowledge, anything is possible. If they fear missing the will of God more than they fear the unknown, then the "everywhere" of the kingdom will come into view.

The way Clay Crosse sees it, all the Christian record companies "and everybody that falls under them, are just acquainted with our industry. We know the bookstores that sell our music—the radio stations that play our music. The rest out there, in the mainstream, is intimidating to us, but it's not intimidating to our parent companies, to Clive Calder (of Zomba) and people like that."[11]

What do we have to fear?

Where have we put our trust?

Not only does Christian music have some of the most talented people in the world in its community; we have every resource at our disposal to accomplish the Christian mission in the world; for nothing less than the divine power of Jesus "has given us everything we need for life and godliness through our knowledge of him who called us by his own glory and goodness" (2 Pet. 1:3). All of us in positions of leadership must remember to lead. "We are not of those who shrink back and are destroyed, but of those who believe and are saved" (Heb. 10:39).

Here at the crossroads CCM leadership must faithfully pray for the wisdom to discern the changes that must be made to faithfully answer the calling to be God's musical people, everywhere and in everything.

CODA

GOOD AND TRUTHFUL MUSIC

Contemporary Christian music is at a crossroads and the stakes are enormous. In one direction there's conformity to an artificial, market-driven definition of what many of us have come to believe CCM should be. In the other, the subject matter and instrumental style of Christian music is allowed—is encouraged—to range over the entire length and breadth of human emotion and experience. Here and now I ask you to consider the second path, a new model of Christian music that embraces the whole kingdom—a path that is absolutely faithful to the other Christian mission as well as the mission to provide the church with good and truthful music. This model of music is not defined by instrumentation or specific lyrical buzzwords, but by the fact that it grows from and points toward a life in Jesus Christ as subjects in his kingdom.

The battle over lyrics shows no signs of ending. There are those who continue to insist on obvious Christian images in any song in the "Christian" camp. But Christian lyrics can't be defined by a list of approved words or subjects any more than poems or sermons can. The subject matter for lyrics is the theater of redemption, the whole of life. We must learn to lovingly and intellectually direct lyric content according to true need and not simply to the satisfaction of consumer wants. We must respect all forms of musical and lyrical artistry, recognizing that God delights in and makes intelligent use of the diversity in his creation.

To All the Earth

If CCM's beginnings back in the 1960s were "something for the kids," its future is for everyone—a witness to the world and not just the youth group. The foundations of CCM were small and enculturated: folk music, the Jesus movement, the Baptist Sunday School Board. Today's new ideas strain against old shackles as they become more and more kingdom-oriented. They are huge ideas, bursting with God-breathed energy because they involve God's musical people everywhere and in everything as salt and light, as roaring lambs. We are coming to learn that our calling is not just "to the kids" but to all the earth, and we will create ways to take our music into the world without asking permission of any gatekeeper save God, and without forsaking our calling to make music for his church.

CCM has never had this kingdom perspective brought to bear on it. Yet it has outgrown the forms and the energy that gave it life more than thirty years ago, and nothing else has come alongside to supplement and renew those sources. This renewal is our task. We need wisdom and experience to accomplish it. We need to be equipped musically and theologically, and we ought to aspire to excellence and faithfulness in both. And pray hard that God will give us strength, discernment, and courage.

A Fresh Start

Stepping out beyond the crossroads is not just about difficult decisions, but about fresh starts as well. The purpose of this book is to encourage you to approach music, ministry, and the music industry in a more comprehensive and faithful manner, one that is informed by the whole of Scripture and the evidence of creation, rather than the insufficient ad hoc philosophy which drove CCM's beginnings and still drives it today.

I hope to move you beyond any private, hunch-oriented ideas about music and ministry that may influence you, to a place where you can consider something far bigger and ultimately far more faithful—God's people creating and enjoying music everywhere and in everything. When you step out from the crossroads, step out into the glorious freedom of the children of God. Acknowledge your God-given freedom to use music for all kinds of purposes—to minister by bringing the gospel in song as well as by creating something of beauty which may or may not be labeled "Christian" by its listeners.

You and I have a choice to make. The music we love is at the crossroads, and it's time to decide which way is forward. There are a few thousand of us in the industry, and some of us consider the path with the light of the kingdom at the end as the only way to go. But the more important decision will come from the millions of listeners, concert goers, record buyers, and request line callers whose actions ultimately define the CCM industry. There's where the power in the choice really is. Together, with God's blessing, let us choose the path that will send his good and truthful music resounding to the farthest corners of creation.

In view of God's mercy we can do nothing less than to live in response to the gospel of grace. This is our spiritual act of worship.

"Open your eyes and look at the fields! They are ripe for harvest" (John 4:35).

May the teachable sinners within the CCM community, artists, industry folks, and members of the audience have the ears to hear.

Afterword

A Certain Tension

by Jars of Clay

To live a Christian life is to be called to live in tension. In order for music created by Christians to grow and mature, we need to wrestle with this idea.

In the spring of 1996, we performed at a club called The Bottom of the Hill in San Francisco, California. As we entered the club, we noticed that the bouncer at the door was wearing a black tee-shirt which read, "My favorite number is 666." Looming above the stage was a goat's head. While we were still unloading our equipment, a fight broke out at the bar. By this time we were feeling totally out of place, and were wondering what we were even doing there that evening. It is difficult to convey the fear and discomfort of four young Christian men in that situation who had been raised in the church and had performed primarily at Christian youth events. But as we played that night, we felt our hearts change from hearts of fear to hearts of compassion—compassion for people in places seemingly neglected by the church. We realized we had somehow stumbled into a very dark place, and for an hour that night, we were given the opportunity to be a spark of light.

Thanks to the mainstream success of our single, "Flood," we were invited to visit radio stations and build some relationships with contemporary rock broadcasters. We quickly came face to face with the painful fact that these people were awkwardly hesitant toward us, as if they were guarding themselves against some religious agenda from a "Christian rock band." Before we could accomplish anything with these encounters, we first had to disarm our hosts of stigmas or prejudices they had toward Christians. We would have to show them that we were four normal guys with a passion for music, and that we were more interested in relating to them as people than in propagating any so-called religious agenda.

We were beginning to realize just how foreign the church must seem to nonbelievers in the world of music. We wondered if we as a church had so distanced ourselves from this particular part of our culture that we could no longer reach them with the gospel. It was then that we began to clarify our vision and respond to a specific calling.

What would it mean to bridge the gap between the church and the music culture? How could we provoke this segment of our society to consider issues of eternity? How would this affect the standard of our art, both lyrically and musically? How would the Christian music industry, with its primary goal to feed the church, respond to this mentality of "musical missions"? As our mission became more focused, we became acutely aware of the diversity needed in the body of Christ to sustain such a vision. For while we didn't want to bury ourselves inside the church, and thereby miss opportunities to reach those in the music industry, we knew that the only way to affect our culture was to be sustained by the church.

Faced with this dilemma, we sought the advice of our pastor, whose godly counsel helped to root us in establishing our vision. As a result, we have grown to understand that the tension that we have experienced is to be expected if we are to act as a bridge between Christ and the music culture. And this tension is not of mere music or ministry. Ultimately, this struggle involves an attempt to understand more fully the person of God, and what he is capable of. After all, God's work on this earth is primarily to build his kingdom, a process which merely starts with the church. And he is, by no means, confined to contemporary Christian music or any other organized ministry for accomplishing his purposes.

With this in mind, it is our hope that the Christian community will accept a more diverse picture of the body of Christ. Even as Jars of Clay may be a hand in reaching out to our generation, we still rely on the rest of the body of Christ to complete the embrace. Rarely do we hear stories of non-believers coming to know Christ through music alone. It is more often accomplished by a partnering of different gifts working together within the Christian body.

A recent concert goer shared his story with us. After hearing "Flood" on a modern rock station, David bought our CD at a local record store. He was not a Christian and seemed to have little or no experience with the church. As he became more familiar with other songs on the record, he began to ask other questions. At a party, he pulled aside a friend whom he knew was a Christian. His friend explained the meaning of the lyrics, and this eventually led to David's salvation. This story is an example of how the different gifts by members within the body were used to further the kingdom. God has designed his church as a body with many parts. We can better understand our purpose when we embrace the struggle of living in conformity with this design.

Paul describes this in Ephesians 4:16: "From him the whole body, joined and held together by every supporting ligament, grows and builds itself up in love, as each part does its work."

Philippians 1:6: "Being confident of this, that he who began a good work in you will carry it on to completion until the day of Christ Jesus." We are a people in process. This is our tension and our hope.

Jars of Clay are Dan Haseltine, Charlie Lowell, Steve Mason, and Matt Odmark

About the Author

Charlie Peacock is an award-winning recording artist, producer, songwriter, and teacher. In addition to his own popular recordings ("One Man Gets Around," "Monkeys at the Zoo"), he has produced recordings by Avalon, Out of the Grey, Margaret Becker, and Sarah Masen. His songs have been recorded by Amy Grant ("Every Heartbeat"), dc Talk ("In the Light"), and Russ Taff ("Down in the Lowlands").

For concert booking information, contact:

Street Level Artist Agency
106 N. Buffalo Street, Suite 200
Warsaw, Indiana 46580
(219) 269–3413

For speaking engagements, contact:
Ambassador Speaker's Bureau
P.O. Box 50358
Nashville, TN 37205
(615) 370–4700
email Wes @AmbassadorAgency.com

To reach the author directly, write to:
Charlie Peacock
P.O. Box 218307
Nashville, TN 37221–8307

Endnotes

Notes for Introduction

1. Robert Palmer, *Deep Blues* (New York: Penguin Books, 1981), 126.
2. David F. Wells, *God in the Wasteland* (Grand Rapids: Wm. B. Eerdmans, 1994), 29.
3. Eugene H. Peterson, *Run with the Horses* (Downers Grove: Inter-Varsity Press, 1983), 161.
4. J. I. Packer, *Knowing God* (Downers Grove: InterVarsity Press, 1973), 104.

Notes for (Chapter 1) Voices at the Crossroads

1. Kathleen A. Ijames, *Letters (Calvin College Chimes,* Volume 92, Issue #16, January 23, 1997), 5.
2. The term *gospel music,* used in this paragraph and others within this chapter, is meant to denote the whole of popular Christian music in America, from Southern Gospel to CCM. While the Gospel Music Association (GMA) continues to perpetuate the term *gospel music* through its literature and events, the bulk of the Christian music industry is commonly known as CCM, or Contemporary Christian Music.
3. *The CCM Update,* Volume 11, Issue #35, September 8, 1997.

4. *The CCM Update,* Volume 12, Issue #26, July 6, 1997.
5. Mark Joseph, *Billboard,* September 20, 1997, 6.
6. Ibid. 22.
7. Deborah Evans Price, *Higher Ground* (*Billboard,* June 7, 1997), 56.
8. Interview with the author, *Gospel Music Week,* April 20-22, 1998.
9. Tom Roland, "Push into Mainstream Triggers Ascension of Christian Music Sales" (*Tennessean,* Volume 94, #44, February 13, 1998).

Notes for (Chapter 2) The Path of the Teachable Sinner

1. Ravi Zacharias, *Can Man Live Without God?* (Dallas: Word Publishing, 1994), 145.

Notes for (Chapter 3) The Source of Truth

This chapter highlights three important areas:

The first idea is what Scripture calls the *kingdom of God.* On this topic I have borrowed liberally from my pastor Scotty Smith's enthusiastic teaching on the subject.

Second is the idea of *the church.* Some of my thinking on this topic is inspired by author Rodney Clapp.

Third is the Christian idea of *calling.* Here I am indebted to Paul Marshall, Ken Meyers, and especially Os Guinness for their scripturally informed thoughts on the nature of God's call to humankind.

1. Source: Quotes taken from pastor Scotty Smith's unpublished sermon notes entitled *Objects of His Affection—Subjects in His Kingdom* (pt. 8), July 5, 1998.
2. Source: Quote taken from the author's study notes of Scotty Smith's preachment, June 21, 1998.
3. Os Guinness, *The Call* (Nashville: Word, 1998), 31.
4. Ibid.
5. Elton Trueblood, *Your Other Vocation* (New York: Harper, 1952), 57.
6. Interview with the author, *Gospel Music Week,* April 20-22, 1998.
7. Interview with the author, *Gospel Music Week,* April 20-22, 1998.
8. Interview with the author, *Gospel Music Week,* April 20-22, 1998.

9. Source: This quote is taken from a mailer that Ken Meyers sent out to his subscription list for the Mars Hill Audio tape series. For the tape conversation "Life Work: On the Christian Idea of Calling," write to Mars Hill Audio, P.O. Box 1527, Charlottesville, VA 22902.
10. John Henry Newman, *Prayer, Verses and Devotions,* quoted in *Christianity Today,* May 19, 1997, 36.

Notes for (Chapter 4) In the Beginning

1. *The "Jesus Movement": Impact On Youth, Church* (*U.S. News & World Report,* March 20, 1972), 59.
2. Ken Myers, *All God's Children and Blue Suede Shoes* (Westchester: Crossway, 1989), 155.
3. *U.S. News & World Report,* 60.
4. Melody Green and David Hazard, *No Compromise. The Life Story of Keith Green.* (Chatsworth: Sparrow Press, 1989), 180.
5. Chuck Smith, *Charisma vs. Charismania* (Eugene: Harvest House, 1983), 127.
6. Hank Hanegraaff, *Counterfeit Revival* (Dallas: Word, 1997), Foreword XVII.
7. Hanegraaff, 109.

Historically, the influence of the two theological positions mentioned under the Charismatic influence on CCM can be traced to the teaching of charismatic-affiliated pastors and leaders such as southern Californians Chuck Smith of Calvary Chapel, Jack Hayford of Church on the Way, and John Wimber of the Vineyard, as well as Don Finto of Belmont Church in Nashville, Scott Ross of the Love Inn community in New York, and later, though no less significant, Louis and Mary Neely of The Warehouse in Sacramento, California.

Notes for (Chapter 5) The Jesus Movement

1. As a companion to Scripture in sorting these issues out for yourself, I recommend a book entitled *Are Miraculous Gifts for Today?* This book, edited by Wayne Grudem, includes arguments for and against the four main views on the gifts prevalent today. While each argument is, of course, biased, the editor leaves it up to readers to decide which view (if any) is most faithful to Scripture.

2. Jonathan Edwards, *Jonathan Edwards on Revival* (Edinburgh: The Banner of Truth Trust, 1965), 87.
3. Ibid. 89.
4. Ibid. 91.
5. Ibid. 91.
6. Ibid. 96.
7. Ibid. 132.
8. Interview with the author, *Gospel Music Week,* April 20-22, 1998.
9. Daniel G. Reid, *Dictionary of Christianity in America* (Downers Grove: InterVarsity Press, 1990), 973.
10. April Hefner, *Don't Know Much 'bout History* (CCM Magazine, April 1996), 40.
11. Ibid. 40.

Notes for (Chapter 6) CCM's History: Of Baptists and Folk Musicals

1. All quotes attributed to Billy Ray Hearn, Ralph Carmichael, and Elwyn Raymer are taken from interviews with the author in July of 1997.
2. Source: *The Billboard Book of Top 40 Hits.*

Notes for (Chapter 7) In Search of Theology

1. Richard Lovelace, *Dynamics of Spiritual Life* (Downers Grove: InterVarsity, 1979), 29.
2. Source for all quotes attributed to Wes King: Interview with the author, *Gospel Music Week,* April 20-22, 1998.
3. Interview with the author, *Gospel Music Week,* April 20-22, 1998.
4. Interview with the author, *Gospel Music Week,* April 20-22, 1998.
5. J. I. Packer, *Hot Tub Religion* (Wheaton: Tyndale, 1987), 12.
6. Os Guinness, *The Gravedigger File* (Downers Grove: InterVarsity Press, 1983), 43.
7. Scott MacCleod, *Snakes in the Lobby* (Nashville: Provision Press, 1997), 44.
8. David F. Wells, *No Place for Truth* (Grand Rapids: Eerdmans, 1993), 290.

9. Interview with the author, *Gospel Music Week,* April 20-22, 1998.
10. Mark Shaw, *10 Great Ideas from Church History* (Downers Grove: InterVarsity Press, 1997), 70.
11. Interview with the author, *Gospel Music Week,* April 20-22, 1998.

Notes for (Chapter 8) Music and the Voice of the People

1. Source for Voice #1 quotes: Steve Camp, *A Call for Reformation in the Contemporary Christian Music Industry* (a poster/essay accompanied by 107 theses made public on October 31, 1997).
2. Source for Voice #2 quotes: The Board of Directors/WAY-FM Media Group Inc., *An Open Letter to The Christian Music Community* (published as a full page advertisement in *CCM Magazine,* April 1996).
3. Source for Voice #3 quotes: Wes King, in an interview with the author, *Gospel Music Week,* April 20-22, 1998.
4. Source: Interview with Seven Day Jesus (Brian McSweeney), *Gospel Music Week,* April 20-22, 1998.
5. Source: Interview with Smalltown Poets (Miguel DeJesus), *Gospel Music Week,* April 20-22, 1998.
6. Source: Interview with Seven Day Jesus (Chris Beaty), *Gospel Music Week,* April 20-22, 1998.
7. Source: Interview with Smalltown Poets, *Gospel Music Week,* April 20-22, 1998.
8. Derek Walker, *Bridging the Gap*, an interview with The W's (Val Hellman) *7ball* magazine, Number 19, July/August 1998.

Notes for (Chapter 11) Lyrics at the Crossroads

1. Interview with the author, *Gospel Music Week,* April 20-22, 1998.
2. *CCM Update,* Volume 12, Issue #3, January 26, 1998, 4.
3. Interview with the author, *Gospel Music Week,* April 20-22, 1998.
4. Interview with the author, *Gospel Music Week,* April 20-22, 1998.
5. Interview with the author, *Gospel Music Week,* April 20-22, 1998.

6. William D. Romanowski, "Where's the Gospel?" (*Christianity Today:* December 8, 1997), 44.
7. *CCM Update,* Ibid.

Notes for (Chapter 12) The Ocean Too Big for the Glass

1. Ray Waddle, "Faithful few wonder if march has lost appeal" (*The Tennessean,* May 31, 1998), 1.
2. Interview with the author, *Gospel Music Week,* April 20-22, 1998.
3. Interview with the author, *Gospel Music Week,* April 20-22, 1998.
4. April Hefner and Gregory Rumburg, "Buying into Family Values," (*CCM Magazine,* Vol. 19, Number 11, May 1997), 52.
5. Ibid.

Notes for (Chapter 13) Stopping to Think

1. J. Alec Motyer, *The Prophecy of Isaiah, An Introduction & Commentary* (Downers Grove: InterVarsity, 1993), 452.
2. Ibid. 457.
3. Ibid. 458.
4. Ibid.
5. Ibid.
6. Interview with the author, *Gospel Music Week,* April 20-22, 1998.
7. David F. Wells, *God in the Wasteland* (Grand Rapids: Eerdmans, 1994), 14.
8. Retail advisor: Michael Wall of Bible Book Store/Solid Rock Christian Music and video, Billings, MT. Quotes taken from correspondence with re:think/EMI April 4, 1997, used by permission.

Notes for (Chapter 14) Defining and Naming: Truth and Consequences

1. Source: Letter addressed to Charlie Peacock from the Awards and Criteria Committee of the Gospel Music Association (GMA) Board of Directors, September 24, 1997.
2. Ibid.

Notes for (Chapter 15) Contemporary Christian Music and the World

1. Steve Camp, *A Call for Reformation in the Contemporary Christian Music Industry* (a poster/essay accompanied by 107 theses made public on October 31, 1997).
2. John Seel, *The Evangelical Forfeit* (Grand Rapids: Baker, 1993), 110.
3. Source for quotes attributed to member of Reality Check: Interview with the author, *Gospel Music Week,* April 20-22, 1998.
4. Os Guinness, *No God but God* (Chicago: Moody Press, 1992), 162.
5. Dick Keyes, *The Biblical Perspective of Ambition* (audio cassette #2), Catalogue no. 2311 & 2312, available from Sound Word Associates, P.O. Box 2035, Mall Station, Michigan City, IN 46360.
6. Os Guinness, *The Call* (Nashville: Word, 1998), p. 178.
7. Ibid. 179.
8. Ibid.
9. David F. Wells, *No Place for Truth* (Grand Rapids: Eerdmans, 1993), 288.
10. The CCM Update, "Plans Forming for 1998 Doves," *Gospel Music Week,* Volume 11, Issue #39, October 6, 1997.
11. Ibid.
12. Jay Orr and Rick de Yampert, "Dove Goes to Deceased Artist," *The Tennessean,* Vol. 94, No. 114, Friday, April 24, 1998, 5A.
13. Mark Shaw, *10 Great Ideas from Church History* (Downers Grove: InterVarsity Press, 1997), 37.
14. Alistar McGrath, *The Mystery of the Cross* (Grand Rapids: Zondervan, 1988), 161.
15. Shaw, ibid., 32.
16. Alister McGrath, *Luther's Theology of the Cross* (Oxford: Blackwell, 1985), 181.
17. David F. Wells, *God in the Wasteland* (Grand Rapids: Eerdmans, 1994), 40.
18. Philip Yancey, *The Jesus I Never Knew* (Grand Rapids: Zondervan, 1995), 76.

19. Ibid. 81.
20. Neil Postman, *Technology* (New York: Vintage, 1993), 13.

Notes for (Chapter 16) Capitalism, the Corporation, and the Record Company

1. Melody Green and David Hazard, *No Compromise. The Life Story of Keith Green* (Chatsworth: Sparrow Press, 1989), 230.
2. Ibid.
3. Ibid. 229, 230.
4. Ibid. 268.
5. Ibid.
6. David F. Wells, *God in the Wasteland* (Grand Rapids: Eerdmans, 1994), 50.
7. Ibid.
8. Ibid.
9. Interview with the author, January 23, 1998.

Notes for (Chapter 17) Music and the Christian Mission

1. Source for all quotes used in Type One Artistry: David Pierce, with Dan Wooding, *They Call Him . . . Rock Priest* (Eastbourne: Kingsway Publications Ltd., 1993), 62, 63, 74, 75, 157, 158.
2. Source for all quotes attributed to Out of the Grey used in Type Two Artistry: Interview with the author, *Gospel Music Week,* April 20-22, 1998.
3. Source for all quotes attributed to Sixpence . . ./Matt Slocum used in Type Two Artistry: Interview with the author, *Gospel Music Week,* April 20-22, 1998.
4. John Fischer, "Consider This: Between a Rock and a Hard Place" (*CCM Magazine,* August 1998), 62.
5. Source for all quotes attributed to Plumb/Tiffany Arbuckle used in Type Three Artistry: Interview with the author, *Gospel Music Week,* April 20-22, 1998.
6. Susan Black, *In His Own Words* (London: Omnibus Press, 1997), 31.
7. Source for all quotes attributed to Peter Garrett used in Type Three Artistry: Stephen Baxter, *The Power Behind the Passion of Midnight Oil (*On Being ALIVE Magazine, reprinted in *Prism,* Vol. 5, Number 5, July/August 1998), 21.

8. Source for all quotes attributed to David Wilcox used in Type Three Artistry: Kirk Webb, "Following the Thirst," *Mars Hill Review,* Number 4, Winter/Spring 1996, 91.
9. Black, *In His Own Words,* 30.
10. Source for all quotes attributed to Don Donahue used in Type Three Artistry: Interview with the author, May 27, 1998.
11. Source for all quotes attributed to Mr. Romanowski used in this chapter: William D. Romanowski, "Evangelicals and Popular Music: The Contemporary Christian Music Industry," taken from Jeffrey H. Mahan and Bruce Forbes, eds., *Religion and Popular Culture in America* (Los Angeles: University of California Press, 1998).

Notes for (Chapter 18) The Truth Is Out There

1. Interview with the author, *Gospel Music Week,* April 20-22, 1998.
2. Source for all quotes attributed to Nate Sjogren of the Insyderz used in this chapter: Interview with the author, *Gospel Music Week,* April 20-22, 1998.
3. Interview with the author, *Gospel Music Week,* April 20-22, 1998.
4. Source for all quotes attributed to Russ Lee and Eddie Carswell of NewSong used in this chapter: Interview with the author, *Gospel Music Week,* April 20-22, 1998.
5. Interview with the author, *Gospel Music Week,* April 20-22, 1998.
6. Interview with the author, *Gospel Music Week,* April 20-22, 1998.
7. Interview with the author, *Gospel Music Week,* April 20-22, 1998.
8. Interview with the author, *Gospel Music Week,* April 20-22, 1998.
9. Interview with the author, *Gospel Music Week,* April 20-22, 1998.
10. Interview with the author, *Gospel Music Week,* April 20-22, 1998.
11. Interview with the author, *Gospel Music Week,* April 20-22, 1998.